QUESTIONING JUDAISM

Cultural Memory

in

the

Present

Mieke Bal and Hent de Vries, Editors

QUESTIONING JUDAISM

Interviews by ELISABETH WEBER

Jacques Derrida

Emmanuel Levinas

Jean-François Lyotard

Léon Poliakov

Luc Rosenzweig

Rita Thalmann

Pierre Vidal-Naquet

Translated by Rachel Bowlby

STANFORD UNIVERSITY PRESS

STANFORD, CALIFORNIA

2004

Stanford University Press
Stanford, California

Questioning Judaism was originally published in German in 1994 under
the title *Jüdisches Denken in Frankreich* © Jüdischer Verlag im Suhrkamp
Verlag, Frankfurt am Main, 1994.

Printed in the United States of America
on acid-free, archival-quality paper.

Library of Congress Cataloging-in-Publication Data

Jüdisches Denken in Frankreich. English.
   Questioning Judaism / Jacques Derrida … [et al.] ;
interviews by Elisabeth Weber ; translated by Rachel Bowlby.
       p.   cm.—(Cultural memory in the present)
Interviews originally conducted in French.
   ISBN 0-8047-4219-7 (cloth : alk. paper)—
ISBN 0-8047-4220-0 (pbk. : alk. paper)
1. Jews—History—Philosophy.   2. Jews—Historiography.
3. Jews—France—Social conditions.   4. Antisemitism.
5. Jews—France—Interviews.   6. Intellectuals—France—Interviews.
7. France—Ethnic relations.   I. Derrida, Jacques.
II. Weber, Elisabeth, date–   III. Title.   IV. Series.
DS115.5.J8413   2004
944'.004924—dc22   2004002493

Original Printing 2004
Last figure below indicates year of this printing:
13   12   11   10   09   08   07   06   05   04
Typeset in 11/13.5 Garamond

Contents

Contributors   ix

Translator's Note   xi

Introduction: The Youngest Children of the Republic   1
ELISABETH WEBER

1. Against the Murderers of Memory   26
   PIERRE VIDAL-NAQUET

2. A Testimony Given . . .   39
   JACQUES DERRIDA

3. Women of Resistance   59
   RITA THALMANN

4. Humanity Is Biblical   77
   EMMANUEL LEVINAS

5. Humanity, Nationality, Bestiality   87
   LÉON POLIAKOV

6. Before the Law, After the Law   104
   JEAN-FRANÇOIS LYOTARD

7. Born in 1943   122
   LUC ROSENZWEIG

Notes   137

Contributors

PIERRE VIDAL-NAQUET, born in 1930 in Paris, is directeur de recherches at the École des Hautes Études en Sciences Sociales in Paris, and researcher at the Centre Louis Gernet de Recherches Comparées sur les Sociétés Anciennes, which is affiliated with the Centre National de la Recherche Scientifique (CNRS). He is the author of *Assassins of Memory: Essays on the Denial of the Holocaust*; *The Jews: History, Memory, and the Present*; *Politics Ancient and Modern*; and (with Jean-Pierre Vernant) *Myth and Tragedy in Ancient Greece*.

JACQUES DERRIDA, born in 1930 in El-Biar, Algeria, is directeur d'études at the École des Hautes Études en Sciences Sociales in Paris; and professor at the University of California, Irvine; at New York University; and at the New School for Social Research. He is the author of (among others) *Archive Fever*; *Memoirs of the Blind: The Self-Portrait and Other Ruins*; *On Cosmopolitanism and Forgiveness*; *Of Spirit: Heidegger and the Question*; *Aporias; Of Hospitality*; *Adieu: To Emmanuel Levinas*; *Points . . . : Interviews, 1974–1994*; and *Negotiations: Interventions and Interviews, 1971–2000*.

RITA THALMANN, born in 1926 in Nürnberg, Germany, is professor of history at the Université Paris VII, Centre d'Études et de Recherche Germanique. She is the author of *Crystal Night, 9–10 November 1938* and *Être femme sous le IIIe Reich*, and the editor of *Femmes et fascismes*.

EMMANUEL LEVINAS, born in 1905 in Kaunas, Lithuania, died in Paris in 1995. His last position was professor of philosophy at the Université Paris IV, Sorbonne. He was the author of *Totality and Infinity*; *Otherwise than Being, or Beyond Essence*; *Alterity and Transcendence*; *Entre Nous: Thinking-of-the-Other*; *Difficult Freedom: Essays on Judaism; Nine Talmudic Readings*; *God, Death, and Time*; *Of God Who Comes to Mind*; *Proper Names;* and *Outside the Subject*.

LÉON POLIAKOV, born in 1910 in Saint Petersburg, Russia, is directeur honoraire de recherches at the Centre National de la Recherche Scientifique in Paris. He is the author of *Aryan Myth: A History of Racist and Nationalist Ideas in Europe*; *Harvest of Hate: Nazi Program for the Destruction of the Jews of Europe*; and the five-volume *History of Anti-Semitism*.

JEAN-FRANÇOIS LYOTARD, born in 1924 in Versailles, died in 1998 in Paris. Until 1989, he was professor at the Université Paris VIII, Saint Denis-Vincennes. He also was professor at the University of California, Irvine; at Yale University; and at Emory University. He was the author of *Heidegger and "the jews"*; *The Hyphen: Between Judaism and Christianity*; *The Postmodern Condition*; *The Postmodern Explained*; *Postmodern Fables*; *The Differend*; *The Inhuman*; and *Lessons on the Analytic of the Sublime*.

LUC ROSENZWEIG, born in 1943 in Villeurbanne, near Lyon, was until 1991 chief of the Bonn bureau of *Le Monde*. Afterwards, he was the director of the European culture channel (Chaîne Culturelle Européenne), ARTE, in Strasbourg, and until 2001 one of the chief editors of *Le Monde*. He is the author of *La jeune France juive*; and (with Bernard Cohen) *Waldheim*. His most recent book is a book of interviews with the Israeli ambassador to France, Elie Barnavi: *La France et Israël: Une affaire passionnelle: De l'affaire Dreyfus à nos jours* (2002).

Translator's Note

Published translations of non-English works cited have been used whenever possible; other translations are my own.

I would like to thank Elisabeth Weber most warmly for her collaboration in the preparation of an English version of this book. Elisabeth Weber joins with me in dedicating *Questioning Judaism* to the memory of Andrée (Lyotard) May (1926–2003).

Rachel Bowlby

QUESTIONING JUDAISM

Introduction: The Youngest Children of the Republic

ELISABETH WEBER

Citizens

On September 27, 1791, following the Revolution, Jews in France were granted French citizenship. The Constituent Assembly thereby made them the first politically emancipated Jews in Europe; and made France, in the words of the historian Théodore Reinach, the "second homeland, moral homeland" for "any Jew of today with a memory and a heart."[1] This constitutional act of emancipation laid down the foundations of "Franco-Judaism";[2] for French Jews it represented the basis of an unshakeable confidence that they would maintain even when anti-Semitic propaganda was at its most intense. Over the course of the next hundred years, for the vast majority of Jews in France, the "second country, moral country" would come to represent the first and only country that had offered them the "chance" of "blossoming."[3]

As the political historian Pierre Birnbaum has recently shown, using previously unpublished evidence, it is no exaggeration to speak of a "cult of the Revolution" taking over from the religious cult, particularly during the Third Republic (1871–1940), a decisive period for the social and political success of French Jews. Where the cult of the Revolution did not take the place of the religious cult, it entered the synagogues. Consider just two of the many examples collected by Birnbaum: in May 1889, in the synagogue on the rue de la Victoire in the 9th arrondissement of Paris, there was a celebration to mark the centenary of emancipation. In his address, the chief rabbi of Paris, Zadoc Kahn, likened the events of 1789 to a "new social Passover" and insisted on the recognition of the "Israelites," whose "devotion to the country of France" had entirely "justified the enlightened generosity of the men of 1789."[4] The same day, the chief rabbi of Bordeaux, Isaac Lévy, recalled the fact that the French Revolution transformed Jews into citizens, paid his respects to the implacable opponent of the Second Empire and republican radical, Léon Gambetta, and "spoke the traditional prayers for the Republic and for France."[5] The centenary addresses published by Benjamin Mossé in 1890 were all enthusiastic and show that the two chief rabbis are not exceptions. For Moïse Schuhl, "the French Revolution can be thought of as the dawn of the Messianic age." According to Émile Levy, rabbi of Verdun, "by proclaiming the rights of man," the Revolution brought back to life "the immortal principles proclaimed on Sinai centuries ago." And if French Jews were asked whether they regarded France as their country and whether they thought they had a duty to defend it, "we would cry out," as Abraham Bloch writes, "unanimously: Yes, to the death!"[6]

For the emancipated Jews of France, Léon Gambetta incarnates the symbol of the "absolute" Republic; he is the "Moses of the land of the Republic."[7] For Rabbi Kahn, the Revolution represents "our exodus from Egypt," "our modern Passover." For Isaac Lévy the loss of Alsace-Lorraine evokes Israel's exile in "Babylon."[8] And even after the shock of the Dreyfus affair—after the amnesty but before the rehabilitation of the captain wrongly condemned for high treason—the deputy Raphaël Bischoffsheim declared, in 1902: "We are all children of the Revolution, faithful observers of the principles of 1789 and of God's ten commandments."[9]

Against this background of a love for the principles of the Revolution and the Republic, always reaffirmed in spite of hostilities, two hundred years of history have been played out, in the course of which the "youngest sons of France"[10] underwent persecution and betrayal under the Vichy government; and if they survived the concentration camps, labor camps, and death camps, they were often—from the fact of having been persecuted and deported *as Jews*—kept apart and forgotten, if not despised.[11] Nonetheless, the principle according to which for French Jews "the real France," as Raymond Aron puts it, is the France of the Republic and the Revolution, cannot be shaken: "A certain France had expelled me from the national community."[12] The Vichy period certainly weakened the desire for "total assimilation," but if Simone Weil is to be believed, the majority thought of Marshal Pétain as an "accident": even at Auschwitz, "we wouldn't have put up with anyone saying anything against France." Right before the departure from Drancy to Auschwitz in the spring of 1942, just as at Auschwitz on July 14, 1944, the deported sang the Marseillaise. Neither Auschwitz nor Pétain could cause French Jews to have doubts about the values of Republican France.[13]

The Routes of Emancipation

For many Jews, emancipation meant first of all the abolition of discriminatory taxes and of restrictions on the choice of where to live.[14] In 1789, the Jewish population in France was about 40,000, of whom 30,000 were part of the Ashkenazi community in Alsace-Lorraine whose first language was Yiddish. Most of them were extremely poor. The 10,000 Sephardic Jews lived mainly in Bordeaux and Bayonne and in Provence. The most visible consequence of the abolition of the discriminatory laws was geographical mobility, which increased rapidly in the nineteenth century and gave rise to new Jewish communities in cities like Lyon, Lille, and Dijon—but especially Paris. Just before the French Revolution, the Jewish population of Paris had been about 500; in 1831 the city was home to 8,000, by far the largest Jewish community in France. After the loss of Alsace-Lorraine through the Franco-Prussian War of 1870, this figure increased substantially. At this time, about two-thirds of French Jews lived in Paris. At the start of the Dreyfus affair, there were about 75,000 Jews living in France, 40,000 of them in Paris.[15] Paula Hyman gives these figures to illustrate the profound changes affecting all French Jews in the nineteenth century, and to shed some light on the ferocious anti-Semitism that broke out with the Dreyfus affair—and ran riot in the press at the time, ever more virulently. Paris was the center of the French press, and also the place of residence for many Jews who were refugees from the lost provinces in the east and immigrants from the Russian Empire: "The former often spoke French with a strong German accent;[16] the latter, with a Yiddish accent or not at all. This situation confirmed hostile observers in their belief that all Jews in France were foreigners and hence not to be trusted."[17]

In reality, a century after emancipation, the assimilation of French Jews had undoubtedly gone further than anywhere else in Europe. Since

Napoleon's reign, Jews had served in the officer corps of the army; after the 1848 revolution, during the short-lived Second Republic, Alphonse Crémieux (later the author of the "Crémieux decree" of October 24, 1870, giving Algerian Jews French citizenship) was appointed Minister of Justice, and Michel Goudchaux Minister for the Budget. For the first time in French history, Jews were occupying top-level positions in politics. Furthermore, Napoleon had introduced the hierarchically structured system of bringing together Jewish communities in consistories placed under the Central Consistory in Paris. Since 1831, the state had been paying the salaries of rabbis and cantors, "as it already did for Catholic priests and Protestant pastors."[18] Consequently until the definitive separation of church and state, in 1905, which had already been advocated by the Revolution, the rabbis were state officials who not only taught members of their communities to love their country, but also encouraged them to do so.

State Jews

For Pierre Birnbaum, what gave French Jews access to civil service careers and helped their rapid advancement in the Republic's institutions was the strength of the state and its institutions, with officials recruited on an egalitarian and meritocratic basis—in other words, based on professional merits and not background or religion. Under the Third Republic, "court Jews," oriented "more toward the world of business or banking" became, as Birnbaum puts it, "state Jews," who showed "from the beginning [that] they were truly enthusiastic about their new roles in public service." As a result, "a phenomenon almost unique for its time came about: Jews attained high government posts without converting to Catholicism and led a public existence as high officials even though, in their heart of hearts, they remained faithful to their own traditions, to one degree or another."[19] Birnbaum contrasts "strong states," whose founding principle is secularism, such as France, with "weak states," such as Britain and above all the United States, where the sphere of private life is more extended. This promotes the formation of numerous interest groups that are tolerated in the same way as the various religious faiths, but whose recognized legitimacy at the same time prevents the secularization of the area of the state.

Birnbaum regards Germany as a special case, where an extraordinarily powerful state depended on "a gigantic bureaucratic machine." In the nineteenth century this state was still "largely controlled by a military-type landed aristocracy," which was decisive in curbing the development of the bourgeoisie and of democracy. This was the "eminently reactionary framework"—without any tradition of pluralism—in which Wilhelm Marr introduced the term *anti-Semitism* into German vocabulary in 1879. "Rejected by the ruling political and administrative circles, despite final emancipation granted in 1869, held in check by an army bound to Christian values which denied Jews access to the higher ranks, and to a very large extent effectively excluded from the state itself until the birth of the Weimar Republic, German Jews were left with few options. They had the choice of converting in large numbers or trying to raise their social position outside the state structure via the business world, banking, or the liberal and intellectual professions."[20] However, Birnbaum argues, specifically political anti-Semitism, "in reaction to the recent and low-key entry of the Jews into the sphere of politico-administrative power," began only with the Weimar Republic. Unlike what happened in France, the institutions of the Weimar Republic— which was trying to "employ the criteria of egalitarian and meritocratic recruitment"—developed alongside, and in the shadow of, the old Prussian bureaucracy. The latter dominated the life of a society "homogenized in this way on a quasi-ethnic basis," and confronted by non-Christian religions, it forgot its declared neutrality toward different faiths. Moreover, the national unity of this state was at best fragile, and not, as in France, established several centuries ago. As a result, "after the defeat of 1918, a state with inadequate strength and legitimacy could not control anti-Semitic political mobilization against this 'Jewish Republic.'"[21]

It is France that seems to be the best example of a "genuinely state integration of Jews." Its institutions were open to anyone, on the egalitarian basis of competence, and independent of social, religious, or ethnic affiliations, enabling an "almost unique" identification with the state. But this is also the reason why a new, specific form of anti-Semitism arose, reaching its climax under the Vichy government—which, in a highly revealing way, abolished at a stroke "both the republican form of the state and, more specifically, its corollary, the emancipation of the Jews and their integration into this vigorously institutionalized state." French anti-Semitism, linked to a retaliatory nationalism, had been more and more forcefully expressed since the defeat of 1870 and right up to the Vichy regime. For Birnbaum, its peculiarity is to be found in the coincidence of two kinds of hostility:

"The enemies of the Republic would be equally the enemies of the Jews, whom only the Republic had been able to transform into citizens. On leaving the ghetto the French Jews entered the Republic: their fate was therefore definitively linked to that of the republican state, sharing its emancipatory ideal which guaranteed both freedom and citizenship."[22]

The Affair

Against this background, the famous Dreyfus affair, and Vichy as well, appear in a different light. Edouard Drumont was "incontestably the inventor of modern French nationalism";[23] his slogan, *La France aux Français* [France for the French][24] is still held dear by sympathizers of groups on the Far Right today. In his inflammatory *La France juive* [Jewish France] of 1886, Drumont presented the French state as a victim of both the Great Revolution and the Jews: "Through the principles of '89, adroitly exploited by the Jews, France is falling apart." Elsewhere, he designates "the Jew" as "absolute master of the society derived from 1789."[25]

The Dreyfus affair erupted in a climate of growing anti-Semitism. On October 15, 1894, Alfred Dreyfus, captain of artillery, was summonsed to the Ministry of War and accused of the crime of high treason.[26] At the end of September a handwritten letter had been discovered, the famous *bordereau* [form, list] listing five secret military documents that were to be passed on to the German embassy. Although the writing on the note could not be definitely identified as that of Dreyfus, who relentlessly maintained his innocence, and although approximations and inconsistencies dominated the enquiry from the start, on December 22 Dreyfus was sentenced, for life, to deportation to Devil's Island, in French Guyana. He was stripped of his rank in the courtyard of the École militaire on January 5, 1895, and sent to the penal colony on February 22. On April 13, he arrived on Devil's Island, whose climate is "unbearable. Tropical heat alternates with a rainy season that lasts five months. Already, under the Second Empire, hundreds of deported men had died there in wretched conditions."[27] In March 1896, Lieutenant-Colonel Picquart received in Paris a document revealing that Commander Esterhazy was a German spy. In August of the same year, Picquart was able to establish that the real author of the bordereau was Esterhazy. Two weeks later, the newspaper *L'Éclair* published a detailed article demonstrating that just before the verdict Dreyfus's judges had had available some documents that had not been brought up in the trial, so that the defense had not had access to them. Lucie Dreyfus, the wife of the condemned, then demanded an appeal, in a petition addressed to the *Assemblée nationale* [National Assembly]. In November of the same year, Bernard Lazare's book *Une erreur judiciaire: La vérité sur l'affaire Dreyfus* [A Miscarriage of Justice: The Truth about the Dreyfus Affair] was published in Brussels. Alfred's brother Mathieu filed a complaint against Esterhazy naming him as the real author of the note. The trial took place but Esterhazy was unanimously acquitted on January 11, 1898, by a military tribunal with seven members. On January 13, *L'Aurore*, whose editor was Georges Clemenceau, published Émile Zola's famous letter addressed to the president of the Republic: "J'accuse."[28] The "cry of my soul" on the part of the most widely read living author in France at the time, printed in three hundred thousand copies, was sold out within a few hours. The Dreyfus court case took on the dimensions of a public scandal, impossible to contain. Conflicts broke out in Parliament, in the press, between friends, in families, in the street. The first anti-Semitic riots took place in towns outside Paris in France and Algeria. Clemenceau and Drumont fought a duel on February 28; on March 4, so did Lieutenant-Commander Picquart and Commander Henry—who, later on, was convicted of perjury and falsifying documents, and committed suicide. In the space of one year (from June 1898 to June 1899), the affair brought down two governments. The anti-Semitic press threw all restraint overboard. On June 11, 1899, a hundred thousand Dreyfus supporters participated in a demonstration organized at Longchamp. A review of the judgement became inevitable. Dreyfus was brought back to France in June 1899 for a new trial that took place at Rennes. On September 9 Dreyfus was declared guilty and sentenced to ten years' detention. On the 19th, he was granted a pardon as part of a general amnesty. Yet he continued to pursue what he called "reparation of the fearful judicial error of which [he was] still the victim."[29] It was only in July 1906 that, after another trial, Dreyfus was fully rehabilitated. In the courtyard of the École militaire—the scene of his dishonorable discharge—he was made knight of the Légion d'Honneur, at the rank of major.

In reality—as Dreyfus's lawyer states in his 1906 defense—this affair, which brought France to the brink of civil war, was not the trial of a person but the trial of a Jewish officer, the application of an anti-Semitic set of beliefs to a judicial case. All the irregularities of the investigation, "all the betrayals, all the crimes against the accused, are simply the result of anti-Semitic ideas, whose unshakable basis is the necessarily treacherous character of the Jews."[30] This conviction was a product of the deep roots of Catholic anti-Semitism, as is shown by caricatures, drawings, and articles of the time that give Dreyfus the surname Judas.[31] For Charles Péguy, the Dreyfus affair was the "last somersault, the death-throes" of republican "heroism," of "republican mysticism." In *Notre Jeunesse* [Our Youth], he describes himself and republican Dreyfus supporters as "fossils, witnesses, survivors of those historical eras" when "republicans were heroic and the Republic had its hands clean."[32] Since then, the memory of the Dreyfus affair has not dimmed in the recollection of French Jews nor in that of French intellectuals. Indeed, the very word "intellectual" acquired a new sense during the affair, because it was taken up positively by those to whom it had been addressed as an insult—a point made by Maurice Blanchot, in 1984: "For the first time, the demand that a rigged trial be reviewed gave rise to an 'Intellectuals' Manifesto,'" with intellectuals defending not only a just cause, but "their Cause: what justified their writing, knowledge, and thinking."[33]

Another Republic?

The rise of Nazism, the collapse of 1940, and the occupation of France were to offer the heirs of the enemies of the Republic that "divine surprise" that gave them the victory they would never have been able to imagine without the decisive contribution of the troops of the Third Reich. As far back as the final decades of the nineteenth century, they had been constantly denouncing republican values as Jewish. And this shameful tradition was not broken with the end of the Vichy regime: before Vichy, it was Léon Blum, leader of the Popular Front government, who for French anti-Semites embodied the unity of the Republic and Judaism; after Vichy, it would be Pierre Mendès France—also a relentless advocate of decolonization—who became the new symbol of the hated alliance between republican ideals and the "Jewish spirit." When these men were in power, "there emerged a vast mobilization of anti-Semitic opinion, which explicitly attacked the 'Jewish Republic'."[34]

At a single stroke, the Vichy government abolished the republican state and Jewish civil rights. In the summer and fall of 1940, it passed a first series of laws against Jewish residents in France. The "Statute on the Jews," passed on October 3, 1940, is in fact unconstitutional. "It assigned, on the basis of race, an inferior position in French civil law and society to a whole segment of French citizens and to non-citizens and foreigners living on French soil."[35] The first article of the law passed that day defined whom the French authorities deemed Jewish;[36] the following articles listed the professional activities now forbidden to Jews: all senior positions in the public services and the army (down to sub-officer) and all teaching professions. They were also refused access to the press, the radio, the cinema, and the theater, and a "quota system" was set up for the liberal professions. The day after, October 4, 1940, Marshal Pétain signed the law on "foreign nationals of Jewish race" authorizing the prefects of each regional department to imprison them in "special camps" or allot them a "compulsory place of residence"—for instance in remote villages. October 7, 1940 saw the abolition of the Crémieux decree, which had granted French nationality to Algerian Jews in 1870. Of course there is no comparison between the Nazis' persecution of the Jews that culminated in the cremations of Auschwitz and the persecution practiced by the Vichy collaborators. Nonetheless, some figures in this regime, such as Raphaël Alibert, the minister of justice, were zealous beyond the terrible demands of the occupier. In their book *Vichy France and the Jews*, the historians Michael Marrus and Robert Paxton have demonstrated this independant responsibility of Vichy.[37]

On June 2, 1941, a second "Statute on the Jews" was promulgated. The texts of these two pieces of legislation are enough on their own to symbolize "the end of the State of Gambetta and Jules Ferry, of Clemenceau and Waldeck-Rousseau."[38] Pierre Mendès France was one of numerous deputies who lost not only their parliamentary seats but also their French nationality.[39] "The coming of the Vichy regime was experienced by Jewish nationals [and not only by them] as a real betrayal of revolutionary ideals" and in their eyes resuscitated the Ancien Régime,[40] and the anti-Semitic laws and the internments and deportations that followed it represented a real betrayal by the state in relation to Jews.[41]

Six of the authors who have made this book possible lived through the days from October 3 to October 7, 1940; Luc Rosenzweig, who was born in 1943, was directly affected by the consequences of this legislation.

Of the 270,000 Jews living in France in 1939, 75,000 were deported. Only 5,000 of these survived. When they returned, they ran up against a wall of incomprehension. One hundred and seven survivor narratives were published between 1945 and 1947 by leading publishers, but none of them made any impact on the public, as Annette Wieviorka demonstrates in an important study—the press hardly did more than mention the publication of this or that book.[42] When General de Gaulle had fifteen corpses brought together around the flame of the Unknown Soldier for a national funeral on November 11, 1945, none among them was a deportee who had died because they were Jewish. "The head of government needs 'champions' who galvanize a country wiped out by defeat, collaboration, economic poverty. Members of the Resistance fit the bill, not the deported. The testimony of theater writer Jean-Claude Grumberg illustrates this: 'As a child I suffered from being the son of a deported man among the children of heroes, the sons of those who had been shot.'" Without ever admitting it openly, France "despised" deported Jews.[43] Simone Weil experienced this herself. Out of the six members of her family, she and her sister Milou were Auschwitz survivors. Her second sister, Denise, returned from the Ravensbrück camp where she had been deported as a member of the Resistance. Simone Weil tells the story: "When I came back to Nice, with Denise, she was invited everywhere. Not me. People wanted to hear the glorious and heroic stories of the Resistance. Auschwitz was of no interest to them." And she finishes with this bitter statement: "For them [members of the Resistance], we were nothing, except perhaps victims condemned to silence."[44]

Suddenly, then, the "equality" of all French people seemed to have been newly reestablished: the specifically Jewish martyr was forgotten as much by the republican leaders like Charles de Gaulle as by communists like the leader of the PCF [French Communist Party], Maurice Thorez, and the Jewish Resistance member Annie Kriegel, who held a senior position in the student communist organization after the war.[45] "Jews came back to France as though they had never been driven out of it," writes Raymond Aron[46]—to be more precise, as though they had never been handed over to the National Socialists by the police and the French government.

Until 1973, in fact, official historiography deemed the National Socialist state to be solely responsible for the deportation of French Jews. That was the year that the French translation of the American historian Robert Paxton's *Vichy France* was published.[47] Paxton's book showed to what extent the French authorities were independent of the National Socialists and how much their politics was guided by a concern for occupying a decisive role in a future National Socialist Europe. "When the Germans extended the final solution to France, in the summer of 1942, the Vichy government did something unprecedented and exceptional in World War II Europe: it handed over Jews for whom it had sole responsibility, in the unoccupied zone."[48]

This painful aspect of French history was also awakened by a debate that began a month before the fiftieth anniversary of the Vél d'Hiv Raid and continued acrimoniously for several months. On July 16, 1942, on government orders, the French police arrested 12,884 Jews and imprisoned them in the Vélodrome d'Hiver [Winter Cycle Stadium], in the 15th arrondissement in Paris. From there, 3,031 men, 5,802 women, and 4,051 children were transported to French camps, including Drancy and Pithiviers, before being handed over to the Germans. In the month of June, 1992, the Vél d'Hiv 1942 Committee, with the support of over two hundred well-known figures, made an appeal to François Mitterrand. The committee demanded that the responsibility of the "French Vichy State in the persecutions and crimes committed against French Jews" be officially acknowledged and proclaimed by the president of the Republic. The appeal stressed that "the French Jews deported and assassinated in the Nazi camps usually appear as victims only of the barbarity of the German occupier, even when they were pursued, raided, and handed over by the French state because they were Jewish."[49] The signatories included Pierre Boulez, Cornelius Castoriadis, Régis Debray, Jacques Derrida, Gisèle Halimi, Michel Piccoli, Marthe Robert, Nathalie Sarraute, Jean-Pierre Vernant, and Pierre Vidal-Naquet. The committee hoped that the appeal would receive a response at the time of the ceremony marking the fiftieth anniversary of the raid, in which François Mitterrand was to participate. Anna Sénik, a researcher at the CNRS [National Research Center], justified her signing in these words: "We had been excluded, which is to say summoned to death, and I have never been able to speak about it. For the silence about Vichy condemns us to the position of victims while preventing us from naming those who drove us toward death." For the writer Viviane Forestier, the significance of the appeal lay in its defining "the persecutions of Vichy as more a French question than a Jewish question. I signed as a French woman, not as a victim, even if that puts me in a complicated situation. I am also asking one part of myself to make its apologies to the other part." The philosopher Élisabeth de Fontenay's description of the commemorative plaque at Drancy summarized a version of history dating back fifty years: this plaque "speaks of the Nazis' victims—although the camp was guarded by French policemen—for Jews who had been raided by the French police." Pierre Le Dantec associated the appeal with the "necessity of renewing the gesture of 1789. . . . An initiative like the one we are asking for will really re-found the Republic."[50] During July, several thousand signatures were collected for the appeal.

François Mitterrand's first reaction to the appeal was to refuse: the French Republic should not be asked to account for crimes committed by a regime that had nothing to do with it. "1940 was the Vichy regime, it was not the Republic." "[T]he Resistance, de Gaulle's government, and then the Fourth Republic were founded on the basis of a refusal" of this regime.[51] However, this response ignored the fact that the "French State" was legitimated by a republican ballot on July 10, 1940, when approximately four hundred and twenty out of five hundred deputies of the National Assembly granted full powers to the "government of the Republic under the authority and signature of Field Marshal Pétain."[52] From a constitutional point of view, the Vichy regime was always a republic. The debate turned bitter when, on November 11, 1992—the anniversary of the 1918 Armistice—in the course of a ceremony he had inaugurated in 1987, François Mitterrand had wreaths laid on the tombs of the French field marshals of World War I, and among those honored there also figured—as happened every year— Field Marshal Pétain, commander of the Battle of Verdun. In the face of the indignation aroused by this gesture, the head of state declared in an interview broadcast by Radio J: "The glory of Verdun, a glory paid for with a great deal of blood and tragedy . . . cannot be forgotten . . . but the shame of 1942 cannot be forgotten either. Here is a fundamental contradiction. I have to manage it."[53] On February 3, 1993, finally, Mitterrand signed an order making July 16 the "national day for the commemoration of the racist and anti-Semitic persecutions committed between 1940 and 1944 under the de facto [thus not legal] authority referred to as the 'government of the French State.'"[54]

Newly elected president Jacques Chirac, on the occasion of the commemoration of the Vél d'Hiv Raid on July 16, 1995, acknowledged the responsibility of the French state in these terms: "The criminal madness of the occupier was seconded by some French people, by the French State. . . . On that day, France was accomplishing something irreparable. . . . In regard [to the deported French Jews] we still have a debt that can never be removed." If François Mitterrand's refusal, which formed part of a tradition going back to 1945, had provoked a lively polemic, the vast majority of reactions to Chirac's initiative, while it did spark a controversy, were favorable, both in France and abroad. The historian Henry Rousso emphasizes the way that this speech, after having acknowledged the "collective fault" and the nation's responsibility, immediately reminds its audience of the existence of an "'other' France" which was "in the Libyan sands and everywhere free Frenchmen were fighting . . . , in London, personified by General de Gaulle . . . present, one and indivisible, in the hearts of the French. In the darkest hours of the torment, as Serge Klarsfeld writes, these 'just ones among the nations' who risked their lives to save three quarters of the Jewish community living in France, gave life to what is best about that country."[55]

Sephardim in Algeria

If, to use the deputy Ferdinand Dreyfus's phrase, already quoted, French Jews are "France's youngest sons," then Sephardic Algerian Jews and the Jews in the old protectorates of Tunisia and Morocco who emigrated to France in the 1960s after their countries became independent, could be thought of as their youngest brothers and sisters. *S'pharad* means Spain in Hebrew. So the Sephardim are the descendants of the Jews expelled from the Iberian peninsula between 1492 and 1497, who settled in the countries of North Africa, in the Near East (Egypt, Palestine, Turkey), in Italy, and also, in the sixteenth and seventeenth centuries, in Holland, England, and France.[56] A broader definition also includes as Sephardic all those who follow the Sephardic ritual, which differs in certain important respects from the Ashkenazi ritual (Ashkenazi is the original Hebrew word for the German cultural sphere).[57] (A reminder that there are two chief rabbis in Israel; one presides over the Sephardic community, the other over the Ashkenazi community.)

In 1830, the French army conquered Algeria. According to André Chouraqui, the travelers' tales of the years leading up to this are unanimous: the situation of Jews under Islamic feudalism was even more pitiful than that of its Arab subjects.[58] Legislation passed by the *Dhimma*, which had governed the status of Christians and Jews in Muslim countries since the ninth century, required Jews to wear distinguishing signs—the yellow turban and the distinctive badge, and to avoid bright colors for their clothes; they were also prohibited from marrying Muslim women and competing with Muslim men: "For instance they are forbidden to mount horses or to build places of worship higher than those of the Muslims."[59] But the oppression and daily humiliations that they suffered were even worse. As a result, the occupation by French troops was welcomed enthusiastically, since it brought them freedom. The Act of Capitulation of July 5, 1830 stipulated "that 'The liberty of the inhabitants of all classes, their religions, their properties, their trade, their industry, will not be violated; their women will be respected. The commander-in-chief assumes this obligation on his honour.'"[60] The traditional hierarchy between Muslims and Jews was abolished; the Act of Surrender constituted "the juridical basis of the equality that had been obtained."[61] However, the arrival of the French was the start of a drama for the Jewish population that was to culminate in the end of Algerian Judaism. The day of the conquest did indeed offer freedom to Algerian Jews, but it also pushed them into the dilemma of "double allegiance": "In the underlying confrontation there was France on one side, with its culture, its social, political, and economic structures, its Christian religion, and Islam on the other, with its traditions, its political, economic, and sociological universe. Battle of cultures, war of religion, conflict of interests that had all begun long before it seemed. In this underlying conflict, Jews were not spectators, far from it, but put in an extremely inconvenient position, at any rate one that had no precedent. In their origins, their past, their language, their way of life, and their habits of thinking, they belonged to the colonized milieu, but without identifying themselves with it. And so, being colonized like Arabs and Muslims, at the end of the day they were bound to find advantages in the French colonial enterprise."[62]

After the arrival of the French, Jewish communities expanded culturally and economically. About ten years after the Crémieux decree, Algerian Jews began to prefer French to Arab as a language, at least for their children's education, and to dress in European clothes.[63] This development was furthered by the Universal Israelite Alliance founded in Paris in 1860. The chief objectives of this political organization were "to work everywhere for the emancipation and the moral development of the Israelites," to support those who "suffer because of their being Israelite," and finally "to encourage all publications likely to bring about these results."[64] When the Crémieux decree granted French citizenship to some thirty thousand Jews, they represented to the French "a richer element, one that was more cultivated and more assimilable than the Arab element,"[65] even if, despite their advanced assimilation to French things, they were much closer to the Arab population than to the colonizers.[66] From this point onwards, the fate of the Jews was linked to the colonizers, which increased the distances separating them from their Arab neighbors and stimulated anti-Semitic feelings.[67] However, the most violent anti-Semitic attacks came from the French colonizers, and the Dreyfus affair provided the awaited pretext. In 1898, there were pogroms in the major Algerian cities. Almost thirty years after it had been passed, French Algerians protested against the Crémieux decree.[68]

This decree was abolished in 1940, in line with the Vichy regime's anti-Jewish laws. All Jewish children (among them Jacques Derrida), all teachers and Jewish functionaries, were excluded from state schools and institutions. In 1942, after the disembarcation of American troops, when General Giraud restored French Republican law in Algeria, he annulled all the measures passed by Pétain, except for the abolition of the Crémieux decree. It was only General de Gaulle who restored to Algerian Jews their rights as French citizens, on October 20, 1943.[69]

On November 1, 1954, when the murder of a French elementary school teacher and a Franco-Arab captain triggered the Algerian War,[70] there were about a hundred and fifty thousand Jews living in Algeria—in other words a fifth of the non-Muslim population.[71] In 1956, the Front de Libération National [National Liberation Front] (FLN) appealed to Algerian Jews to "condemn outright the dying French colonial regime and to proclaim their choice of Algerian nationality."[72] The Front expressed the feelings of many Jews when its leaders declared to them in 1959: "You are an integral part of the Algerian people: for you it is not a question of making a choice between France and Algeria, but of becoming actual citizens of *your real country*."[73] But the situation was more complicated. Since the founding of the State of Israel, there had been a tense relationship between Jews and Arabs; in 1948, there had been anti-Semitic rioting in some North African cities.[74] While there were Jews fighting on the side of the pro-independence nationalists as well as on the French side, "the vast majority of the community remained as though petrified by the unresolvable conflict it was going through and sensed, more or less vaguely, that it would die of it in the end."[75] In the month of December 1960, the main synagogue in Algiers was vandalized, and the scrolls of Scripture destroyed. In Oran, the Jewish cemetery was desecrated. By the time of the declaration of the sovereign Algerian Republic, on July 3, 1962, the majority of Jews had left the country, leaving almost all their belongings behind them.[76] Between a hundred and twenty and a hundred and thirty thousand French Algerian Jews arrived in France during 1962, as well as ten to fifteen thousand Tunisian Jews.[77] French Judaism, which had been mainly Ashkenazic up to then, underwent a fundamental change.

Witnessing

It was important to go back over these major stages in the history of French Jews, so as to bring out better against their background the specific historical imprints of the interviews in this volume. These are "micrological," to use the language of Theodor W. Adorno. The interviews do not seek to "represent" French Judaism; and the participants are not "representative" of a community that, in any case, has no single and homogeneous existence. On the contrary, the project of this collection can be traced to the multiple possibilities and multiple ways of reflecting on the Jewish tradition, on the relations between Jews and non-Jews, and on the very fact of being Jewish. All the same, the choice of interlocutors cannot hide editorial predilections and subjective interests, nor is it meant to; but these are not its only source. Responses, whether affirmative or missing, to the invitation to have a voice in this book, have also shaped it.

However, the question of representation emerges in a much more demanding and fundamental sense, which puts in doubt the very possibility of representativeness. Whether we understand "representation" by relating it to the imagination, to the mind's faculty of representing something to itself, or else by relating it to presentation, to making visible, to "showing," this question kept on returning in the course of the interviews. Using their own particular approaches, the interlocutors of this collection debate the very possibility of remembering, of imagining, of representing. And if this possibility is the angel of history, the writings of the witnesses who speak here (for they are all witnesses) admit that the fight with this angel has left them limping, but without guaranteeing them the blessing that Jacob, at the dawn of day, was able to obtain in exchange for his wound. The period that has profoundly marked this fight saw not only innumerable massacres and catastrophes, which there is no question of relativizing, but also the murder of five million European Jews for the sole reason that they were

Jewish. If the program of what was called the "Final Solution" had as its aim the extinction of the Jews and of all traces that could keep the memory of them, it was also seeking to abolish the "witnesses of witnessing"—a name that, for Jean-François Lyotard, could be given to the Jews, since witnessing always means bearing witness to the other, witnessing always means humility before another—and even the traces of these witnesses. The architecture and the economy of the writings of those who speak here are marked from the beginning to the end by cracks where remains accumulate that cannot be assimilated by the sovereignty of logic, dialectic, reason, or even of the work of mourning—or the work of negativity, for Hegel the cause of progress in the development of the mind. These are remains that, in their excessiveness, slip away from representation, from presentation, and even challenge remembering. And this is precisely why they have never ceased to demand testimony.

History, philosophy, literature, and art all find themselves affected by this demand. In Jacques Derrida's texts, the obsession with following remains, what is excluded from the system, finds an echo in the way that the reflections of a historian like Pierre Vidal-Naquet speak for the silent witnesses of history. Claude Lanzmann's film *Shoah* gave a first cinematographic expression to something that has also had a deep influence on the approaches of every contributor to this collection: in order to bear witness, what is necessary is not only the exact narratives of victims, eye-witnesses, historians, and, as in Lanzmann's film, the executioners themselves, but also the testimony carried from that place—impossible to inhabit—at the intersection of the "intransmissible" and the "impossibility of telling this story."[78] Writing and thinking have to be situated around this point of deafness or silence, around this blind spot, this incandescent place. And this is not so as to secure the healing of this painful spot, restoring it to itself, but to multiply, in the work, in the writing, the critical moments where the continuity of reading, life, and forgetting is suddenly interrupted before a word or before a sentence, as before "a burning tomb in the middle of the grass" (Derrida). If there is anything "in common" among the seven very different contemporaries who offer their thoughts in the course of these interviews, perhaps that might be recognizable before this burning place: for them all, it is about testifying to the impossibility of its representation.

Hostages

In Emmanuel Levinas's important work, *Otherwise than Being or Beyond Essence*,[79] which opens with two dedications to the victims of National Socialism, "responsibility" is defined in terms that are no longer concepts in the traditional sense of the word: "persecution," the "condition of being hostage," and "trauma." Responsibility, or the response given to the appeal of the other, which cannot be represented, only escapes the domination of consciousness—in other words the supremacy of the self's interests—as traumatic responsibility. It is because it inflicts a trauma that the appeal of the other is unrepresentable. What the interviews in this book have in "common" might be expressed in Jean-François Lyotard's formulation that to be Jewish means to be hostage to the unrepresentable: hostage or witness. To be hostage or witness to this unrepresentable is to have been exposed to an appeal which the understanding that is given over to the present cannot reclaim for itself. For the present is the eternal temporality of philosophical judgment, a judgment that operates through categories identifying alterity with sameness. At the heart of the eternity of this present, the possibility of trauma, of the irrecuperable shaking up of the sovereign serenity of consciousness, cannot even be envisaged. But contemporary paths in philosophy no longer seek the realms of this kind of eternity of presence. Shot through with history, its grief and its catastrophes, shot through with psychoanalytic ways of knowing and political experiences, philosophical reflection is no longer unaware of its sites of powerlessness, its interruptions, and its silences. Of course, it is inevitable that philosophical discourse, but also every other form of discourse, as Derrida put it on one occasion, "has to 'deal,' so to speak, with traumatism. At the same time discourse repeats it—when one repeats a traumatism, Freud teaches us, one is trying to get control of it—it repeats it as such, without letting itself be annihilated by the traumatism, while keeping speech 'alive,' without forgetting the traumatism totally and without letting itself be totally annihilated by it. It is between these two perils that philosophical experience advances."[80] Nonetheless, if, as Levinas has it, persecution may be characterized as "the precise moment in which the subject is reached or touched without the mediation of the *logos*," or as that which "breaks off every justification, every apology, every *logos*,"[81] then that "obsessive meditation" that is writing tries to approach this breaking off, tries to bear witness to it—and so in the last analysis goes back to "meditat[ing] constantly on what renders unreadable or what is rendered unreadable." Pursuing indefatigably the trace of the unreadable, writing's meditation becomes a meditation on the "absolute weakness" of the victim.[82]

Suspecting and Betraying Dogmas

The debate that started in relation to the revisionists, such as Robert Faurisson and Henri Roques,[83] shows that efforts to render history unreadable still have to be counteracted. If the pathetic desire to render an event unreadable can eat up months and entire years of a history that has taken place, and for whose memory new words must always be found, then it is not enough to denounce the political and ideological motives of such an enterprise. Faced with the danger that future generations might see the revisionist negation of the Shoah as one thesis among others, writing, representation, and memory are required to question themselves about their inner paradoxes. Pierre Vidal-Naquet emphasizes that it was only after the mass distribution of the film *Holocaust* that revisionism definitively took off. Which then means that forms of remembering exist that are capable of engendering an even more harmful forgetting than the kind that comes from time passing and the death of witnesses.

However, the memory selected by the authorities in power and celebrated for their own purposes also leads to a relativization, a wearing away, and even a misuse of what happened, and so condemns it to a systematic forgetting. So the historian has to follow routes which can seem paradoxical and which, as Vidal-Naquet puts it, are those of a "traitor." "The historian, free man par excellence, is not to be divided. Even at the sharpest point of a polemic, he can only remain a historian, meaning a traitor, in the face of all the dogmas—theological, ideological, and even would-be scientific. Which goes against his own prejudices that form part of his baggage as well as against the more visible prejudices of others."[84] Fidelity to what is unreadable and what risks being rendered unreadable, fidelity to what is unrepresentable and to what has been distorted for ideological, political, or religious purposes, is only possible through the "betrayal" of the current dogmas.

In some cases, not only are the dogmas articulated in widespread doctrines or commonplace articles of faith, but they hide behind words whose usage seems to be obvious. Thus Léon Poliakov, at the start of the

German translation of his *Histoire de l'antisémitisme* [History of Anti-Semitism], draws the reader's attention to the problematic aspects of the concept of *anti-Semitism:*

As is proven by today's discussions and publications, scientific as well as non-scientific, a great deal of semantic caution must be shown when one is speaking of a "history of anti-Semitism," and even, as in my case, when one writes one: for the expression *anti-Semitism* was only coined in the last quarter of the nineteenth century and designated hostility toward a certain "race" of human beings who, it was constantly being claimed, were endowed with utterly sinister spiritual and moral characteristics. This concept of "race" dates from a relatively recent time: it was unknown to the detractors of Judaism during Antiquity and the Middle Ages, in the same way that our grandchildren, probably, will have ceased either to be familiar with or to utilize this kind of idea of "race" . . . [85]

But because of the international use of this term to mean "all kinds of anti-Judaism from every period," it was inevitable, for this author, that it should be taken up again. Even if nowadays, as Poliakov again stresses, the term *Semitic* is used only to designate a linguistic family, it is appropriate to remain wary in relation to a word that has harbored one of the fundamental dogmas of the largest destructive machine known in history, according to which "there are races." Yet this dogma only existed in close association with another one, that of the hierarchy of the races. This is why Poliakov also questions the concept of *racism*: "For it seems, because of its semantic connotations, to contribute to the perpetuation of the situation it denounces as well as to that of the injustices that it condemns."[86] Nationalisms are reappearing today, especially in the states freed from communist dictatorship, but also in western democracies, including the German Federal Republic and France, as proved by numerous indicators—not the least of which is the attraction to parties of the extreme right. In this situation, it is urgent that concepts like *anti-Semitism* and *racism* be subjected to an intransigent critique, even if, up till now, we have not had any satisfactory terms available to substitute for them.

Breaks

Pierre Vidal-Naquet makes the idea of *betrayal* emblematic; and through it another question emerges, which is a particular issue for modern Jewish historians. This finds its anchor in what the American historian Yosef

Hayim Yerushalmi has called "a recognition of the chasm that separates modern Jewish historiography from all the ways in which Jews once concerned themselves with their past." But in order for this recognition to be possible, "the modern Jewish historian must first understand the degree to which he himself is a product of rupture."[87] For as Yerushalmi says, "only in the modern era do we really find, for the first time, a Jewish historiography divorced from Jewish collective memory and, in crucial respects, thoroughly at odds with it," because "nothing has replaced the coherence and meaning with which a powerful messianic faith once imbued both Jewish past and future."[88] While this rupture can be glimpsed on numerous occasions in the interviews collected here, it also opens the space for a political reflection expressing, for Luc Rosenzweig for instance, an obligation to the Jewish tradition. Rita Thalmann grants a preeminent role to the political dimension of a feminist historiography. An alliance of this kind—between political reflection and feminist perspectives—remains faithful to one of the traditions, probably the most "hidden" one,[89] of modern Judaism, namely that of the political commitment of Jewish women who were persecuted as Jews while fighting for their equal rights as women. When Rita Thalmann describes "the wall of silence and anonymity" surrounding the women combatants of the Resistance in general, and the Jewish Resistance in particular; when she refutes the widespread prejudice that has it that women's role in the Resistance was limited to auxiliary functions and assistance, with male comrades "providing what is conventionally called 'active resistance,'"[90] it becomes clear that, after the break with religious tradition and after the entry into political struggle, the barriers raised on the road to real emancipation were far from being all surmounted for Jewish women. Here too, dogmas still hold sway today, made of prejudices and ignorance, transformed into dogmatic silence and forgetting. Women historians like Rita Thalmann have begun the task of dismantling them.

In a television broadcast on June 11, 1991, entitled "Être juif" [Being Jewish/Jewish Being], during a discussion that was largely about religious questions, the historian Lily Scherr stressed that Judaism is based on an ethics of openness and universality. "When you have a law . . . raising respect for the other to such a height that even God cannot forgive an act of aggression toward the other, then none of us has the right to condemn those who take other routes [than the religious one]. . . . We still speak of the revolt of the Warsaw Ghetto. The man who defended the honor of the Jews of the Warsaw Ghetto, Mordechai Anielevicz, was a Marxist atheist. And for me, he was the one carrying the Torah."[91] Mordechai Anielevicz, commander of the Jewish combat organization during the revolt of the Warsaw Ghetto, was twenty-four when he was shot, on May 8, 1943. Rita Thalmann reminds us that in the fight against the National Socialist enemy, there were women, often very young, who risked and often lost their lives; in this fight they were the ones who carried the Torah.

Fidelities

Pierre Vidal-Naquet characterizes his work as turning on "*moments* of condensation and rupture" in the history of the Jewish people, and it is "moments of condensation and rupture" like "emancipation, assimilation, destruction, the nationalist breakthrough, the confrontation with Palestinian nationalism" also represent points of crystallization in these interviews. However, there is another rule that should be mentioned: "No moment in this history" can "be interpreted through a consideration of its Jewish aspect alone."[92] Questions concerning Judaism and Jewish tradition and history always concern other traditions as well. Thus Rita Thalmann is also opposed to a "ghetto history," be this Jewish or feminist. At any rate, a "ghetto history," like any "ghetto thinking," would compromise fidelity to an indeterminable and indeterminate other, a fidelity in a way comparable to the stubbornness which, for Jean-François Lyotard, characterizes the "soul" insofar as it is haunted or "inhabited by something to which no response is ever given." Inhabited or haunted in this way, it is "led in its undertakings by an arrogant fidelity to this unknown guest to which it feels it is hostage."[93] The oeuvres and the routes of thought whose traces this collection pursues often break with tradition: they are deployed in what can be considered the margins of this tradition. "Don't forget you are the kernel of a break," a sentence reads in *The Book of Questions* by the poet Edmond Jabès. Not to forget this is not to forget *tout court*. It is to obey the commandment: *Zakhor*,[94] "Remember," of which the Bible is always reminding the people of Israel, even if the content of this memory no longer coincides with that of tradition. In the postscript to the 1989 English edition of his book, entitled, "Reflections on Forgetting," Yerushalmi tells how, in May 1987, his friend Pierre Birnbaum had sent him a page from *Le Monde* that had a survey on the question of whether or not Klaus Barbie should be tried.[95] "The central question was as follows: 'Which of the following two words, *forgetting* or *justice*, better expresses your attitude to the events of this period of the war and the Occupation?'"[96] This is Yerushalmi's comment: "Could it be that the journalists had hit upon something more important than they realized? Is it possible that the antonym of forgetting is not memory but justice?"[97]

"It is well known that Jews normally reply to a question with another question."[98] The interviews collected here multiply the questions instead of delivering replies. This book marks a route across multiple ways of thinking whose complex architecture each time remains faithful to the Jewish custom that says that anyone building a house should leave a corner unfinished, with no paint or coating. Elsewhere, the meaning of this custom comes down to keeping alive the memory of the destroyed Temple. Here, in the writings of the philosophers, historians, and journalists who have contributed to this collection, it could take on the meaning of a methodical renunciation of totality, an openness that does not fear being without shelter, a humility that has learned to do battle.

Acknowledgments

The interviews collected here took place between March and December, 1991. My warm thanks go first of all to my interlocutors, whose patience and generosity made it possible to bring this book to completion.

I would like to take this opportunity of thanking Emmanuel Brassat and Joseph Vogl whose friendship accompanied the project, adding other, invisible conversations to the ones collected in this volume. Without the dedicated help and unwavering friendship of Isabelle Châtelet, this book would not have come into existence. I am deeply indebted to her.

Note for the 1996 French Edition

This book first appeared in German translation from French in 1994, published in Frankfurt by Jüdischer Verlag, for a German readership. Clarifications in relation to the preface, to particular notes, or to references to current events have been added, without fundamentally altering the original text. (This procedure was also followed for the English translation.—Tr.)

Since 1991 many events have happened in the Jewish world, in France and elsewhere, and have radically changed it. It is not possible to list them here, but readers are asked not to be surprised that the interviews make no mention either of the agreement between Israel and the Palestinians, who voted for the first time in January 1996 in relation to the autonomy of the Gaza Strip and the West Bank, or of the assassination, on November 4, 1995, of Itzhak Rabin, one of the principal artisans of this peace that had seemed so unlikely only a few years before.

On December 25, 1995, the death of Emmanuel Levinas in Paris, at the age of ninety, deprived those to whom he had given his hospitality, his generosity, his wisdom, and his humor of a shining presence. The person conducting the interviews in this collection was fortunate to experience the pleasure of exchanges with him for almost ten years. As Jacques Derrida wrote in the "Adieu" he addressed to him, Emmanuel Levinas disrupted the "landscape without landscape of thought; he did so in a dignified way, without polemic, at once from within, faithfully, and from very far away, from the attestation of a completely other place. And I believe that what occurred there . . . is a discreet but irreversible mutation, one of those powerful, singular, and rare provocations in history that, for over two thousand years now, will have ineffaceably marked the space and body of what is more or less, something else at any rate, than a simple dialogue between Jewish thought and its others, the philosophies of Greek origin or, in the tradition of a certain 'Here I am,' the other Abrahamic monotheisms. This happened, this mutation happened, *through him*, through Emmanuel Levinas, who was conscious of this immense responsibility in a way that was, I believe, at once clear, confident, calm, and modest, like that of a prophet."[99]

This collection tries to be attentive to both the obvious signs and the subtle traces of this "mutation," to be listening for this disruption and to be faithful to it.

January 1996

Note for the 2004 English Edition

On April 21, 1998, Jean-François Lyotard died at the age of seventy-three. The thinker of irreconcilable differends communicated to his students and interlocutors an indelible joy, a lightness that never mitigated the *address* of his thought—the call it always addressed not to a third person, or a neutral agency, but to *me*. The sheer joy of thinking does not, in this philosopher's oeuvre, contradict or expel melancholy—the former is, rather, the secret messenger of the latter. In its joy and lightness, Jean-François Lyotard's thought is testimony to a secret messenger who has taken us hostage and to respond to whom is still our debt. His thought has left its traces on this collection in more ways than through the presence of the conversation with him.

I wish to thank Rachel Bowlby for her careful translation and her patience with this book.

I also wish to thank my research assistant, William Robert, for his invaluable help in preparing the manuscript for the English edition.

Elisabeth Weber
Santa Barbara, California
November 2003

1

Against the Murderers of Memory

PIERRE VIDAL-NAQUET

ELISABETH WEBER: You are a historian who specializes in the history of ancient Greece, but you work on plenty of other subjects, and always with great commitment. So much so that this saying of Henri-Irénée Marrou's could apply to you: "Historical work is not the evocation of a dead past, but a living experience in which historians engage the vocations of their own destinies."[1] Your numerous writings on the Algerian War and torture, on the student commune of May 1968,[2] on the debate about revisionism, and other subjects to do with the past and the present—all these amply prove that your work as a historian is inseparable from your destiny.

This work as a historian is constantly accompanied by a meditation on memory. In the preface to your book *Les Crimes de l'armée française* [The Crimes of the French Army], you describe memory as a highly socialized phenomenon, deeply bound up with the culture of a period or society, and therefore like a given that is in no way "natural," in no way a matter of course. The "social function of historical work" is to "supply frameworks and points of reference for collective memory." On the other hand, you claim that "our society, the classes and groups that control it, function exactly the other way around. Everything, from television to handbooks to advertising, is designed to stop us from remembering, to prevent memory from being transmitted, to install forgetting—selective forgetting, of course."[3] Does this mean that the historian's work can only be done *against* the wheels and the mechanisms of the society we live in?

PIERRE VIDAL-NAQUET: Yes, I do tend to think that the historian is a traitor par excellence. I wrote a piece called "The Right Way to Use Treason,"[4] and the right way to use treason is by writing history. Why traitor? Because history is in an awkward position in relation to all doctrines, ideologies, and previous standpoints. It is also, in one way, in an awkward position in relation to memory. You quoted a text which I don't in any way repudiate, but I've written others since in which I stress two things that slightly contradict each other. And this is the main object of the second volume of my book *Les Juifs, la mémoire et le présent* [The Jews, Memory, and the Present].[5] First, the historian not only has this responsibility for collective memory, but I'd say that he or she also has to be responsible for individual memories. And I summarize this in a formula when I say: "The historian has the duty of integrating Proust into his own work." Proust, the little madeleine, the uneven paving stones—well, whatever, the shock, the memory of the Saint-Marc basilica, etc. All that has to be integrated. My thought has taken here its point of departure from Marek Edelman's two texts on the Warsaw Ghetto.[6] It was when I was thinking about that, thinking about what made the difference between Marek Edelman in 1945 and Marek Edelman thirty-five years later, thinking about films like *Le Chagrin et la pitié* [The Grief and the Pity][7] and then about films like *Shoah*,[8] that I said to myself: "Our duty, the duty for us as historians, is to integrate memory." But in the particular case of Jewish memory, since that was your starting point, I would say that the famous commandment "Zakhor," analyzed so well by Yosef Yerushalmi,[9] is an obstacle to history. In Jewish tradition, memory means fixing, once and for all—"Remember"; and so it constantly mixes up the fall of the Temple in 586 B.C. with Titus' taking of Jerusalem on the Ninth Av,[10] and if it was possible to make the Ninth Av coincide with the expulsion of the Jews from Spain, that would be done too, and if a date was also found in World War II that also corresponds to the Ninth Av, that would be done too . . . All that operates against history. On this, I'm a faithless and utterly treacherous Jew, by which I mean that I'm in favor of opposing the obsession with remembering, and also in favor of integrating the work of memory with the work of the historian.

E. W.: Perhaps I should make my question more specific: doesn't the historian work more against the mechanisms of the state?

P. V.-N.: Yes, you're right. Still, it's not only the mechanisms of the state, but also the mechanisms of society. It's not only that the state is based on forgetting—this is obvious and to some extent it's necessary—it's the problem of amnesty. A number of German intellectuals asked me questions about this for the *Tageszeitung*,[11] in connection with East German criminals.[12] The text you began with is less about the state than about society, in other words the fact that the media get hold of something, bring it alive for a week or two, and then move on to something else: we live in a permanent kaleidoscope. And in one way historical work is about rebelling against that, making it possible for the long term to show up, even in the here and now, if I may put it like that.

E. W.: Yes. I was also thinking of your preface to Miguel Benasayag's book on human rights. You write: "Everywhere . . . the state is present . . . and everywhere, 'totalitarian' or not, the state proceeds masked."[13] You have experienced this yourself a number of times, I believe, especially as witness and historian of the Audin affair.[14] In an interview with Jean-François Lyotard, you speak of a "fundamental melancholy" in relation to the meaning of bearing witness. To Lyotard's statement, "Consciousness of the infinity of a task [namely, that of bearing witness] is one thing, consciousness of its absolute uselessness is another," you replied in 1989: "I don't see this as a major difference."[15] Would you still hold to this?

P. V.-N.: It's hard to say. In the case of the Audin affair, I had an extremely strange experience of a kind that historians rarely have, because I had studied this affair on the basis of a certain number of documents that the lawyers had given us, but that represented only a fraction of what could be known and guessed at the time. I made a number of inferences. At the start of the Mitterand presidency, when Robert Badinter was minister for justice, I was able to have access to the files kept at the chancellery, and could then—and again, this is a pretty rare experience—make a review of this affair, not in total, since I had not had access to the files kept by the war minister (M. Charles Hernu had refused me permission to consult them),[16] but I could at least see how the legal authorities of this country had treated it. And I realized that the dismissal of the case had been prepared well before the end of the Algerian War and not, as I thought, when Chenot was minister, but earlier than that, when the minister was Michelet.[17] This was a shock, and I did that new edition of *The Audin Affair* which, by the way, attracted no attention at all. No one, or practically no one, took any interest, and this was a bit of a disappointment.

E. W.: Your response to Lyotard's sentence, "Consciousness of the end-lessness of a task [namely, that of bearing witness] is one thing, conscious-ness of its absolute uselessness is another" astonished me, coming from you.

P. V.-N.: I said I don't see this difference because I think that, in one way, a certain amount of uselessness is included in what Montherlant called "useless service," in the endlessness of bearing witness. Meaning that you no longer believe . . . I went into this affair with a Dreyfusard obses-sion, with the idea that we were going to sort something out, that we were going to bring Audin's murderer to justice. If I hadn't lost this illusion, I would have made very little progress in life. So now, yes, I think that these two things, consciousness of the endlessness of a task and consciousness of its absolute uselessness, are linked.

E. W.: At any rate, this fundamental melancholy is confirmed in the same interview when you say that your book on the Audin affair is above all a testimony to powerlessness. That made me think of an earlier text which also has to do with the Algerian War, *Les Crimes de l'armée française* [The Crimes of the French Army], where you said: "The worst ruse of the dominant class is to impose its own methods of struggle and organization on its adversaries. 'If you want to conquer the lion,' said a fisherman from the Sorgue to the poet René Char, 'you will be the lion's slave. What's needed is to put fire between you and it.'"[18] And your conclusion then was: "This little book is meant as a fire curtain between us and the French army."[19] Even if it is impossible to conquer the lion, books can still be "fire curtains" . . . But is it impossible to conquer the lion?

P. V.-N.: In very rare cases, you conquer it. Since the fall of the Berlin Wall, a whole network of dictatorships has collapsed that many doctrinaire types thought of as eternal. So the lion can be conquered when the lion is tired. But we can always wonder whether thousands of little lions don't pop up once the lion is conquered. With the Soviet Union, we saw an enor-mous despotism collapse. It took two years to collapse, but it did collapse. It's not absolutely certain that the nationalist rage that is in the process of gripping Eastern Europe isn't also going to create a lot of problems. The different nationalist ambitions make me think of that well-known Jewish story: In a Belgian barracks, the recruiting sergeant says: "Walloons to the left, Flemish to the right," and Private Abramovitch says: "And where do the Belgians go?" At the moment, my sense is that with the rise of all kinds of nationalist ambitions we are dealing with a proliferation of lions. But yes, now and then it is possible to conquer the lion.

E. W.: And do you think of your books, sometimes, as "fire curtains"?

P. V.-N.: Not all of them; some.

E. W.: In the past few years, that "fundamental melancholy"—and it's not unwarranted, I think—has found ample matter for confirmation in the publications of the revisionist enterprise that denies the Hitler gas chambers.[20] I think that one of the greatest dangers here is that the revisionists have succeeded in sowing a doubt, especially among those born after the war. As you write: "Now we are obliged, ultimately, to *prove* what happened . . ."

P. V.-N.: What happened to *us.*

E. W.: Yes. "We who, since 1945, have *known,*" you say, "here we are expected to be proving things, to be eloquent, to use the weapons of rhetoric, to enter into the world of what the Greeks called *Peitho,* persuasion, which they made into a goddess who isn't ours."[21] What can we do so as not to become slaves of Peitho who in this instance, I would say, is the lion's goddess?

P. V.-N.: Not really: Peitho is a Greek divinity who figures a lot in tragedy and is an ambiguous divinity. There is holy Persuasion, which comes up at the end of the *Eumenides;*[22] but there is also a trickster, lying Peitho—so it's an ambivalent divinity. What terrified me about the revisionists' enterprise—and this is why I fought against it with the thought that it was possible to conquer it and with the will to conquer it—what terrified me is the idea that maybe one day, in fifty or a hundred years, there would be people saying: "After all, there are two hypotheses, which is the good one and which is the bad one?" And that I can't accept, it's an idea that strikes me very violently, that shocks me. For instance, take a series of extracts of letters from Michel de Boüard published by the revisionists. Michel de Boüard was my first dean. He was a historian, a medieval historian. He gave a kind of support to Faurisson and his friends.[23] And the most extraordinary thing is that at the same time when he was writing to Henri Roques and a few other individuals of that type that they were quite right,[24] that all that was most illuminating, Michel de Boüard was writing the opposite to me—which goes to show that there was something that wasn't working in the brain department, to put it a bit crudely. What I have always fought against is the theory of two hypotheses, two theories, and I also fight—and this puts me against people like Jean-François Lyotard—of whom by the way I am very fond—against the idea that with this affair, in the end, we are in the area of probability not certainty. For a historian, this was an important experience, because though I always write that truth mustn't have a capital letter, that doesn't stop historians—and I am myself a historian of myths, of the imaginary, and so on—from all the same having to be practitioners of truth, including truth in the most traditional sense of the word.

E. W.: In this connection, you bring up a crucial point that gets neglected too often, I think. Let me quote from your book *Assassins of Memory*: "Revisionism is an ancient practice, but the revisionist crisis occurred in the West only after the widespread broadcast of *Holocaust*, that is, after the turning of the genocide into a spectacle, its transformation into pure language and an object of mass consumption. There lies, I believe, the point of departure for considerations that will, I hope, be pursued by others than myself."[25] Is memory possible in a society of the spectacle, as ours indubitably is? We are a long way from the prohibition of images. How can memory be transmitted to a wide public without Auschwitz being transformed into a "commodity,"[26] into an object of mass consumption?

P. V.-N.: I think the answer to that question is the film *Shoah*. I'm not an unconditional admirer of Lanzmann, and at any rate not of his political views on the Middle East. But he showed through *Shoah* that it is possible to do the opposite of *Holocaust*. *Holocaust* had made me very angry and I'd written a short piece about it in *Esprit* called "The Turnip and the Spectacle," when the film was being shown on French television, in which I expressed my anger and my disgust.[27] *Holocaust* was a success because it provoked a participation phenomenon: in a way the whole thing happened at the level of the family—two families, the history of two families—and it provoked a sort of identification which for me, when this sort of thing happens without precautions, is a very dangerous phenomenon. *Shoah*, by contrast, is in my opinion the great historical work on the integration of memory and history that I was alluding to before. And it is all the more remarkable that with *Shoah*, one is both in a work of art in the Proustian sense of the term—at the end of *Remembrance of Things Past*, when the narrator says, "I have decided to build a work of art"—and in pure memory, since, with one exception, not a single document is quoted in the film or the book. It is people speaking and remembering; they are on site and not in archives.

E. W.: Let me come back to melancholy, which I mentioned earlier . . .

P. V.-N.: Perhaps the reason I wrote about it was because I had just read *Saturn and Melancholy* . . . [28]

E. W.: It seems a bit less strong in the first sentence of your preface to the translation of Arno Mayer's book on the Final Solution, when you say: "The historian is a free man . . . " You continue that, in spite of the opinion that sees the historian as "a slave, slave to facts . . . slave to documents," the "real work—and with it the freedom—begins afterwards, when the last document has been read . . . : it is then that the work of the interpreter begins." And, you go on, "No history is possible where the state, a church, a community, even respectable ones, impose an orthodoxy." The end of this preface picks up the same idea again: You point out the book's English title, *Why Did the Heavens Not Darken?* (which was "borrowed from a Jewish chronicle of the massacres that took place in the Rhineland during the First Crusade"), and you say: "Why indeed? Allow a historian to venture a response. It is not for theologians to take this on."[29] Where, for you, do the dangers lie in this kind of theologization of massacre?

P. V.-N.: I think I partly replied to this question already when I spoke about the Ninth Av. To my mind, the person who has given the best response to this question is Amos Funkenstein, in his study of the religious interpretations of the Shoah, which was published in French and English in the volume *L'Allemagne nazie et le génocide juif* [Nazi Germany and Jewish Genocide].[30] After you get the theologians to intervene, there are two choices. Either you think, like the *Neturei Karta* sect,[31] that the Shoah, and I say Shoah rather than Holocaust advisedly, was the punishment for the sins of the Jewish people. Or you think that the Shoah was a sort of religious catastrophe of the kind that happen from time to time, and that it calls for a sort of permanent watchfulness on the part of the Jewish people. In the first case, we are in the realm of pure theology; in the second, that of theo-politics—and in both cases I think it's dangerous. This links up to the question raised by Weiler's book on the absence of a political dimension in Jewish thought.[32] This is a fundamental point because for a very, very long time (it's already operating to some extent in the work of Flavius Josephus) Jewish thought has indeed delegated the task of doing politics to others; and that, Weiler shows, is true of Flavius Josephus, but is present also in Isaac Abravanel. And Spinoza's role in the development of political thought was not because of the synagogue, but because, on the contrary, he was excluded from it. So, just as it is time to integrate memory and history, so too I think it is time to integrate Spinoza into Jewish thought. This is what is not done by, for example, the contemporary Israeli rulers who reason in terms of essentialism. The chief danger of the interpretations deriving from the theologization of the Shoah lies there: it is in the refusal of politics. Arno Mayer's book is one that I have extensively discussed. My preface is an extremely critical preface. He was loyal enough to accept it without a problem. But it is a critical preface. You know, I've written a lot of critical prefaces. The earliest one appeared in 1964; it was the preface to Wittfogel, reprinted in my book *La Démocratie grecque vue d'ailleurs* [Greek Democracy Seen from Elsewhere].[33] And when I say "The historian is a free man," then that does temper the melancholy a bit. As you say, it means that an interpretation like Arno Mayer's can be defended, it isn't the truth with a capital T.

E. W.: In this same preface, but also in other texts, you deplore the fact that whereas the wiping out of European Jews by Hitler's Germany is "denied by some, it has been sanctified by others, to the point that it has become the object of services, celebrations, a whole religious orchestration. The historian knows how to recognize the sacred as an object of study; he couldn't participate in it without being an impostor." Would this kind of sanctification be as destructive for memory as the attempt at denial? Because faced with the monstrousness of what happened, isn't the need for this kind of sanctification in some sense just as comprehensible so as to be able to undertake what we might call the "work of mourning"?

P. V.-N.: Clearly it's comprehensible. I say so in the same text you are quoting from. But let me tell you a little story. The first time I went to Israel, when I came back, I had written a journalistic piece and an article. Both are in volume 1 of *Les Juifs, la mémoire et le présent* [Jews, Memory, and the Present]. Before I go on, I would like to draw your attention to the illustration I chose for the cover of volume 2: Klimt's *Judith*[34] . . . which was scandalous for some people, because this very scantily clad lady, a bit of a tart in fact, represents the Viennese style of modernity. Why did I choose her for the cover? Because it was a summary of the title. Judith is a character of memory. Naturally, this character never existed. When you say to the Israelis that neither Judith nor Esther ever existed, they are very surprised. But Judith is a character who has been endlessly reinterpreted, reviewed. And to present a Viennese Judith is to point out that I am a man who remembers, but I am a man of the present who looks at the past. So, to reply now to your question—yes, I do think that the sanctification is comprehensible, but you have to resist it at all costs. I don't claim that this is easy. And Arno Mayer himself, in his rationalist, sometimes over-rationalist book, which even manifests certain features of hyper-critique, does have to acknowledge that faced with the sites of pure massacre, in other words Sobibor, Chelmno, Belzec, and Treblinka, you have to come to a halt. Isaac Deutscher, in his study of "The Jewish Tragedy and the Historian," said that it is something that can be dealt with through tragedy more easily than by the historian.[35] As a result, I am extremely aware of all that. So I go back to my little story because it is typical of this. In this newspaper article, I was speaking of the shock I had felt in the Golan Heights when I saw a young man from Nice, who had left there two or three months before, who felt he was at home. And that was not at all a problem for him. And afterwards I got a letter telling me about the kibbutz in question and saying: "Your article was read here on the day of the ceremony in honor of the dead of the Shoah, and it led to additional mourning." The fact that a straightforward reaction like that can be integrated into the process of mourning—that, in my view, is where there is something dangerous, and far from facilitating the work of mourning it blocks it. And, believe me, the question of mourning—I have been confronted with it just like everybody else. After all . . . One day my wife told me that I had said to her, and I'd completely forgotten this, when I was speaking about my parents: I wasn't even able to say goodbye to them. And in fact a few years ago there was a book published with the title *Je ne lui ai pas dit au revoir* [I Didn't Say Goodbye].[36] I am deeply aware of this question of mourning.

E. W.: In your "Theses on Revisionism" (1985), you go even further: you speak of "the *everyday instrumentalization* of the great massacre by the Israeli political class" and the "paradox of a use that makes of the genocide at once a sacred moment in history, a very secular argument, and even a pretext for tourism and commerce."[37]

P. V.-N.: Yes, because one day in Israel I came across a tourist leaflet about the "Holocaust Cave" which shocked and angered me very much.

E. W.: In this article you stress that the "permanent exploitation" of the years 1939–1945 "toward extremely pragmatic ends deprives them of their historical density, strips them of their reality, and thus offers the folly and lies of the revisionists their most fearsome and effective collaboration."[38]

P. V.-N.: Yes, yes, I believe this very strongly. If every time a Palestinian throws a stone we say it is the continuation of the Holocaust, that's as far as we will get. I'm thinking, in this context, of the quite remarkable book by Simha Guterman, *Le Livre retrouvé* [The Rediscovered Book].[39] The book is centered on a manuscript two Polish men found in a bottle one day at Radom [near Plock] in Poland, which they brought back to the Jewish Historical Institute—a manuscript found in a bottle, written in Yiddish. It was obvious that the author of this manuscript had written others too, but what we had there was a narrative of the period from 1939 to 1941 as it had been lived by a Jew at Plock. As well as this manuscript, the book also contains Nicole Lapierre's account of what happened to this family. The author of the manuscript was killed in Warsaw in August 1944, but his son survived, went to Israel, also had a son, and this son was killed in front of Beaufort Castle during the Lebanon War in 1982. I have a clear image of Beaufort Castle, because when I went to Israel, just before that war, a colonel showed it to me, and I said afterwards that he had a sort of lustful look. An exchange of letters between Menachem Begin and the father of this boy appears in the book, the father who is the son, and the father is angry that his son died to conquer Beaufort, which Begin had solemnly given to an Israeli colonel with the words "I give you Beaufort." Begin replies that no war in the history of the Jewish people has been more justified than the "Peace in Galilee" operation. What we have there, in a kind of typical form, is the instrumentalization of Hitlerian genocide in the service of something secular, the utilization of the sacred for very secular ends.

E. W.: You mentioned your parents a moment ago. Who saved you from the same fate that your parents suffered? You dedicate *Les Assassins de la mémoire* [The Murderers of Memory] to the memory of your mother.

P. V.-N.: Who saved me? My classmates and my high-school teacher who stopped me going home.

E. W.: And the following years you spent . . .

P. V.-N.: . . . with my family. I have uncles and aunts, but both my parents left for Auschwitz.

E. W.: I would like to come back to your relationship to Israel. You have for instance analyzed what you call an "ideological reading" of history that is evident in the Israeli state's use of the story of the famous fortress of Masada. Flavius Josephus's account of the siege of Masada and the resistance of the Jewish combatants is interpreted by official historiography along the lines of a heroism whose resistance reaches the point of collective suicide. You show that in reality what Flavius Josephus describes is the absurdity of this kind of collective suicide. A type of official historiography in Israel depends on this myth: "Before Masada's name could be restored and before it could be endowed with the symbolic quality it has since acquired, the advent of Zionism and the formation of the modern state of Israel were required."[40] Does the founding of a state always need a myth or a mythical narrative of this type?[41] Does it always need the guarantee of the "beautiful death," as analyzed by Lyotard in *The Differend*, in that it is "the 'reason to die' [that] always forms the bond of a 'we'"?[42] But it is precisely this we, for Lyotard, that is impossible after Auschwitz. Wouldn't the state of Israel be an exception here? Is there a political possibility of escaping from what you call the "infantile illness which is just what identification with the nation-state is"?[43]

P. V.-N.: Well, the "beautiful death" is a Greek notion mainly elaborated by one of my former students, Nicole Loraux. Lyotard knows her well. Her work on funeral orations is on this topic, as well as other things she has written.[44] Now certainly, every state lives off myths, it's absolutely clear, and every state has its founding myth. What makes the Israel business complicated, long before Auschwitz, is that it's an *Altneuland* [Oldnewland], and that's where it's paradoxical. That title of Theodor Herzl's is a kind of hallmark for Israel. In targeting Masada, I wanted to do away with the misunderstanding that made Masada into pure *Alt*. I showed that it was *Neu*— and even, relatively, very *Neu*. I'm not the only one, because I learned in Israel that there were theses being written about the founding myths of the state of Israel. Once again, the paradox of Israel is that everything has happened, everything can happen very very fast, you have both the highest technology and, in a certain way, the highest mythology. Things will calm down when all that becomes a museum piece in the way that our kings' crowns are museum pieces or the basilica of Saint-Denis. But that is not for the immediate future.

E. W.: So it really is an infantile illness . . .

P. V.-N.: Yes, it is partly an infantile illness, but an infantile illness which is suicidal.

E. W.: This is a question now for Germany since its reunification.[45] You outlined it in your 1990 foreword to the French translation of Karl Jaspers's book, *German Culpability*, as follows: "Europe's future will be different, fundamentally, according to whether the Germany of tomorrow accepts the break or claims imperial continuity."[46] You wrote that sentence in August 1990. Since then, the remains of the two kings of Prussia have been transferred to Potsdam. You have made a connection between the problem of identification with a national state and the "quarrel of the historians":[47] in some of the contributions to this debate, it was possible to glimpse an attempt to downplay, even efface, the break represented by National Socialism in German history, mainly because of the destruction of the European Jews. Doesn't this transfer of the remains mean a clinging to imperial continuity?

P. V.-N.: Absolutely, very much so. But in the same foreword, since you mention it, I say how one day I saw a performance of Aeschylus' *Persians* put on by a theater in Stuttgart. It was a very, very fine performance in which the calling out of Darius' shade took place at Potsdam, while Darius was Frederick the Great in relation to Hitler. The play was based on the idea of a radical opposition between Xerxes-Hitler, if you like, and Frederick II-Darius. On the other hand, the question put in historical terms by Arno Mayer and a number of other historians in Germany, such as Mommsen, is whether the same forces symbolized by Potsdam might not have made Hitler's work easier. That is pretty well condensed in the famous celebration organized by Hindenburg and Hitler at Potsdam, and which the crown prince honored with his participation. On this crucial point, I am absolutely with Habermas. And I consider that all those whose attitude toward the revisionists, in the German sense of the term, has been conciliatory—including, for instance, a historian like my colleague Christian Meier, who is president of the German historians—have been wrong, I think.[48] I edited a historical atlas, which was translated into German and published by Bertelsmann.[49] Without me being told in advance, some pages were added on the division of Germany and also a double page on exiles, the banished, in contemporary Europe—in fact essentially on refugees in Germany. It was clear that the intention of this double page was to put the exiles and expulsions of contemporary Europe on a par with the Nazi persecutions between 1939 and 1945; it is clear that this is the influence of Nolte and Hillgruber,[50] and I don't agree. It's impossible not to get anxious, in fact, when we see signs like these. So everything depends on the reply we will give this question: shall we make the king of Prussia into anti-Hitler or shall we make the king of Prussia *and* Hitler something that fits with national normality? The future remains open.

E. W.: In an interview you did for *Libération* during the Gulf War, you explained why you had abandoned your initial opposition to this war. It's a very detailed argument, which I won't attempt to summarize here, but the last sentence surprised me. You quote a bitter sentence written by Maxime Rodinson, one of your fellow travelers campaigning for Algerian independence: "Ultimately, pacifists have always worked for war"; and you conclude: "Sometimes I wonder if he wasn't right."[51] What is your position now?

P. V.-N.: I will start by telling you that I have evolved a little, retrospectively, in this matter. What I said to *Libération* was what I thought at that point in time, naturally. What would I say today?—and I have said it, what's more, in a short piece that appeared in the bulletin *France-Palestine.*[52] In that piece, I wrote that perhaps, or probably, we made a mistake about the objective. It would have been better to kill Saddam Hussein and spare the Iraqi people. Now what we did was to kill a lot of Iraqi people and spare Saddam Hussein, when what we should have done was the opposite. Having said that, I was shocked by some aspects of the pacifist movement that seemed Munich-like to me. Denis Langlois's arguments—and he's a man I admire in other respects—seemed to me to be participating in the spirit of that 1938 conference. He said: "No war is acceptable." My job has taught me that there are some wars that have to be fought. Whether that particular one needed to be fought is another problem. I found that there was a Munich-like dimension in the attitude of some pacifists.

Paris
September 11, 1991

2

A Testimony Given . . .

JACQUES DERRIDA

ELISABETH WEBER: In your first text on Emmanuel Levinas, you read in his writing the mark of a "truth to which the traditional logos is forever inhospitable": "Unthinkable truth of living experience . . . [that] cannot possibly be encompassed by philosophical speech without immediately revealing, by philosophy's own light, that philosophy's surface is severely cracked, and that what was taken for its solidity is its rigidity." This writing would thus be marked by a "wounding of language."[1]

From your book on Hegel and Genet, *Glas*, to your text "Circumfession," by way of *The Post Card* and "Shibboleth," you have been meditating on circumcision, turning around it.[2] In "Circumfession," you cite an unpublished text of 1976: "Circumcision, that's all I've ever talked about, consider the discourse on the limit, margins, marks, marches, etc., the closure, the ring (alliance and gift), the sacrifice, the writing of the body, the *pharmakos* excluded or cut off."[3] Later on, a text from 1977: "[C]ircumcision remains the guiding thread of what makes me write here, even if what hangs on it only hangs by a thread and threatens to be lost."[4] While this is about an "unthinkable truth of living experience" and of experience that is absolutely unique, in "Shibboleth" you also link it to the most universal: every man is "circumcised by language . . . therefore so is every woman."[5] But what we have there is something unthinkable for the logos, and which puts it in danger. Perhaps none of your books has exposed the "wound in language" as much as this text, "Circumfession."

JACQUES DERRIDA: How can I reply here without vibrations of pathos? To do it in as neutral and, to begin with, as cold a way as possible, I will point out, going back to your first words, that there is a paradox in *turning around.* It signifies obsession but also avoidance. As if you couldn't detach yourself from what obsesses and, at the same time, as if you were avoiding getting too close; there is thus a contradiction in *turning around,* in the two senses of this expression; and above all in turning around something that remains a wound: that has taken place, that has already taken place inside the body. And how can you turn around a wound which in one way is your own? From a topological point of view, this already resembles the logical game of an impossible geometry: you can't turn around your wound. A wound has already taken place that marks an incision in the body; it forbids you this distance or this play which consists in turning around. The game is no longer possible. And yet this hopeless challenge— that's what it is, in fact—which takes the form of an unbelievable topology or phoronomy, of an impossible displacement, perhaps engages precisely what is going on, at any rate what describes the figure, very difficult to represent, for me as much as anyone, of *my* experience or the experience of my relationship to . . . I don't venture to say Judaism—let's say, to circumcision. But you have described this very well yourself—for me "circumcision" could mean on the one hand the singular alliance of the Jewish people with their God, but just as well, on the other hand, it could figure a sort of universal mark that we find not only in men but also in women and in all the peoples of the world, whether or not they have thought of themselves as chosen or singular. I can't even say if this figure, so very unlikely, of "turning around" a wound translates for me an experience of or an approach to Judaism. There remains the question of knowing what Judaism as a figure is, in fact; and what circumcision as a figure is. And basically, however I interpret or one interprets the fact that, I'm told, I was born Jewish or am circumcised, I always find once again, I always find *myself* once again confronted with a problem of figure, a *cas de figure,* as we say in French. It's not only a problem of rhetoric, a case of figure, if at the same time Judaism is an absolutely singular trait not shared by all men and all women, but represents itself, as Judaism, as the figure of the human universal. This exemplary "logic" holds from people to people, from sex to sex, from nation to nation, and so on. I have always struggled within what looks like a logical paradox—and when I say "struggled," that means that I have also battled against the misuse by some groups, Jews in particular, but not only them, of this figure of exemplarity. It is this figure that makes it possible to say "I am Jewish," which means: I am testifying to the humanity of human beings, to universality, to responsibility for universality. "We are the chosen people" means: We are par excellence, and in an exemplary way, witnesses to what a people can be, we are not only God's allies, God's chosen, but God's witnesses, and so on. And then, a paradox that is not supplementary, but lodged within this one—which moreover makes this logic of exemplarity a bit crazy: Once the self-identity of a Jew or of Judaism consist*ed* in this exemplarity—in other words in a certain non–self-identity, "I am this," meaning "I am this and the universal"—well, the more you break up self-identity, the more you are saying "My self-identity consists in not being identical to myself, in being foreign, the non–self-coincident one," etc., the more you are Jewish! And at that point, the word, the attribute "Jewish," the qualities of "Jewish" and "Judaism" are caught up in a bidding war. It makes it possible to say that the less you are what you are, the more you are Jewish and, as a result, the less you are Jewish, the more you are Jewish . . . The logical proposition "I am Jewish" then loses all certainty; it is carried off into an ambition, a claim, a bidding-up of value with no basis! Everyone would like to be the best example of identity as non–self-identity and so an exemplary Jew. From this point of view, Jews—I don't want to say "actual" Jews, because that no longer means anything—Jews who base their Jewishness on an actual circumcision, a Jewish name, a Jewish birth, a land, a Jewish soil, etc.—they would by definition be no better placed than others for speaking in the name of Judaism. Who can speak in the name of Judaism? In all the circumstances or all the texts that you mentioned just now, I found myself (not in the sense where you find *yourself* or re-find or recover yourself, but where you find yourself thrust out there, beside yourself, without finding yourself or recovering yourself—I "found" myself) in this unease which did not simply consist in *not being Jewish enough* or *being too Jewish* all the time, but in trying to think through this paradoxical logic, without being able to master it. But yes, trying to think it through! To endure the experience of it. And so always accompanied by an element of making claims on behalf of an accepted Jewishness, but also a kind of bad temper, and a mistrust— suspicions in relation to those who too readily accommodate themselves to that logic and who sometimes abuse it. Not only in the texts you mentioned, but in everything I may do or say, there is an "Of course, I am Jewish" and "Of course, I am not Jewish"—there, you are in denial from the outset!—and a slightly inept and ironic way of living both of these at the same time, the condition of the Jew. So much so that, referring only to what I immediately remember of "Circumfession," there are quite a few remarks tending this way, which are both ironic and serious. They may seem intolerable to those for whom the position of Judaism is something obvious and straightforward, to those who think, who believe they know—who maybe do know, I don't know!—what it is to be Jewish. For instance, when I say in a particular way—and of course, it's all in the tone of the thing—"I am the last of the Jews,"[6] that can have more than one meaning (and actually I do mean it in various ways)—both "I am a bad Jew," as we say in French "the ultimate such-and-such"—this is the last Jew to deserve to be called a Jew, he really is a traitor and a bad Jew; but also, "I am the end of Judaism," and so the death of Judaism, but also its one chance of survival, I am the last one to be able to say that, the others don't even deserve to say it, they've lost the right to, because in order to say "I am Jewish" you perhaps have to say how difficult it is to say "I am Jewish." There is also a painfully ironic way of giving a "final" lesson (what's the end, the last, the eschatological in general?), of giving a lesson in Jewishness to all those who accuse me of not being Jewish enough and calmly think that they are themselves. And the finicky reasonings I used just now when I was talking about this impossible utterance "I am Jewish" can themselves be seen as an ancestral inclination; rabbis short of overinterpretations can go on doing the hermeneutics and the philology and the rhetoric, in some sense, of the utterance "I am Jewish," and in every way, allegorical, metaphorical, metonymical, etc.

E. W.: You bring up the proximity that exists in Hebrew between *miilah*, "circumcision," and *milah*, "word": give or take a little yod, it's the same word.[7] That makes me think of some lines from a poem by Paul Celan that you comment on in "Shibboleth": "Diesem/beschneide das Wort, diesem schreib das lebendige/Nichts ins Gemüt . . ." [to him/I opened my word/ . . . /for this one,/circumcise the word,/for this one,/for this one/write the living/Nothing in the heart,/for this one . . .].[8] For your writing, might circumcision be a figure of the gift of speech? And also to the extent that the recipient has no memory of it, which is the very condition of the gift, as you write in your book *Given Time*—the condition without which the gift would immediately be ruined.[9]

J. D.: When I was interpreting Celan's writing in that way, the allusion to the circumcision of language or the word *circumcised* was unrelated, at least in my mind, to the play in the Hebrew word. Being incompetent, I took risks on the basis of second-hand explications. My ignorance of Hebrew and my lack of culture in relation to Judaism aggravate the uneasiness I was speaking of just now. This lack of culture, which is a fact, which is of my making, which is in some sense my doing, and singular (it happens that I don't know Hebrew, or hardly any; I am very unfamiliar with Jewish history or the texts of Jewish culture)—this lack of culture obliges me not to settle down, but to move about in the metaphorical, rhetorical, allegorical dimension of Judaism. That of circumcision, for instance. Perhaps it's because of my ignorance and the fact of my not belonging in Jewish culture that I come to consider that, basically, circumcision is there where there isn't any and that what it marks, namely belonging to a community, alliance, wounding, the relationship to the father, the symbolic, etc., is something that happens in all cultures, in all languages: the straightforward fact of speaking establishes us from the outset in the alliance of circumcision, in general. It's the paradox of "All poets are Jews."[10] The poetic relationship to language is the experience of what makes us born into language, to language's already-being-there, to the fact that language precedes us, governs our thought, gives us the names of things, etc. This poetical experience of language is from the outset an experience of circumcision (cutting and belonging, originary entrance into the space of law, non-symmetrical alliance between the finite and the infinite). And so, in quotation marks and with all the necessary rhetorical precautions, a "Jewish experience." Therefore, the sudden irruption of the gift, the gift granted or the gift received, can be closely related to this universal circumcision of language. If the gift presupposes impossibility, the gift, if there is such a thing, as I always think I need to say—you neither can nor should ever be sure that there is giving—the gift, *if there is such a thing*, presupposes the impossibility of appropriation or reappropriation. I can only give if I don't know what it is I am giving, if I cannot calculate what I am giving, if I am not ultimately expecting the thanks or the commerce of gratitude, if I can't even know that I am giving, if the other cannot know that they are receiving. In this sense there would be an initial and radical expropriation at the origin of the gift. And in this sense, language is a gift! Because you don't first of all know who is giving it, who is receiving it, it is there before there is anyone there to give or to receive, and every time there is giving, language is at stake. Every time there is language, there is giving, to the point that it is impossible for the circle to close itself up again. But here I always prefer to speak in terms of trace, rather than language.

To take a step backwards for a moment: In a word, the compulsion of "turning around" is also the experience of an impossible circle or circulation: the impossibility of closing the circle. You turn around because you can't bring the circle to a halt. It can't come back to itself. The impossibility of a coming-back-to-oneself, in the sense of reappropriation, but just as much in the sense of consciousness—in French we say *revenir à soi*, "to come back to oneself," meaning "to recover consciousness, become aware again"—the impossibility of recovering, of recovering oneself, of coming back to oneself, that's what it is, the openness of the gift, *if there is such a thing*. If it were possible to recover, recover oneself, come back to oneself, the gift would be calculation, programming, reappropriation, thanks. These paradoxical motifs of being Jewish, the gift, and circumcision, are indissociable for me. In order for them to be indissociable, for them to form a chain in some way, the main thing is that it mustn't come to a halt and that you can't assign an identity, a stable self-identity, to one of those notions. If you think you know what it is to be Jewish, what giving is, what circumcision is, you can be sure that there won't be any more of them: that there never has been any of them!

E. W.: Would you be taking a distance here with regard to a psychoanalytic interpretation of circumcision? When you speak of the "universal circumcision" of language, that might make one think of the psychoanalytic account of language, in Lacan for example.

J. D.: That depends on the way you interpret it. You can't just do without psychoanalysis. It all depends on how it is determined. If psychoanalysis claims to be a knowledge in the position of metalanguage in relation to all that, then at that point circumcision escapes psychoanalysis and everything we've just been talking about is instead a challenge to psychoanalysis, as it is to knowledge in general. Because it is *also* their unthought condition. If we call another gesture psychoanalysis, another gesture that takes account of psychoanalysis without fastening it into a knowledge, then at that point, instead, I think everything we have just said perhaps opens up onto the unconscious another way of thinking the symbolic order, of thinking how language precedes the subject, and so on. *This* is the direction in which I try to analyze dissemination as well as circumcision: by showing where, so to speak, they resist a logic of the signifier and of castration.

E. W.: You have devoted a number of texts and a number of years of teaching[11] to Jewish German philosophers: Hermann Cohen, Franz Rosenzweig, Walter Benjamin, Gershom Scholem. The Judaeo-German alliance, for all it might seem necessary, unavoidable, and exemplary, was nevertheless impossible. What is it that always makes you come back again to this unavoidable and impossible alliance, to the Judaeo-German psyche?[12]

J. D.: In a slightly elliptical way, I am tempted here to insist most of all on this paradox: not being German, not being Jewish except through the complicated protocols we were talking about just now, I have still considered it unavoidable to turn around this Judaeo-German couple. Why? Once again, impossible to enter into the content of things. Let's say this: I'm not simply Jewish, certainly, but I am Jewish, and although I'm not German, I was raised in a culture and a philosophical tradition for which the German inheritance is inescapable, in a century or half-century where what happened to or through this couple not only concerns the universe, but concerned me, no doubt less seriously than others, but still in a way that was close, vivid, and harsh. Bearing in mind what happened not only in the 1920s and 1930s, and in this [twentieth] century and even in the nineteenth century, it is urgent to think about the history of philosophy, quite simply about history, in its most terrifying traumas. It is a duty to try to understand how all that was possible, without being content with the images and the conventional concepts that circulate on the subject of the Shoah, the genocides, etc. Naturally, you cannot claim to have thought about this even in seminar series lasting a year or two, but I have tried not to "turn around" too much, here in the sense of pure and simple evasion.

E. W.: What seems striking to me is that every time you have worked on the Judaeo-German psyche, we have been confronted by a double aspect of the texts which means that we are constantly being sent back and forth between the "German" side and the "Jewish" side, to the point that we can't really distinguish them precisely from each other any longer.

J. D.: In one way, even in *Glas*, whether it's about Genet or Hegel, the Jewish question was present, all the time. But in the case of the seminars on the Judaeo-German psyche, and where the first year was about

Kant and Hegel, it's true that I was constantly finding myself in the situation you describe: you are dealing with two and one at the same time, there is a mirror and so a speculation in which, as a result, the images go back and forth, and attach the Jew and the German together, both face to face, looking at each other, not able to see each other, interiorizing each other, unto death! And yet in this specularity and this reflection, a certain heterogeneity, a certain infinite alterity, comes to make speculation and specularity impossible. It's the paradox of an image in which the two identities are caught up in mutual fascination and where, at the same time, however, transcendence and "foreignness," the heterogeneity of each of them, remain intact. The German Jew is fascinated by the German, the German is fascinated by the Jew, it's a terrifying couple: and at the same time, no identification is possible. The Jew remains absolutely foreign, infinitely foreign, to the German. There are many signs of this double fascination, particularly in Scheler, Cohen, Rosenzweig and Buber, in Scholem, in Benjamin and Adorno, etc. For instance we find a double fascination, a desire for alliance and appropriation, for an "I am more German than the German" in some Jews—and this is true of Hermann Cohen—who claim a degree of German patriotism. There are signs of this in Adorno, even in Benjamin. This double fascination, this desire for appropriation, has not been simply an intellectual, cultural, theoretical mirage, but has given rise to what has been lived to the death, so to speak, lived to the point of that monstrosity that you know. Not that, it seems to me—and this is obviously a slightly outrageous hypothesis—not that this has been radically thought through up till now by anyone. Obviously, there's a burning and dangerous prohibition there; I am well aware that I have sometimes come close to it, perhaps a bit dangerously; to speak of specularity here can appear an act of extreme violence, to the point—and this is a step which of course I won't ever take—to the point of making the German Jews complicit in their own misfortune. Not only do I not take this step, but in a text on Benjamin, I noted how sometimes an affinity between the discourses of some Jewish thinkers and those of German thinkers at one moment of German history—in particular during the Weimar Republic or the rise of Nazism—ran this risk of opening up an interpretation that would make the Jewish people responsible for or guilty of what was going to happen to it, which would be interpretable as a kind of punishment.[13] I believe that the attempt to think about what happened there takes account of the need to break this enchantment—there is an enchantment, there is a specular fascination, there's an impossibility of detaching oneself from it!—of the need to break the fascination of this couple. It's a history, and it happened! It's a history with points of emphasis, of course, it happened in an especially knotted-up way, knotted tightly under Nazism, but the knot was already tied in the time of Nietzsche and Wagner, a knot that had itself got started in another knot at the time of Jewish emancipation. (I have moved very swiftly from the *mirror* to the *knot*, but in fact what it is is a *specular link*, a specularity that knots, attaches, interlocks in its very delusiveness). But you can't give an account of the history of this knot, as Hermann Cohen himself shows, and this is why I did a close reading of his text *Deutschtum und Judentum*, without going back to the Reformation and to Plato, to Platonism, to the origin of Christianity, to the Hellenistic period, and so on.[14] It's a history with rhythms, nodal points. Each knot has a definite singularity of its own, but you have to pull the whole string! If we want this fascination to be interrupted—or, at any rate, no longer to give rise to murder as we have lived it in the most intolerable form—we must try to think that through! It is also a political duty. Of course, I am very far from having done it, but this is the direction, I think, in which we should undertake to go.

E. W.: In *Glas*, you ask the question: "Isn't it always an element excluded from the system that assures the system's space of possibility?" And you summarize Hegel's judgment on the Jews: "Their own nature remains foreign to them, their secret secret: separated, cut off, infinitely distanced, terrifying."[15] Would it then be the foreign own nature, the secret secret, the separation, or cutting off of the Jews which would organize the space of possibility of the Western philosophical system?

To put it another way, might there be in Western philosophy, and perhaps in Hegel above all, a "crypt—one would have said, of the transcendental or the repressed, of the unthought or the excluded—that organizes the ground to which it does not belong"? On the other hand, "what speculative dialectics means (to say) is that the crypt can still be incorporated into the system."[16] So doesn't your writing constantly suggest crypts of this kind? Crypts of the kind that are inadmissible for Western philosophy?

J. D.: I want to reply to all your questions with a single word: yes! So, I would say "yes," you have replied on my behalf. I would just add a codicil. We will have to go back to the beginning of the interview. This excluded element that makes possible the functioning of the system—a very general formulation—in your question you identified this excluded element as the Jew: excluded from Hegel's system, excluded, let's suppose, from German culture, and so on. Fine. But for the reasons mentioned just now, it can also be something else, it can also be the woman, for instance. The example I give of this transcendental or quasi-transcendental structure is just as much the sister, in Hegel's case. It can be the non-European in general, it is all the figures of the other! And one of them can—even must—become the figure of the other. The Jew can be an exemplary figure, but all the other examples are also exemplary figures, all those excluded. It can be the woman, the non-European, the immigrant, it can be anything that comes into the position of a crypt excluded on the inside.

E. W.: Women have an extensive role in your writing. They intervene in your texts, they interrupt your writing. But before intervening explicitly, they perhaps already dictate the style of your writing. I'm thinking in particular of another passage in *Glas*, where you give a short account of the place Hegel assigns to women: "Human law, the law of the rational community that institutes itself against the private law of the family, always suppresses femininity, stands up against it, girds, squeezes, curbs, compresses it. But masculine power has a limit—an essential and eternal one: the arm, the weapon, doubtless impotent, the all-powerful weapon of impotence, the inalienable shot [*coup*] of the woman, is *irony*. Woman, '[the community's] inside enemy,' can always burst out [*éclater*] laughing at the last moment; she knows, in tears and in death, how to pervert the power that suppresses."[17] Couldn't these last two sentences be read as a sort of program for your writing?

J. D.: The word "program" always makes me anxious. But if "program" there were, it's a program that I wouldn't have established myself, or formalized, that I wouldn't have set for myself. It's a program that programs me, it's not a project.

E. W.: Yes, that's why I said "dictate."

J. D.: Yes, it is a dictation, a prescription that I try to submit to, if I can put it like that, that I try to understand and listen to. The fact is that the figure of the Jew and the figure of the woman have often been associated. In *Spurs*, I speak about a text of Nietzsche's on this subject which treats the Jew and the woman in the same way;[18] and indeed the association of these two figures can be interpreted in a way that is in some sense valorizing, it can be taken in good part—or, on the contrary, denounced with contempt. Which might give rise to a sentence like this: "The Jew is only a woman, the Jew is the feminization or the femininity of society, the threat to all the virile values that govern a community, an army, a nation, and so forth." In the figure of the Jew and the woman there is also an oscillation between the two values. With this symptom in mind, we should interrogate not only anti-Semitism of the kind that has emerged in European societies or nations, at the times when they have exalted the values of roots, the army, force, virile and fraternal qualities, and so on (we could find lots of examples of this, some old, some less old, some completely contemporary), but we should also ask the question of every nation and every state, including Israel (of the inside of that which, in the Jewish tradition, has been able to give rise to nation, state, army, fraternity, and so on). What becomes of the woman there? What becomes of the value of femininity? I am not claiming that there is homogeneity on this, for instance in the state of Israel. But there are diverse movements of which some can be analyzed or suspected with these schemas as a starting point. There are a number of ways of thinking about the state or the nation of Israel, a number of ways of thinking about the army, the purpose of the Israeli army, a number of ways of thinking about the relation to the woman in this society, in this religion, but also in its army. I have no ready conclusion, but I wanted to set out the problem.

E. W.: In *Mémoires: for Paul de Man,* you describe deconstruction as follows: "Deconstruction is not an operation that supervenes *afterwards,* from the outside, one fine day; it is always already at work in the work. . . . Since the disruptive force of deconstruction is always already contained within the architecture of the work, all one would finally have to do to be able to deconstruct, given this *always already,* is to do memory work."[19] Memory work to recall the crypts and to shake up the solid architecture that dissimulates them. . . . However, we run up against a paradox. *The Post Card* several times mentions the destruction of the correspondence of which that book is in a sense presenting the "remains." And several times, also, there is talk of "burning it all," of "holocaust," of "catastrophe."[20] The publication of these letters could mean their destruction; whereas to burn the correspondence would protect their secret.[21] Through this question of the "publication" of this postcard correspondence, we are thus constantly being confronted with the paradox or the essential double bind of memory: remembering, keeping, risks coming back to better destroying. This question is sharply topical for historiography, in face of the attempts at destruction, censorship, falsification, denial. Doubtless we would also have to take account here of the role of the media today. Total archiving can destroy memory. Might it be possible that one of the deconstructions that, you say, only exist in the plural, would therefore consist in the construction of crypts? Not, this time, crypts to bring about the disappearance of what disturbs the functioning of the system, but crypts for what must be protected from the blinding light of representation, in other words, crypts for the *gaps* in memory?

J. D.: Yes, you are right. In the first passage you quoted, when it was said that deconstruction had only to do memory work, I was not speaking directly in my own name. I was describing an interpretation of deconstruction, in particular that of de Man in some passages. It consists in saying (what I only half believe) that basically, in literature, deconstruction is already going on, in Rousseau for instance. So we would have nothing to add, it's already been done. At that point, I remember putting a question to de Man, in the form of a virtual objection: if that's the way it is, there's no longer anything to do; how are we to interpret the fact that now, in spite of everything, deconstruction is becoming a theme, that it marks events, and that something is happening? Whence the necessity and the double bind you have outlined, the necessity both of taking account of the fact that, yes, deconstruction is always already at work, but that nonetheless the act of remembering does not consist only in unveiling and making explicit what is already there. You have to produce new events. Deconstruction is not a memory that simply recalls to mind what is already there. The act of memory is also an unpredictable event, an event that calls forth a responsibility and also gestures and actions. But that "doing" is caught in a double bind. The more you remember, the more you risk deleting, and vice versa. Deconstruction cannot get out of this aporia, this double bind, in a secure way. I don't think there's a rule or imperative here that could give us an assurance. We always run the risk of deleting when we remember, and the other way around.

We then get to your unusual question: should we construct crypts, almost deliberately, on purpose, so as to shelter archives in a slightly more secure way? In other words, should we set up things like safes within safety-chests, hiding places, sort of, where the double-bind machine can no longer do its work by committing memory itself to forgetting? It's a highly paradoxical and appropriate way of putting the problem, but here too, I have no answer. Of course, you have to do that, to try it, but by definition, crypts being places of unconsciousness, places that escape the will and the deliberate memory, you cannot calculate. You can try to calculate and when you can, you must do it. But at the point when you want to construct guaranteed crypts against forgetting, contracting forms of insurance, setting up cast-iron chests as is sometimes done in a wholly concrete way for archives (for documents that in principle ought to be available for millennia to come, you try to put them miles away, or else in cement, sheltered from an atomic explosion), you know very well it's no longer about memory. It would be all very well to protect an archive from destruction (but the very finitude of the earth prevents us from having an absolute insurance here), we can dream of an absolute insurance; but if we reached the indestructible, if we constructed a blockhouse, an absolutely indestructible chest, the very fact of its invulnerability would make it a present monument, a present stone that would have no relationship to memory. You would risk destroying precisely because you had wanted to save at any price. The salvation of memory cannot be an insurance against forgetting. The salvation of memory or by memory, for memory, implies an absolute risk, the act of faith that must remain a testimony on display. It will never be a proof. You cannot and should not avoid the risk of forgetting if you want to remember. Memory without risk of forgetting is no longer a memory. It's dreadful, but that is finitude itself, the limit and the chance of what comes, of the other and the event: the gift.

E. W.: In *Memoirs of the Blind*, you sharpen this double bind of memory: while the blind man in antiquity or as a biblical figure is, through his blindness, "the best witness, a chosen witness," a witness, for his part, "is always blind. Witnessing substitutes narrative for perception. The witness cannot see, show, and speak at the same time, and the interest of bearing witness, like that of the testament, stems from this dissociation. No authentication can show in the present what the most reliable of witnesses sees—or rather, has seen and now keeps in memory, provided that he has not been carried off by fire. (And as for the witnesses of Auschwitz, as of all the extermination camps, what we have here is an abominable resource for all "revisionist" denials.)"[22]

J. D.: Yes, this terrifying structure of testimony is indeed the one that our testimony is caught in too, in particular with regard to Auschwitz, to keep this example that is both singular and exemplary. The debates with revisionists, with all revisionisms, the fights against revisionism, will not be won simply by science. We need science! And so, beyond testimony, we need to try to bring proofs. Testimonies are not proofs. And proofs are not testimonies. We need to bring proofs, and we need to do everything that can be done to bring proofs and, consequently, to leave the scientific debate open by responding to it as scientifically as possible, so without ever interrupting it in the name of some authority or dogma or other. And we need to struggle just as scientifically against the revisionists. But knowing full well that at the end of the day the decision—what we can hold on to in this debate—will never be the result of a proof, because in that case revisionism might always win—not scientifically, but for the cause that it wants to defend, whether or not it admits it. So it is through speaking—in other words, through a commitment that goes beyond seeing—that we can beat the revisionist denial. This will never be a battle of figures, of victim counts, of extermination techniques; it's about something else. And with this something else, it's speaking that counts, and not proof. In other words, it is testimony. But "testifying" doesn't mean simply having seen, or getting together people who have seen the things; testifying means nowadays testifying against the project of Auschwitz, whatever the numbers and the techniques. And testifying against the revisionist desire. So, it's a certain way of putting yourself in this paradox that comes from the divorce between seeing and saying. From this point of view faith is blind. We certainly should not yield to obscurantism, we should not give up seeing, give up science and knowledge, but we need to know that there is also that which is beyond science and knowledge and, therefore, a speech that is all the more telling for not being tied to sight.

E. W.: Toward the end of *Of Spirit*, you stage a fictional interview between Heidegger and a Christian theologian, a Messianic Jew, and a Muslim theologian. This conversation shows that in the quest or the "return towards the land of pre-archi-originarity," there are echoes between the discourses of each of them. One claims to speak from a more originary position than the other. They all join "in the concert or the hymn" of appealing "to this entirely other in the memory of a promise or in the promise of a memory." In other words, in a conversation like this, "the places can sometimes be exchanged in a disturbing way." The "abyssal" "power" presaged in all these versions of "pre-archi-originarity" "in all rigor exculpates none of the discourses which can thus exchange their powers. It leaves no place open for any arbitrating authority." The political significance of this diagnosis lies in your observations that Nazism "was not born in the desert," but "in the shadow of big trees, in the shelter of their silence or their indifference"; and, in all these cases, "in their same soil," in the shadow of trees whose "bushy taxonomy" would bear "the names of religions, philosophies, political regimes, economic structures, religious or academic institutions."[23]

If you reconstitute the possible voices that join in this concert, you don't simply mingle your own with it; even if it participates in this concert, it remains dissonant. Might the strident sound of the "voice" of your writing arise from the demolition of the quest for origins?

J. D.: No, certainly not "demolition" or "denunciation" of the quest for origins. In the fictional scene you mentioned, it's not a matter of dismissing the cases of all the interlocutors, or of saying that they are all the same and all caught up in the same fantasy, the same way of upping the bids, the same pretense. It's about pointing out that there really is no arbitrator here and so, when you say my voice is mingled in it, Yes! I don't believe in the possibility of an overarching position in relation to those three voices—or others either. By analyzing and formalizing a sort of program, this time, an upping of the bids from which no one escapes, I am trying to point out the way formalization itself is caught up in this connection, in this knot. This is also to point out that there really is no arbitration: there is no innocence. Even the agencies represented by these voices, whether we call them Christian, Jewish, or Muslim, are not innocent in the culture and institutions I mention a little earlier in the text. There are no innocents. I think that to seek to exculpate is a delusion. To seek to judge, to isolate a guilty person, is a mystification. Not that we should give up courts, trials, all the preliminary reports or all the official inquiries. Not all responsibilities are the same: the law, human rights, international law, the denunciation of war crimes—none of these should be given up. But as long as we are well aware that there is a point at which these judgments are fallible. And that if this law is fallible, it can be perfected. Judgments are dispatched from a place that is not a place of innocence. Judges are always parties. This is what I wanted to point out. Of course, there is an ironic tone in the way of describing these theologians going beyond or outdoing each other: Heidegger in discussion with a rabbi, a Christian theologian and a Muslim; but in the end, since their escalation consists of referring the matter to the absolute other, to the absolute originarity of the other, it is such that any claim to place oneself on the outside would consequently be ridiculous, would deserve the most cutting irony. This fictional scene is thus, finally, a way—a humble way, I would say—of reminding us all the same that there are programs and that no one here holds an absolute privilege. And in the deciphering of history that remains to be done, of the history of European culture that for instance brought Nazism and brought the Shoah, we need modesty and the feeling of non-innocence, as much in the historian's work as in all the evaluations and all their consequences. That must not make for a loosening of rigor but, at a given moment, it ought to prevent this rigor from draping itself in the authority of the absolute judge and the good conscience.

E. W.: Beyond or before this pursuit of the origin, you put forward the notion of *différance*.[24] While this is implicated in the Judaeo-Graeco-Christian program, it seems to me nonetheless to belong as it were out of synch with this program. It doesn't exactly hang together. On several occasions, in *Of Grammatology* as well as in *Speech and Phenomena*, you speak of the "closure of knowledge" and the "opening of an unheard-of question that opens neither onto a knowledge nor onto a non-knowledge as knowledge to come. In the opening of this question, *we no longer know*."[25] In "Circumfession," you describe yourself as "eschatological . . . in the extreme, I am the last of the eschatologists."[26] What distinguishes the notion of *différance* from an "eschatological" concept that would turn back into a concept of origin?

J. D.: It is distinct from it imperceptibly, I would say, in a furtive or fleeting way. The archi-origin is both more and less than an origin. When you speak of archi-origin, of what is before the origin, in one way you give the impression of intensifying the originary quality of the origin, but you are also referring just as much to something that is not at all of the order of the origin. It's the paradox of *différance*. On the one hand, *différance* is set going by a desire, a movement, a tendency toward an origin that is constantly delayed, toward the future or the past, toward the *eschaton*, which means the extreme (that's exactly what "eschatological" means, that which has the quality of last), but at the same time *différance* is that which in a sense bars the origin. The extreme, then, is neither the end nor the origin. The slightly ironic sentence, "I am the last of the eschatologists," like "I am the last of the Jews," means, I am the last of the last. The eschatological is the last! Meaning, I am the most last, so the least last. There is no last! Just as there is no first, no origin. Obviously, to be logical, to say that there is no origin, is to put something before the origin and, as a result, according to what can look like antinomies of the Kantian type, constantly to dissolve *and* to restore the originary. It is the space of margin, the opening that enables the endless escalation of arguments among the three theologians! All of them leapfrogging over each other, claiming more alterity and more transcendence, more originarity. It's the *différance of* the origin, the origin is *différ/ant*, it is separated from itself, it is not what it is. If there weren't this dislocation of the origin, this gap of the origin in relation to itself, and so this non-originarity in the origin, there would be nothing! No speech, no debate, no escalation of arguments, no transcendence. Which means that nothing is more incompatible than originarity and *différance* but, at the same time, they are inseparable, according to a *différantial* logic that is both economic, meaning that it functions like the restoration of the same in alterity, and, at the same time, an-economic, like absolute heterogeneity. Absolute *différance*.

E. W.: In "Circumfession," but also already in *The Post Card*, you mention that in 1942 you were excluded from your high school "and from Frenchness."[27] Could you say something about that?

J. D.: I shouldn't place so much emphasis on this episode in my life—perhaps I already have a bit too much. Of course it was painful, with pain that can't be measured, since all pain is immeasurable. All the same, I shouldn't do it, because measured on the scale of the pains, wounds, and crimes of that time—because you do have to measure as well—it would be indecent to stress it. Just a word to comment instead on your reference to Frenchness. What was going on in Algeria at that time, although it has some historical relation to what was going on in occupied France, nonetheless went back to a purely French initiative! The French people who had passed the anti-Jewish laws of this period in Algeria were in no way forced to do so by the Germans! It was all accompanied not only by all kinds of persecutions, small or large, but also by a loss of French citizenship that no one on the German side was demanding. Somewhere in our book, Bennington cites some documents I had given him, a reminder that from the educational point of view the anti-Jewish laws passed in Algeria were even more serious than what was ever done in occupied France.[28] Obviously, my consciousness was not well informed at the time, but in fact this was something I experienced not from Nazism and the Germans, not even directly from Vichy, but from the French who surrounded me at the time. For me, it was France, some French people, and not history with a capital H, or Germany or Nazism, that were responsible for what was happening then. This probably had strange and complicated effects on my relationship with French culture, and with the French language.

E. W.: In "Shibboleth," you speak of Paul Celan's affirmation of Judaism in terms of "accepting the memory of a destination that was not chosen." Commenting on Celan's "Conversation in the Mountains" which speaks of the Jew as someone who possesses nothing "that is really his own, that is not borrowed, taken and not returned,"[29] you conclude: "The Jew is also the other, myself and the other."[30] At the same time, Judaism is absolutely unique, absolutely "distinctive," so that in "Circumfession" you speak of "the last of the Jews that I . . . am."[31] Here Jewishness seems to me so profoundly present, in its absence, that it carries within it the vanished Temple: all the walls become wailing walls when you write: "[E]very time that I am walking in the streets of a city I love, in which I love, on whose walls I weep myself and was weeping myself again yesterday . . ."[32] But even this wall is in a way "lent": its name, "Wailing Wall," originates in the mockery on the part of the Jerusalem Christians who saw Jews of the city weeping in front of the only wall of the Temple that remained . . .

J. D.: I won't give a lengthy commentary on what you say, but I will keep the motif of mockery. A sentence like "I am the last of the Jews," like all the sentences in "Circumfession," is both a sentence that I am signing, in one way, but also a sentence I am putting in quotation marks as typical or stereotypical. There is a sort of hubris in this sentence (who do you think you are when you say "I am the last of the Jews?" Christ could have said that! Christ was the last of the Jews, in one way, in all the senses of this term). So, there's both the signing of an outrageous declaration, taking it on yourself, and at the same time showing it, quoting it—it's a quasi-quotation. And so a moment of mockery, but also the citational staging of mockery itself. This *mise-en-abyme* is writing itself. I wanted to show the way that mockery repeats, responds to, a stereotype or prototype. To say "I am the last Jew" is also to say "I am the best Jew," the *Urbild*, at the same time the archetype or the ultimate example, so the best example of the Jews. It's not necessarily the anti-Jewish irony of those who laugh at the Wailing Wall, but it's perhaps also the irony of the Jew speaking of himself, listening to himself speaking about himself, telling Jewish stories, thumping himself on the chest and showing himself off with a "Here's what I have to say, here's another one saying that," and so on. So, in all sentences of this type there is both the utmost seriousness and the least possible seriousness; that is true of all the sentences in "Circumfession": the most confidential are at the same time the most on show, like postcards or snapshots.

As to the wall—I will take your quotation as a pretext to link back to what we were saying a little while ago about testimony and blindness, about the wound that deprives us of sight, but also of hearing, of hearing ourselves speak. Perhaps you have noticed that the wall against which I weep myself, I weep or weep "myself," is the wall of the rue de l'Abbé-de-l'Épée. It's a true story. I was coming back after a trip to England where I had met up with Geoff Bennington—and I speak to him at that point in the text—I was returning from Roissy airport, I got on the train that took me to the boulevard Saint-Michel stop, from which I went back along the rue de l'Abbé-de-l'Épée to go and get my car. So it's a true story, I can vouch for it. But, obviously, I also "chose" this street because it's the street of the wounds I was talking about just now, of the institution for the deaf and mute.[33] One thinks about what the prayer of the deaf and mute might be, and about all those who only have eyes to weep, in a way. So, in one sense, it's to do with a wailing wall . . . it's a coincidence, because it's true, that did happen on the rue de l'Abbé-de-l'Épée, which for a moment became the Wailing Wall, but for no other reason than my own wandering as a traveler or a Jew and a blind man.

E. W.: When you say that every sentence in "Circumfession" is marked by mockery, there is perhaps one kind of sentence that doesn't include: the sentences on weeping. You write: "For like SA [St. Augustine] I love only tears, it is only through them that I love and speak"; and "I have spent my life teaching so as to return in the end to what mixes prayer and tears with blood."[34] Would this be returning to the unreadable, for instance to the unreadability in a circumcision? Might this text, "Circumfession," be the enactment of a sentence from *Memoirs of the Blind* which says: "A work is at once order and its ruin. And they weep for one another."[35]

J. D.: Yes. I will just go back to the word "mockery." Mockery is a certain kind of laughing. I endorse all you have said and I am even ready to take on the word mockery as I've already done, but perhaps while trying to delete what remains close to sarcasm in mockery. Mockery is a type of bad laughter. So, in everything we've just been speaking about there's something that laughs, smiles, is ironic—I wish that there was no mockery in the sense of sarcasm (but perhaps it's inevitable, whatever we do). So, if instead of mockery we say a certain kind of laughter—in *Ulysses Gramophone*, I try to distinguish among several kinds of laughter which are very close to each other[36]—a certain laughter which is not negative, which is not far from affirmation, I'm not sure you have to choose between laughter and tears. Good tears are not necessarily free of all smiles. It is possible, as one says, to smile through your tears, to laugh while crying. The tears this text is about ought to rule out mockery, but not necessarily a kind of laughing. On the contrary.

Ris-Orangis
September 13, 1991

Women of Resistance

RITA THALMANN

ELISABETH WEBER: You have devoted your career as a historian to Germany and Nazism, but also, and probably just as much, to questions that relate to the lives, the status, and the activities of women in German-speaking countries. In addition, you are the author of a number of works on the living conditions and the persecution of German Jews in the first half of the twentieth century—or more precisely, up to 1943. It seems to me that there is a deep connection between these two areas of enquiry in your work—into the situation of women, and the situation of Jews. For instance, in your book *Être femme sous le IIIe Reich* [Women Under the Third Reich] you mention the well-known "thesis of the incompatibility of female emancipation [which Hitler called a 'Jewish invention'] and motherhood." For "Gottfried Feder, that obscure founder of what became the NSDAP,"[1] Jews "stole the women" from German men "by the forces of sexual democracy."[2] This is a very frequent theme in Nazi ideology. In the same book, you speak of "the analysis of the similarities between racism and sexism."[3] You refer to Gunnar Myrdal and Simone de Beauvoir.[4] Would you say that there are also similarities of this kind between anti-Semitism and sexism? In other words (perhaps the question is either a bit bold or a bit simplistic), is it possible—and including women in this—to be anti-Semitic without a deep hatred of women?

RITA THALMANN: It's a difficult and complex question, but Weininger shows well the link between antifeminism and anti-Semitism. But racism, anti-Semitism, and sexism also need to be differentiated. I have done this, starting from Léon Poliakov, who didn't go the whole way but clearly indicated the direction.[5] The basis is that fixed binarism in relation to genotypes (man = architect, builder; woman = passive, vegetative), which then, afterwards, gets applied to peoples and ethnic groups. So the basis is similar. Of course, you have to add some nuances because we are well aware nowadays that right in the heart of minorities, women are also oppressed by the persecuted, especially in the Arab world, in colonies or ex-colonies, and so on. So there is a link, but one should not do what some young Germans I won't cite have done, which is to go so far as to speak, for instance, of a Final Solution of women under Nazism.

E. W.: Yes, we will come back to that.

R. T.: It's a very important point. I think you have to keep your cool. So I had to warn a young German historian in relation to a catalog we had produced for the Berlin exhibition on women at Gurs,[6] especially women artists.[7] She writes: in 1939, women and men emigrants from Germany were arrested in the course of a "Night and Fog" action. First of all, this is false because women weren't arrested right away; but second, to speak of a "Night and Fog" action, a name which refers to a later Nazi decision to exterminate, seems to me extremely serious because it trivializes Nazi crimes. Personally, I am against these verbal and even conceptual excesses on the part of some feminists, even though I'm a committed feminist.

E. W.: I would like to insist on this point because I think it is a very tricky one in the German feminist movement. I have found something like it in a woman like Maria Antonietta Macciocchi,[8] whom you quote in your book—in particular this sentence, from January 1979: "We are already navigating in the estuary of post-feminism with our sails slack." Now this admirable woman, who is a feminist of the first generation, seems to me to resort to a type of identification that appears very problematic. In her book *Les Femmes et leurs maîtres* [Women and Their Masters], she describes an attack against the women of Radio Città Futura in January 1979, and writes: "The women of Radio Città Futura, targets of the visceral hatred of male racism—woman as Jew—were attacked and hurt with submachine guns."[9] A few pages on, dedicating her book to "generations of laughing women, protagonists of the future," she writes: "For them, I here transcribe the Nazi curse *on women and their newborn babies* against the mania for minimizing the madness of the gas chambers, against the lies that circulate today in Paris and that seek to efface an atrocious historical truth,"[10] and later on, she transcribes a fragment from one of Himmler's speeches, given at a Nazi rally and considered as the "clearest and most explicit declaration on the extinction of the Jews."[11] It is true that she doesn't deny the specificity of Jewish genocide, but a disturbing tendency does appear here, even if Macciocchi doesn't give in to it. Some strands of feminism, however, do give way to this temptation, which comes down to maintaining, directly or indirectly, that the annihilation of the Jews was also aimed at women as women.

R. T.: Yes, here you have to be very careful. At a recent conference at the Goethe Institute in Paris, organized by Léon Poliakov, he stressed that in order to avoid some people's exasperation because we only speak about Jews in this matter, we need to show the general problem—whence the conference title, "Hitler's Racial State."[12] It is necessary to show the different aspects. And Léon Poliakov had pointed out that in 1929 Hitler was saying: if Germany produces a million babies a year, if there are only three or four hundred thousand left, that will be enough for the vital force of the German people—which, in fact, his subsequent policies partly disproved. It was at this conference that I first developed the idea of a hierarchy in the treatment of women, an idea that has been knocking around in my mind for some time, since I teach a course at my university called "Sex and Race" where we work with a multidisciplinary team of young men and women historians on these questions. I developed this aspect in a piece that was solicited by the political studies department at Bonn, especially Professor Bracher. The editors called my piece "Zwischen Mutterkreuz und Rüstungsbetrieb" [Between the Motherhood Cross and the Armaments Industry], a very dubious title but a striking one.[13] In reality, the *Mutterkreuz* was only introduced in 1938, and the *Rüstungsbetrieb* only became obvious to most people in 1939, with the war, whereas everything had begun in 1933, perhaps even earlier. In this study I developed the theme of the Goethe Institute conference by showing that right from the start the Nazis were aware that you couldn't do without women. Alfred Rosenberg said in his book of 1930—and I quote this in my book about women under the Third Reich—that what caused the loss of the Teutonic knights was their vow of chastity, whereas the Slavs had a very high birthrate.[14] So they needed women, and Himmler was against what he called *Scheidenpinselei*, or vaginal daubings—artificial insemination; so you needed women for repro-

duction. I also showed that the whole hierarchization of women derives
from their racial as well as genetic evaluation. Thus there were what Goer-
ing called the *Kulturträgerinnen* [culture bearers] who were at the top of
the scale and led a relatively privileged life. So we shouldn't declare that
women were generally victims, without taking account of their hierarchization. It's an idea I pursued in the book: women like Emmi Göring,[15]
the aviator Hanna Reitsch, and Leni Riefenstahl were not victims. In addition, there was a whole intermediate category of the wives of high-up Nazis
or the privileged of the regime, often jumped-up petits-bourgeois who
were even exempted from war service (there is a heated debate over this
point, which I describe). Then there were the *Arbeitspferde* [workhorses].
All this the Nazis said quite clearly themselves. Finally, there were the "sub-
women" who weren't superior to the "sub-men" since they were destined
for extermination: there too there was a hierarchy, since, contrary to what
is often said, the Slavs were "sub-men," whereas the Jews were only "para-
sites," which is not even a category of "sub-men." So what we have
amounts to an actual typology that is specific to women, but parallel to the
hierarchy of men. So it is unacceptable to mix everything up together. It is
also unacceptable to consider a woman who has lent her hand to the ex-
terminations in the camps as a victim—an example, at Auschwitz, is Irma
Grese, nicknamed "the angel of death"—although on the other hand, I did
get very angry with a French journalist, Pierre Durand, who wrote a book
called *La Chienne de Buchenwal* [The Bitch of Buchenwald], Ilse Koch's
nickname.[16] He had to be reminded that the dog of Buchenwald, the hus-
band, was the leader of the camp at Buchenwald. Hierarchy has to be
taken into consideration: even the infamous "angels of death" were under
men's orders. Birkenau, which was a women's camp, was run by a man.
Obviously, there were women who agreed to serve this system, and nowadays, in Germany, the expression used is *Mittäterinnen* [active coresponsible women], even though, with the exception of Irma Grese, none of them
was condemned as a war criminal, which is symptomatic.[17] I think you
have to keep a cool head and not make generalizations. What you quote
from Macciocchi is that kind of temptation to conceptual sliding which,
personally, I prefer to avoid.

E. W.: That's what I thought. I'd like to insist on another important
point that you stress: the demands of radical feminists at the turn of the
[twentieth] century—meaning the demands for abortion rights, contracep-

tion, the right to vote, sexual freedom—are associated by their enemies, male and female, with what is called the "Judaeo-Bolshevik perversion" threatening the *Volksgemeinschaft* (the community of the people, "based on Christian and German tradition, over and above conflicts of class and sex"[18]). In his Nuremberg speech of September 8, 1934, Hitler exclaims: "the message of women's equality is a message that only the Jewish spirit has been able to discover."[19] But on the other hand, in a book of 1917 a nationalist, racist "feminist" like Mathilde von Kemnitz,[20] who later became an influence on Pia Sophie Rogge-Börner,[21] accuses the Jews of the opposite— "of having been the principal instigators of women's legal incapacitation" [*jüdische Entmündigung*].[22] Whence the passion (because I do think it is a sort of passion) with which questions to do with women's freedom or lack of freedom are linked to the Jewish question, directly, on both sides?

R. T.: There I think we are touching on a fundamental problem which is the rejection of the other. Today, through psychoanalysis—which I draw on prudently, but still . . . —we know that the hatred of the other is also self-hatred. If you can't stand the other, you can't stand yourself. Personally, I came to feminism through my experience as an excluded Jewish woman, so through a double exclusion. Which perhaps protects me from the deviations you mention. I don't believe in superwomen or superintelligent women.

Our research team published a second book, a collective study about various countries, since unlike German women we are working toward an international history of women. I find it very shocking to see that German women working on women's history concentrate essentially on German women's history, as if these women hadn't had connections with women from other countries. But we know that the beginnings of feminism, at least, were marked by a significant international dimension. I have no conception of a national feminism. And that is why a few of us created the Women's International Scientific Association, the WIF (*Wissenschaftliche Internationale Frauenforschung*) which, as the name suggests, is international. And that is also why a few months ago I took part in an international conference in the United States on the emigration of Third Reich women. To come back to your question, the second collective book we published, *La Tentation nationaliste* [The Nationalist Temptation], shows that in the history of German feminism this temptation has always been there. One of our Italian experts showed what the situation was in that country, another woman did the same for Spain, another for France, and the forms of this temptation vary greatly according to the culture of the country concerned. But what jumps out at you in Germany, especially in the aftermath of World War I, is this emergence of Social Darwinism among women in the *Frauenbewegung*, the women's movement. Basically, we find not many progressive women and a few Jewish women opposing this tendency—I very much like women such as Lida Gustava Heymann and Anita Augsburg,[23] they are my role models—one was Jewish, the other not, but a progressive. As for Helene Stöcker,[24] my appreciation is much more qualified there because she was much influenced by Nietzsche and even by Social Darwinism. But a woman like Camilla Jellinek,[25] from the fact of having studied law, was opposed to this Social Darwinist tendency. In my opinion, this is one of the great dangers faced by the German feminist movement, which sometimes goes back to tedious myths, the myth of a matriarchy, for instance, and sometimes—you touched on this a moment ago—this movement follows in the footsteps of some American women in saying that Judaism is the root of all prejudices against women, when they are so ignorant of history that they don't know—and you cited this—that the emancipation of women is always assimilated to the emancipation of the Jews. Basically, there is a whole strand that doesn't accept the other, the one who is different, although among Jews as well, the ones who are different are a minority. A minority that wants change, that wants progress, that wants emancipation; which isn't all Jews. I show, for instance, in the essay I alluded to just now,[26] that very few Jewish women emigrants from the Third Reich were involved in political struggle, which is a sign of the bourgeois minds of German women. There are far more among Austrian emigrant women. And the majority of women participating in the French Resistance were of Jewish origin—Russian or Polish. You find some exemplary figures among them, particularly girls of fifteen. One of them, when she was taken by the Gestapo, jumped from the sixth floor at the Porte d'Orléans in Paris, to avoid informing against her friends.[27] But this kind of thing is very rare among German Jewish emigrant women because they are bourgeois German women. Sure, they must have had to work hard. A woman like my mother was a member of the support committee for Republican Spain. She would send us round to collect milk and clothes; it was my first lesson in international solidarity. But this was very unusual. I think in the German tradition, the progressive tendency is basically very weak and not interna-

tionalist enough, and that's still true today. In saying that I don't mean
French feminism is fabulous, but let's say it's much more oriented toward
international problems.

E. W.: In Germany there are feminist theologians who study the Bible
in order to expose what would be, as they see it, pure and simple antifeminism. But let me make the link right away by a question to do with the book
from which you have just quoted. In "La voix du silence" [The Voice of Si-
lence], your contribution to *La Tentation nationaliste*, you write that "Hitler's
assertion, denouncing the demand for women's rights as an invention of intellectual Jews, was not entirely groundless," given the fact that "German
Jews were mainly from the lower or middle ranks of the liberal bourgeoisie
in the cities, and they encouraged the advanced education of girls, which is
an indispensable condition for a secure future, more than the majority of the
German population."[28] Leaving aside the existence of supportive economic
conditions, for you there are presumably elements in the Jewish tradition, as
opposed to the Christian tradition, Protestant or Catholic, that favor the liberation of women? And in spite of the fact that Christianity, at least at the
beginning, was able to seem to be a message of liberation for women, since
it granted them some rights in the religious community.

R. T.: I think your question has to be given a more sociological angle, rather than a religious one. If we take Judaism as a religion, we will find
that, as in all monotheistic religions, women have only a very minor place
in it. After all, the great man of Christianity, St. Paul, the Rabbi Shaul,
converted to Christianity, uttered declarations of exclusion and marginal-
ization that nothing since then has equaled! But in the Jewish tradition, so-
ciologically this time, there is a different experience, that of marginaliza-
tion, and situations of exclusion or emigration. The Jews have a long
experience of the difficulty of living. I have always disputed the thesis of
some feminists on the supposed virtues or innate good qualities of "the"
woman, in quotation marks: for me there isn't "the" woman, there is
women, there are women. On the other hand, I believe in there being
qualities intrinsic to a specific social status. When the day comes that
women really are men's equals in society, this aspect will tend to disappear.
For the Jews, it's a constant, since they have been persecuted throughout
history. I know this from my own family. In France, my mother had to sell
to private customers, to sell door to door, as the phrase goes, because she

knew French better than my father, being of Swiss origin, but she was absolutely determined that her daughter should get an education. I went to the local school first, then high school, and it wasn't her fault that the war interrupted my education and I had to go back to it afterwards, but with the conviction firmly anchored in the family tradition that you get an education to get somewhere, to manage, even if you have to eat contaminated beef while you are waiting. So it is more a historical, sociological tradition than a religious one. I think you do have to keep the two distinct, and I blame these feminist theologians for not doing so. There are exceptions: my friend Leonore Siegele-Wenschkewitz, who represents our WIF in Germany, organized a counter-conference, since she is a theologian, against these so-called feminist theologians, to show that Judaism is no more guilty of excluding women than Catholicism or Protestantism.[29] It's generally true of monotheistic religions. But you have to distinguish religion from sociology. So, coming from an actively practicing family, and having learned Hebrew, today I am strongly non-religious. This is a development for me, because historical Jewish culture in general, to which I am most attached, I keep separate from religious practice, which I am detached from and which, in my opinion, is an obstacle to women's emancipation. This really does have to be very clear. Unfortunately, in Germany it isn't. It's a blessing for France to be a secular state, but I always point out that when France was doing badly, under Vichy, the state was no longer secular, it was a reactionary clerical state. Even if nowadays communism is in its death throes, I persist in saying that the opium of the peoples remains what we might call an ossified religion. Not that all the values that religion broadcasts are bad: I believe in ethical values, but not in obscurantism, which is still so much in evidence in the world of today.

E. W.: It is very telling that it was radical feminists who "refuse[d] to join in [the] war fever" of 1914, as you tell the story in your book.[30] On the other hand, this wasn't true of a woman like Gertrud Bäumer. At the beginning of the book you write that you have spontaneous sympathies for feminists and that you try to practice "empathy toward others, without exclusion."[31] That seems to me very difficult for women like Gertrud Bäumer,[32] for instance . . .

R. T.: I would say that one develops . . . My books take me an average of six or seven years. That book was published in France in 1982; take away six years, that makes 1976. I think today I would reason differently because the more you go into the role of someone like Gertrud Bäumer, the less empathy and sympathy you can have. Still, I had already shown that she and her companions secured the transition to National Socialism and that at one point she was in favor of the *Gleichschaltung* [elimination of opponents], in contrast to others. It even appears that today we are downgrading our views of women like Agnes von Zahn-Harnack,[33] who I thought was better than Bäumer. History evolves, and true revisionism is not the denial of something but the focusing that comes after exhaustive research. Some German feminists were seeking to rehabilitate Gertrud Bäumer. A few years ago, I received an emergency call from Alice Schwarzer asking me to write a piece on this for her journal *Emma*, in which I laid out the issues.[34] Because, as I have said, in Germany I still find a certain sympathy for a national line. And since the notion of nation has never been well developed in Germany, this is dangerous. For, as my friend and colleague Rudolf von Thadden says,[35] the concept of a nation constructed on the basis of the idea of land and blood and not the idea of a chosen citizenship,[36] as is the case in France, or at least it has been up till now, is disturbing.

E. W.: To go back to Gertrud Bäumer. She founded the *Nationaler Frauendienst* [National Women's Service] in 1914, encouraging "German women of all backgrounds and all classes to *serve their country*, in the armaments industries as well, until October 1918," and she also admits to "hating even the word 'sexuality.'"[37] Unlike radical feminists, she is not a pacifist. You can find a certain echo of this much later, in 1978, when Maria Antonietta Macciocchi writes: "The sexual illiteracy of women is part and parcel of institutional feminism. The refusal of pleasure, of sexual liberation."[38] Doesn't all this lead to the following conclusion: any liberation of women takes place *first of all* via sexual liberation?

R. T.: No. That seems too categorical to me. Liberation, sure. I remember how, when we started the *Choisir* [Choice] movement in France,[39] of which I was national secretary before going on to the international movement, we fought against the women who would brandish placards at demonstrations with slogans like "My womb belongs to me," or "My body belongs to me," and I shouted "So does my head!" I don't think you can separate sexual liberation and intellectual liberation. Without endorsing the excesses of *Sex-pol*, I was very influenced by Reich at the beginning because he never separated the political and social dimension from the sexual dimension.[40] Sex for sex's sake, no. What have we seen showing up in the Eastern European countries liberated from communism? The first thing to be introduced is the sex business: women dancing naked to earn their living is not sexual liberation. For women who aren't intellectually capable of the power of knowledge, there is no sexual liberation; the two things are closely linked. In France as well I have noticed the same drift. We have succeeded very well with things that are obvious in the view of most women, like the freeing up of contraception and abortion. Then, when it was a question of rape and violence against women, it was still okay, but when it comes to fundamental political rights, everything remains to be done. How many women are there in the National Assembly?[41] How many women leaders in the political parties? It's true that in Germany now quotas have been introduced, but for instance, at the WIF congress at the Evangelische Akademie Arnoldshain near Frankfurt, in the presence of the women's rights delegate for Hesse who, at the time, was a member of the Christian Democratic Union (CDU) (before that she was a Green, in fact it was she who had invited us), I criticized the low proportion of women in senior university positions (and I got flak for doing so).[42] In this regard, France is more advanced. It's the power of knowledge that determines everything else. I don't think it is possible to be sexually liberated without it. I have lived with someone without being married, and ten or fifteen years ago I wouldn't have been able to take on this position without at the same time making sure of my social situation. Today, in France, it's easier. I'm a professor (it's a coincidence—not quite—that I became one when a great number of women were promoted in the *Année de la femme* [Year of Women], 1975, when Giscard D'Estaing promoted women to the rank of university professor). And you mustn't forget the women who haven't got there yet and pull the ladder away when you're at the top of it. In the same way I protest, and I said this as well in front of that congress in the US, against a ghettoized history of women. Women's history is not an annex of history, but it is *in* history. It's always the same problem: you have to insert these questions into a social context, preferably international.

    E. W.: You try, in your work as a woman historian, to "develop reflection and the scientific cooperation of women with regard to the alterity which, without excluding men, nonetheless goes against the norms of a 'male order' of the world."[43] You say you want to "contribute to international feminist research";[44] and you do so . . . You are president of the Women's International Scientific Foundation, the WIF . . .

R. T.: President-delegate, yes—we don't have a president.

E. W.: Could you tell us some more about what research of this kind, or thinking in this spirit, consists of?

R. T.: At the International League Against Racism and Anti-Semitism (LICRA), which wasn't desparately feminist—it's a pluralist organization that's been in existence since 1927 and changed over the years; first it was the League against the pogroms, then against anti-Semitism; it's the oldest world organization of this type—I got a committee set up a few years ago to look at "Historical Memory and Human Rights." I did this at a Strasbourg conference where the delegates had visited the Struthof camp where several prisoners were gassed and where there were victims of the "Night and Fog" actions. People were so shaken by this visit that I succeeded in creating this committee, with the support of our panelists whose comment was: "It can't be enough to attack those who deny genocide, we must educate." For instance, we are starting to teach the problems of racism and anti-Semitism as part of the syllabus for university colleges training teachers. As I see it, the past is not a museum piece, but must become a weapon, a dyke, to avoid slippages of the kind we have in France with Le Pen. That doesn't only go on in Germany. This committee includes both men and women—I say that to show you that I'm not a ghetto feminist. In the same way, my research seminar "Sex and Race" alternates the subjects. The subtitle is "New Forms and Discourses of Exclusion in the Nineteenth and Twentieth Centuries." It covers several countries—at present, mainly in Europe—and different forms of exclusion. For instance, I have just invited a specialist in freemasonry because freemasons were pursued under the Nazi occupation of France. But we deal in rotation with problems concerning women, Jews, and so on—this year for instance one theme will be the attitude of the Austrian Church. I edited a journal special issue on Judaism, anti-Judaism, and anti-Semitism in Austria.[45] So I have also tried to bring a feminist dimension into milieux that aren't particularly feminist, that aren't sensitive to it, by showing its links with the different forms of anti-Semitism and racism, as we were discussing at the beginning. I think it's a mistake for feminism to concentrate itself in what are like ghettoes. It reminds me of the communists who stayed among communists and who didn't see what was going on around them, until one day they were in such a minority that they no longer had any power. You have to watch out that you don't construct ghettoes. And it's a tendency in Jewish circles. For instance, I'm a member of the Jewish Academics' Committee in France within a larger Jewish organization (*Fonds social juif unifié*) and I often have to warn against this ghetto tendency: I also address it in my paper on Jewish women in emigration. The lesson I've drawn from it personally is that without the solidarity of non-Jews, I wouldn't be speaking to you at this moment. And you have to hold on to this lesson . . . Jews on their own or women on their own . . . let's say feminists on their own will never succeed in obtaining anything. Moreover, we know that many women suffer from self-hatred, like some Jews suffer from self-hatred.

As for cooperating with German colleagues, it's not always easy. For instance, at the Arnoldsheim WIF conference I mentioned a little while ago, I had a difficult discussion with a German ecologist philosopher who had spoken of *Heimat* [native land]. I said without hesitating: when will it be *Blut und Boden* [blood and land]?

At the first WIF conference, in December 1983, in Salzburg since it [the organization] is based in Austria, there was a very serious incident. A German woman—I won't give her name—thought the photographs of naked Jewish women shot dead by the Nazis were not of Jews but of Polish women workers, that it was a mythologization, upon which I called her a "German Faurisson."[46] My German colleague's remark had shocked one of the participants, an Austrian Jewish woman, who is now an eminent psychiatrist-psychoanalyst for children in Vienna, so much so that in the evening she came to my room to say: "I'm leaving, I'm not giving my paper tomorrow." I replied, "That's not the right attitude—we must sort out the problem. Tomorrow, before you give your paper, we will discuss this question." And there was indeed a very lively discussion—with no agreement though, but at least we debated it in depth. This wasn't simple, but all the same it was more positive than what I experienced at a history conference at the Catholic University of Eichstätt in Bavaria, where a young German researcher in history, to whom I was pointing out that you didn't "die" in a concentration camp but you "perished" or you were "murdered," which are terms that exist in German too—*umkommen* and *umgebracht werden*—said to me: "In your language I suppose you would call Hitler a murderer." I said: "What else would you call him?" What shocked a number of the foreign participants was that none of the organizers, men this time, Germans, protested. We simply went on to the next thing. With the feminists, at least we were able to have a discussion. All the same, feminists still have a long way to go to reach a political consciousness, political in the broad sense of the term.

E. W.: As you know, in 1986 there was a dispute and division among West German intellectuals, called the *Historikerstreit*, on the question of the uniqueness of the annihilation of European Jews by the National Socialists.[47] Those who deny that the Shoah cannot be compared to other massacres blame their opponents for concealing the actual relativity of history and obscuring or at least ignoring other atrocities in the shadow of the barbarity committed against the Jews—for instance, the terrors under Stalinism. This battle brought about the open explosion of a deep-seated crisis in the discipline of history, a crisis that confirms that all historical research has moral implications, whatever color they may be. Among other things, this crisis showed how historicism, which claims to narrate the facts of history with a supposedly strict objectivity, ends up, through the relativization of crimes, contributing to the rehabilitation of a national narcissism and, in the last analysis, an exculpation. There were heavy repercussions for the discipline of history. What conclusions would you draw from this affair?

R. T.: I did, of course, protest at the time of the *Historikerstreit*. We happened to be holding a convention of the International Federation for the Resistance on the historiography of Nazism and oppression in the war and the Resistance—a very interesting conference because for the first time there were as many historians from Eastern Europe as from Western Europe; and since I was representing France in the organizing committee of this conference, I very much wanted it to be in Vienna, whereas the German delegates wanted it to be in Bonn because of the *Historikerstreit*. I wanted it to be in Vienna because of the Waldheim affair, which seemed to me both serious and important.[48] I met a historian from the Academy of Sciences in the USSR, Ilja Kramer, who waited until we were on our own to say: "I think, my dear, that we are of the same religion," which I confirmed. And when I congratulated him on Gorbachev coming to power, he said: "Wait a bit, we have been through the Krushchev experience, it's not certain that it will succeed." This was 1986. So already at that time we had seen what I would call a historiographical thaw in the East, leaving aside a few slower countries, East Germany in particular. But I think the problem is much wider than the crisis in historiography. Because basically, what is scientific objectivity? As a feminist and a Jewish woman, I have to contest the notion of objectivity. Georg Simmel had pointed the way a little bit when he said: "Male subjectivity has been set up as objectivity." There has been objectification. In general, the human and social sciences, unlike the natural sciences, are not exact sciences, and even the natural sciences are always needing revisions. But having said that, you have to see what is implied by any notion of subjectivity in history. You were right to say that there is a dimension that I would call ethical. In the same way that a doctor needs to have a code of ethics, I think we have to look after our professional ethics. And let me repeat what I was saying was needed just now, when you put the question about Judaism—a distinction between a faith and the sociocultural dimension: meaning that we need to take great care over the subtle differences. To put the genocide of the Jews in the same category as the massacres of history in general is to forget a specific dimension. But that isn't to say that the genocide of the Armenians didn't take place. I began my research with a dissertation on Franz Werfel's *The Forty Days of Musa Dagh*, a book of 1939 that tells the story of the massacre and resistance of the Armenians. As a young student I was extremely sensitive to this superb novel of Werfel's. [Stressing the specificity of the Jewish case] doesn't mean that you forget or neglect the other genocides, but you have to make sure you don't lump them all together.

E. W.: In the 1988 preface to the German edition of your book *La Nuit du cristal* [The Crystal Night], you write: "Especially at this time when there is so much talk about how the past is dealt with (*Entsorgung der Vergangenheit* [the disposal of the past]), it seems necessary to us to awaken memory."[49] How do you estimate the risks of this kind of *Entsorgung* or disposal after the reunification of Germany?

R. T.: It's one of my main preoccupations. In June 1991, at my suggestion, we had a debate at the Universal Israelite Alliance with Alfred Grosser and Rudolf von Thadden.[50] Katharina von Bülow was chairing the debate, with a mostly Jewish audience. I must admit that I didn't wholly share the optimism of someone like Alfred Grosser. Von Thadden was more qualified. He began by saying that one of the conditions for things going well—a condition that hasn't been met up to now—was that Germany should finally adopt the notion of a citizenship not based on ethnic origin. We don't know where Germany will go. I continue to think that the choice of Berlin as the capital will already tend more toward a German leadership in Eastern Europe, economically and culturally to begin with. And so a decentering in relation to the West. That affects cultural life as well as the economy. I continue to believe—and I don't say this in a spirit of superiority—that Germany needs Western influence to keep it on course. What always strikes me when I go to Germany, which I do often for lectures and panels, is the weakness of the political culture. It's not enough to have a democratic system; every citizen needs to have a political consciousness in the broad sense of the term, and it is lacking. In the editor's preface to a special issue of the journal *Matériaux pour l'histoire* on the theme *Allemagne, an 1 de l'unification* [Germany, Unification Year 1], I write that one of Germany's big problems is how it will come to terms with its history.[51] For example, as if by chance—and, I think, not entirely by chance—the wall came down on the day that was the anniversary of the Crystal Night.[52] In 1990 it was the first time for thirty years that I had not been invited anywhere in Germany to give a lecture on the Crystal Night. There were already problems in 1989, the year the wall came down; they wanted to postpone the lecture. I replied: "Even if only half the number of people turn up, I am keeping to the date." But in 1990, nothing. And then look what happened because of the Ravensbrück camp: they wanted to open a supermarket there on the pretext that "life must go on."[53] Can't life go on if you put up a supermarket somewhere else? This controversy was barely over when they wanted to set up the tax office in the central administration buildings of the Nazi camps at Sachsenhausen![54] Then there was the transfer of the ashes of King Sargent and Frédéric II, honoring the virtues of these sovereigns.[55] But King Sargent was after all the personification of militarism. It didn't bother me that their bodies should be transported to Potsdam, which was indeed where they should have been buried. But with military honors, and Chancellor Kohl—please! The Germans have a real problem about coming to terms peacefully with their history. It irritates me when Napoleon is celebrated in France, but after all there are enough other democratic traditions to compensate. So, let him remain in Les Invalides and let's say no more about him, at least. Sometimes there is an exasperating nationalism in France, but there are also safeguards, counter-weights, because of this tradition of citizenship. Despite there being some problems, let's say that history is better accepted. What I fear in Germany is the weakness of the political culture. The Germans have a tradition that is difficult to inherit. One day they will have to learn . . . Let me put another question that von Thadden in fact began to raise: "How will we celebrate May 8, 1945 in the Europe of the future?" Von Thadden gave us different possible definitions, year by year, in Germany. In France it's clear, it's the Liberation. Couldn't it be admitted in Germany that it isn't November 9, 1989 that marks Germany's liberation? As it was for all countries, May 8, 1945 was the day of the German people's liberation from the yoke of National Socialism. Daniel Mayer, who isn't unknown in France— he has been vice-president of the Constitutional Council and an eminent socialist leader—said: "To please our German European partners, are we going to cancel the May 8 celebration?"—which is what Giscard d'Estaing did, and we protested. These aren't only symbols. The *Historikerstreit* is not alone in showing up the uneasiness. And by the way, very few women had a voice in this debate: my friend and colleague Anette Kuhn, from Bonn, made a stand, but I didn't see many others. Where are the feminists in this battle? We come back to the problem of political culture. One day, in front of a conference of pacifist feminists in Paris, I said I wasn't unconditionally a pacifist. In Nuremberg at the age of six I learned to throw myself on the ground to take cover from SA shooting.[56]

E. W.: You were born in Nuremberg?

R. T.: Yes. So when I was six, I was there at the SA's siege of the *Tagespost* building—the *Tagespost* was the Social Democrat newspaper. And I will never forget the Social Democrats who were there shouting "Brüder, kein Blut vergiessen!" [Brothers, don't shed any blood!]. That kind of pacifism is not for me. There are times when you have to know how to fight. And that was something I learned physically.

E. W.: When was it you came to France?

R. T.: In 1933. Right after those events, because my father was a personal enemy of Streicher's.[57] We fled in the space of a single night, me with my mother first of all and my brother, each holding a little suitcase in hand, to Basel, in Switzerland, where my mother's family was, and my father followed as and when he could. But we couldn't stay in Switzerland because my father was German. Streicher arrested my uncle instead and sent him to Dachau. So my grandmother wrote to Hindenburg to tell him my uncle had received the first-class iron cross. Hindenburg had him freed. He was part of the convoy of Jews going from Baden to Gurs, and it was there that the Germans caught him again, because he was handed over for deportation with one of my aunts and both of them died—we don't know if it was at Lublin or at Auschwitz. As far as pacifism is concerned, I had a fairly heated debate about it in the German city of Aachen. It was during the Gulf War. I said I wasn't one of the pacifists and that I would have liked them to be as energetic as that against the manufacture of gases threatening Israeli Jews, who had already experienced some a number of years before. There are contradictions that you have to know how to take on. I am not an unconditional pacifist.

E. W.: To come back to France: 1947 saw the publication of Adorno and Horkheimer's *Dialectic of Enlightenment*, including a chapter entitled "Elements of Anti-Semitism." They say there: "The destruction of cemeteries is not a mere excess of anti-Semitism—it is anti-Semitism in its essence."[58] What is your impression or your judgment of the current situation in France with regard to a possible resurgence of anti-Semitism, especially following the desecration of the Jewish cemetery at Carpentras?

R. T.: It is unfortunate that this affair provided an opportunity not just for the far right, but also for intellectuals like those on the journal *Le Débat*, which has nothing far right about it, to ask themselves disturbing questions.[59] Basically, in France anti-Semitism is linked to economic and social crises, that's clear, and the fact that four million French people, even a bit more, vote for Le Pen is pretty worrying.[60] And indeed whereas at first Le Pen advanced on tiptoe, he's no longer embarrassed to be attacking the Jews, the freemasons, the communists—that goes without saying—and now he wants to de-Marxify France. Le Pen's real followers are the category of people who partly used to vote communist out of economic and social confusion. It's true that anti-Semitism and xenophobia are on the increase in France—perhaps more than racism, which is primarily directed against North African immigrants. But still, there are democratic safeguards in France. There are organizations, and even in government departments there are plenty of people, and of all persuasions, not only on the left, who fight anti-Semitism. I don't think there's a very serious danger. But having said that, we have to be very vigilant. And our battle, which is why I am also in the LICRA, is a constant one. But in France, at the moment, there is no serious, threatening drift. The big problem will be immigration, but in my opinion that's the big problem for the end of the twentieth and the beginning of the twenty-first century all over the world, not just for France. And problems are going to be more and more interdependent. What worries me more in Germany than in France is the weakness of political culture. I'm not saying France is a model of democracy, but there is a secular, republican, democratic tradition that is still alive for many French people.

Paris
August 26, 1991

4

Humanity Is Biblical

EMMANUEL LEVINAS

ELISABETH WEBER: In one of the last series of seminars you gave at the Sorbonne, called "Death and Time," published in the *Cahiers de l'Herne* special issue on your work, you were saying: "In death, as pure nothingness, as foundationlessness—which we feel more dramatically, with the acuteness of that nothingness that is greater in death than in the idea of the nothingness of being . . . we arrive at something that European philosophy has not thought."[1] This statement may seem surprising. Even if Western philosophy can be considered as a long meditation on death—we might think for instance of the saying of Socrates repeated by Montaigne, that to philosophize is to learn how to die—there would be something in death that this meditation had not grasped hold of. One of the main ideas of your seminars is that "every death is a murder, is premature, and there is the responsibility of the survivor."[2] While taking part in mourning for someone close, there would be a kind of suffering owed to remorse.

EMMANUEL LEVINAS: The straightforward idea of nothingness is not in itself a more difficult idea than the idea of being. And this is no doubt because a being fully a being feels itself on the edge of nothingness.

It happens quite otherwise with death. There, it's a question of what is lived directly. It is as though death were a murder that you didn't know how to avoid. In other words, death includes some murder. A murder that is not simply an event like all the events of nature but that, in a way that is incomprehensible—meaning foreign to the categories of European secular, nonreligious thought—concerns me, me as survivor.

E. W.: In other words, in relation to your earlier writings,[3] you are pushing the notion of responsibility further.

E. L.: Yes, the idea of responsibility, which is central and doesn't begin with me, but which is awakened in the face of the death of the other and which is in the consciousness of guilt that colors all compassion. I refer finally to a common feeling, the feeling it is common to experience at any burial: as if it was me who had killed.

E. W.: Then one could wonder whether the responsibility taught us by your thinking doesn't in that way become not only an infinite responsibility, but also a hopeless responsibility?

E. L.: The idea of charity, the idea of commitment with regard to the other, is reinforced by each mortal event. Obviously, all that I have just spoken about constitutes a provisional weakness in European philosophy, a weakness that has not been clarified. In the idea of being there is a kind of wrong from the very fact that this being is doomed to die, but the important thing is, as soon as I see someone else, *bin ich schon schuldig*: I am already "guilty." Perhaps this modality should be thought through today, above all after Auschwitz: the guilt of survival. But think about compassion too. In compassion for a wrong—however slight—there is something like guilt. For me this is a fundamental category of sensitivity, a category I would like to insist on here. As soon as I see the face of the other, *I am already guilty*, at least under an obligation. As though any vision—and for me this is an essential structure of time—any encounter with another, was the encountering of an obligation preceding our encounter. So that, in the structure of time, the "ecstasy"[4] of the past is the encounter with the other. Already, I owe him, and I owe him without having ever borrowed. As if, in encountering the other, there was a past that has never been present. To put it in different terms, there would be a first "ecstasy" there in the very constitution of time.

E. W.: You describe death as "the very event of passing" (indeed the phrase is "he passes away"),[5] but a much earlier text associates this "very event of passing" not directly with death, but with an "irreducible absence," with what you call *la passée*,[6] the immemorial passage of the Wholly-Other.[7]

Between this *passée* or immemorial passage and "the very event of passing" which is what you say death is, there is presumably a link. Would you say that what European philosophy has not thought through has been more deeply thought through in Jewish tradition?

E. L.: I don't know. I would like to stress this word immemorial. It is an immemorial past that does not refer to a present anterior. As a result, it is essential in the constitution of becoming as such, in temporality as such. I sought a similar situation for the future, for the ecstasy of the future. The meaning of the future is that there is meaning in spite of my death. Within religion, that is quite simple: it is the whole story of the resurrection. Here, on the other hand, thanks to the child, and as a result thanks to femininity, I can have this possibility of dying in a world that has a meaning. A meaning after my death is not simply an acceptance, a giving up, a sacrifice, but all that is meaningful in sexuality and in paternity, in the other. So what we have is an attempt to describe a temporality very different from the one analyzed by Heidegger.

As to the present, there is an eloquent and revealing word in the French language, the word *maintenant*.[8] It's what I take, what I understand. All the optimism of knowledge is due to this priority of the present where the hand [*main*] not only touches, but grasps, tries to understand.

E. W.: Yes, in German it's *begreifen*.

E. L.: And you have *eingreifen* . . .[9]

E. W.: . . . . which makes the violence of the intervention explicit. . . .

You ask the question: "Doesn't the trauma of the other come from *someone else*? Isn't the nothingness of death the very nakedness of the face of the one near?"[10] In other texts,[11] you link the face of the other first of all to an appeal that precedes any appeal that is heard, any concrete language: you link it to the openness of language. The death heralded in the face of the other and the openness of language that happens through the encounter with the other—would these be, if I can put it like this, "co-originary," or rather, to pick up one of your terms, each as "an-archic" as the other?

E. L.: But language is not a threat of death. Language is not grasping the other, not taking another. To speak to another is no longer to threaten them, to be no longer threatened by them. It's the idea of peace. *Shalom* is "hello"! When I meet a stranger, I involve myself in their life by saying "hello!" This phenomenon of peace, outside any religion, starting from the present, starting from the other, starting from the encounter, is essential.

E. W.: My question was also pointing toward a certain proximity with Heidegger who, especially in the texts written after *Being and Time*, makes a link between language and *Sterblichkeit* [mortality].

E. L.: It's a different meaning that matters to me. I can't help thinking of Heidegger. But there, we encounter the question "What is phenomenology?" It's not at all a reconstitution of being on the basis of the phenomenon, but a recovery of the horizon, in Husserl's sense of the term, that gives meaning to the essential. For Husserl, the horizon is very frequently what is on the margins. But what is on the horizon is determining for being and for the development it includes. For me phenomenology, in general, is the evocation of the horizon, a reminder of the horizon, even for the word *maintenant*. What is on the horizon gives the tonality, gives phenomena their different meanings, which subsist in their contradictions.

E. W.: In an interview you said: "My philosophy rests on a prephilosophical experience, on a terrain that is not derived only from philosophy."[12] Can you speak about these experiences?

E. L.: There is philosophy because, first of all, there's a heap of things on the horizon that have no meaning, that aren't felt, that are barely human. So, why is there philosophy? It's so that things will signify. It's the beginning of meaning.

E. W.: To what extent are political experiences part of these prephilosophical experiences?

E. L.: In my thinking, the political has a completely determined meaning. It is a fact that we are not two, that we are at least three. Straight away, in addition to the initial charity, since the relationship between two is a form of charity, there is "calculation" and comparison. In multiplicity, all faces count, and all the faces negate one another. Each one is elected as if by word of God, each one has a right. Each face is also responsibility. Starting from the third one, I have to compare, compare the incomparable of the face with all possible "decency." The justice of comparison necessarily comes after charity. It owes everything to charity, but it constantly denies charity. That is already the political.

Whence the great questions: why is there evil, why can politics absorb all forms of activity, why does the *conatus essendi*, the effort of being, become the fundamental effort?[13]

E. W.: To what extent have political experiences influenced your thinking? Such as experiencing the forms of totalitarianism in the twentieth century and, in particular, that of National Socialism? Your book *Otherwise than Being or Beyond Essence* opens with a commemoration of the victims of National Socialism . . . This book would then be an attempt to put into memory a catastrophe that is almost unnameable . . .

E. L.: . . . . which happened in history and which has a motivation, a meaning.

E. W.: Your book is unique because through notions such as "trauma," "obsession," and "persecution," it tries to preserve the memory of something that Western philosophical concepts cannot make out or recollect at all.

E. L.: There is another direction in my thought as well: realizing that man's humanity is not reducible to the freedom manifested in politics, but signifies goodness, the possibility of what the writer Vassili Grossman calls "small goodness"—in a book that is fundamental to me, *Vie et destin* [Life and Destiny].[14] It's a kind of goodness that doesn't manage to conquer evil, but nor does evil manage to wipe it from memory or to conquer it, either. That is where reflection on National Socialism leads, if one can put it like this.

E. W.: Is that how the experience of twentieth-century totalitarianisms has marked your thinking?

E. L.: Yes, that is how it has determined it. "Gut sei der Mensch . . ." [Let man be good . . .].

E. W.: Are you thinking of Goethe's "Hilfreich sei der Mensch, edel und gut" [Let man be a helper, noble, and good]?

E. L.: Yes, except that *edel* contains the word *Adel*, nobility, and that can hide many things. In the Hitlerian version of authenticity, in *Eigentlichkeit*, there is this bad *Adel* which at the very least is extremely ambiguous.

E. W.: I would like to embark on a more specifically Jewish subject. The notion of election, in particular, has considerable importance in your philosophy. In the *Le Monde* interview with Descamps, you say: "Election does not grant privilege. Election has only a moral sense. The moral person is the one in a gathering who does the thing that has to be done. In that, he elects himself." Is this the sense in which "being Jewish is not a particularity," but "a modality"?[15]

E. L.: It is a human modality. I think humanity is biblical. The alliance was made with Abraham, because the human wasn't "working" too well before that . . . The Bible has an important place in the discovery of the meaning of the human, its importance equals that of the universal destiny of Greece. The rise of Greece signifies the appearance of the political. And that happens very early on. So then you are dealing with a people, and no longer with a person. This moment is inevitable. Thinking the meaning of the human means also thinking the future without me that opens up through sexuality and the otherness of woman. I have developed this in the short text *Le Temps et l'autre* [Time and the Other].[16] That remains essential for the idea of the future, for the ecstasy of the future.

E. W.: You mention Kafka who, you say, "describes a guilt without crime, a world where man never understands the accusations brought against him. We see there the beginnings of the question of meaning. This is not only 'Is my life just?' but rather, 'Is it just to exist?'"[17] Which leads to the notion of "substitution" which you introduce in your thinking,[18] as well as that "dying for" which, you maintain, Heidegger was unable to think . . . [19]

E. L.: *Eigentlichkeit* is the *Adel* [nobility] of sword and blood! I have often said so. Crime can hide in that *Adel*. This Heideggerian ambiguity is a fundamental ambiguity!

E. W.: Speaking of "dying for another," on one occasion you referred to Moses' words proposing to God that he should allow an exchange and let him give several years of his life . . .

E. L.: Yes, there is a commentary on that verse in the Midrash. In Exodus (32:32) Moses says to God: "Blot me out from the book that you have written."[20] It would be possible to read this as: "Blot me out of history." But it is always read as: "Blot me out from my future, my destiny." Textually, Moses does not say: "Take my life in exchange," he says: "Blot me out from the book that you have written." This is a lot more! And more important: he wants to give his life on condition that pardon be granted to the others.

E. W.: Which reminds me of a text where you write: "If patience has a meaning as inevitable obligation, this meaning becomes a sufficiency and institution if there is no suspicion of non-sense beneath it. So in the I's egoity there has to be a risk of a non-sense, a madness." "Thus passivity is possible only if a pure madness can be suspected at the very heart of sense."[21]

E. L.: Yes, without the risk of this madness, meaning is fixed and consolidated in a norm or ideal where everything fits together.

E. W.: I'd like to talk about your Talmudic readings. At one point you cite a passage from the Talmud that says: "The words of wise men are like burning ashes." Then you add: "Why not fire rather than ashes? Because you have to breathe on them to rekindle them."[22] You often stress that the Talmud and the Bible, in spite of all their differences from Greek thought, respond to an approach that is not at all irrational. How would you establish the differences between this breath that rekindles the words of wise men and the study of a philosophical text?

E. L.: I wouldn't establish the difference, instead I'd maintain that in both cases there is a breath of the spirit. I'm not so much speaking about the way we interpret a page of Kant or Hegel or the legitimate way it is renewed in the course of history or again the way this interpretation renews the course of history. Rather, what matters to me is the spiritual value of lay interpretation in which its spiritual meaning is revealed. That is how interpretation resuscitates. And I even think that the ecstasy of the future is always that: it is a renewal because there is breath. I don't consider that a specialty of the Talmud. I would say rather that it is the very order of the activity of the spirit: the spirit is always that breathing. Obviously philosophy and the Talmud are not dealing with the same truths. But I think there can be an element of spirituality in any breath. Even when Heidegger interprets one of the philosophers of history. It is a renewal. There is no distinction there between the pure and the impure. Yet what is admirable is that people who had no access to Greek culture grasped that in their reading of traditional texts.

You also need the breath to rekindle the text when it comes to translating. To give you an example, in the prophet Micah (6:8) it is said that God required of us the love of love. But these two words are not the same in Hebrew.[23] In translation, that would come out as the charity of love. The word love seems to be repeated. How should this be translated? The

Benedictines, translators [into French] of the Jerusalem Bible, translate as *amour délicat* [tender love].[24] Chouraqui translates it as *amour du chérisse-ment* [love of cherishing].[25] Personally, I prefer Pascal, even if this isn't an exact translation of the verse in question—Pascal the good Christian who speaks of *amour sans concupiscence* [love without lust]. Love's second word speaks of gratuity, gratuitous love, without reciprocity. Buber didn't get as far as love without reciprocity. But it's in the Bible.

E. W.: It was the encounter with the Talmudist Chouchani that started off your interest in the Talmud.

E. L.: That was a big event in my life that I often recount. It was an extraordinary encounter. I had a very distinctive Jewish education. I was born in a family where Russian was spoken with the children. But when I was six, my father hired a Hebrew teacher. So I learned to read Hebrew, to read and study the Bible in Hebrew without weighing it down with Talmudic commentaries. In my time, that went on in an atmosphere that was more Zionist than Talmudic; I was learning what is called modern Hebrew. In my book, the Bible commentaries were written in modern Hebrew. There was no biblical criticism, of course, but the spirit of these commentaries was completely rational. I was not given a Talmudic education. It was in France, when I was thirty-five, that I met this extraordinary man who was a genius in the true sense of the word. On the outside, he looked like just anyone. It was he who got me to feel the breath in the Talmud. You couldn't find his equal. He could suddenly find a wonderful unity among a thousand contradictory things—which isn't easy! What is more, he also knew philosophy, even if he didn't talk about it. And he was full of admiration for mathematics. He was a difficult man to talk to, but the force of his intellect was frightening.

E. W.: Did you study with him for a long time?

E. L.: Yes, for a number of years. He gave me the spirit of the thing. He is dead now.[26] Anecdotes can't do justice to the dazzling effects of what he said. Despite appearances, white became black, red became every color!

E. W.: You have written a number of articles on the question of the relationship between Jews and Christians. Many Christian theologians refer to your thought; especially in Germany, this reception of your work is very important. How would you evaluate the relationship between Christians and Jews today, in particular after the Shoah?

E. L.: During the Hitler period, the attitude of many Christians was extraordinary. Of course it wasn't everything it could have been, if it had been organized, but ultimately it was fraternal, and I owe them much.[27]

And then, as you well know, Christian scripture comes from the Bible! As a result, in ongoing exchanges it is often possible to speak biblical language. I take the Christian reading seriously. Anti-Semitism I put down to obscurantism. When I say that Europe is the Bible and the Greeks, I am not only thinking of the Jewish Bible, but also the Bible as it has been known and spread by Christianity. As in the Jewish Bible, the three principal characters of humanity are the widow, the orphan, and the foreigner. Of course, I can't forget the persecutions and the obscurantisms, but the doctrine of the Old Testament, especially as it is read nowadays, agrees with Jewish hermeneutics. The great difficulty, nonetheless, is to show that everything is already there in the Jewish Bible. The Hebraic Bible should not be neglected.

I am skeptical with regard to a literature that seeks to show that all humanity is one, since I would not build the future of humanity on exotic cultures. Whereas whenever you open a Christian book, you find the same language again, in the end. And that is true in spite of the memories of the persecutions, which cannot be forgotten.

E. W.: Would the criterion be monotheism?

E. L.: The criterion is the Bible.

E. W.: . . . . which is not quite the same in each case . . .

E. L.: The Christian Bible contains the whole Jewish Bible, no book is excluded from it. And then I don't take literally all the mysteries and miracles, indeed not in Judaism either. It's not miracles that I find striking, but the meaning miracles have to be given. Christ has been very badly treated!

E. W.: When was your first encounter with German language and culture? Was it in the country where you were born, Lithuania?

E. L.: Yes. I would like to tell you the story of Dr. Mosche Schwabe. He was a German Jew of long-established allegiance, completely assimilated to the West and of high Greek culture. As you know, in the 1914–1918 war the German armies advanced a very long way into Eastern Europe. So it was during this war that Dr. Schwabe, who was conscripted as a soldier, first saw the faces of Eastern European Jews. He was very interested in their destiny. When peacetime came, he took up a post as head of a Jewish high school in Lithuania where the language of instruction was still for the time being Russian and where I was a pupil. In the year before the final exams, he taught a German class. He read *Hermann und Dorothea* with us, that was all.[28] It was dazzling. He said: "Make an effort, if it goes well you'll have a fever of 102 degrees and we'll read an act of *Faust.*" We didn't read *Faust,* but today I still know some passages of *Hermann und Dorothea* by heart. Among the most impressive are the dialogues *mit dem Pfarrer* [with the pastor] about France and the French Revolution. It's an extraordinary book. Then, instead of bringing *Faust,* he came with *Dichtung und Wahrheit* [*Poetry and Truth*]. He read out the pages describing the period when Goethe was living in Frankfurt, when he was a young boy, in his father's house, and where he mentions all the paintings that decorated this house.[29] We, the pupils, were a bit disappointed: the artists were unknown. Not Michelangelo, not Raphaël, not Rubens! Whence my question: how had he managed it for there to be only unknown artists? Dr. Schwabe's reply: "Er hat sie in seine Unsterblichkeit mitgenommen!" [He took them away with him into his immortality!]

Certainly the same could be said of Montaigne, Descartes, Shakespeare, Pushkin, or Dostoevsky. The West—the West in all its glory—is contained in this. These are the minds in contact with *Unsterblichkeit,* with the absolute, and that we could understand at any rate. In our high school innocence, we missed a Europe we were longing for. At any rate, in my class, everyone understood that these people Goethe allowed into his oeuvre belonged among the living greats.

In 1952 I went to Jerusalem. And I saw Dr. Schwabe again. He had emigrated and was teaching Greek there at a university! I don't think he is still alive. But I would really like it for his children one day, in Israel, to find my story.

Paris
August 7, 1991

5

Humanity, Nationality, Bestiality

LÉON POLIAKOV

ELISABETH WEBER: In your autobiographical book, *L'Auberge des musiciens* [The Musicians' Inn], you write: "If it is true that all one does is to write the same book over and over again, then my case is a blatant one."[1] However, even if your monumental *Histoire de l'antisémitisme* [A History of Anti-Semitism] can be considered as your main book,[2] you have worked on many other subjects, which are certainly linked to the huge question of anti-Semitism, but at the same time distinct from it. Here, by way of example, I'll just mention your research on the forms of totalitarianism or on sexual difference. How would you describe the link that exists between your work on anti-Semitism and your thinking about totalitarianism?

LÉON POLIAKOV: It's a fairly common approach for Jews. Since the history of the Jews appears unique of its kind, I looked for parallel cases, and I found one that was very distinctive and very little known, on which I published a book: this is the example of the *Altgläubige*, Russian traditional believers.[3] The role they played in world history is totally unknown. Like so many other persecuted groups, they specialized in the areas of finance and trade. Compared with the majority of Russian businesses (there were also many foreigners, but let's stick to Russian Russians here), they were much more dynamic than Russian orthodox people and, with the help of their ancient grudges, they contributed in many ways to Lenin's victory. Lenin was supported financially by the richest of them, Savva Morosov. So it can reasonably be argued that without the role they played, the course of world history would have been different.

But on the other hand, everyone develops in their own way. Perhaps you notice that while speaking French I have kept a Russian accent. In a way, I have always felt Russian. Which explains my interest in Russian things generally.

E. W.: So the link between the two questions would be persecution?

L. P.: Yes. And also, in the past, many Jews, after fighting for their own emancipation, joined the struggles for the rights of blacks or some other group!

E. W.: You have worked a great deal on racism and the notion of racism. Since the Cerisy conference "Ni Juif, ni Grec" [Neither Jewish nor Greek],[4] you have been putting the term racism in quotation marks, the idea being that since this term is derived from the physiological concept of "race," it would suggest that "race" had something to do with racism. You contrast to this a *sociological* meaning: "racism" understood as *belief* (and this term belief needs to be stressed) in a common, specific origin, a belief which, fairly often, implies a hostile or pejorative attitude to some other group.[5] How would you situate yourself in relation to the distinction utilized by Vladimir Jankélévitch between, on the one hand, racism as a superiority complex (for instance of the white person in relation to the black person) and a hatred of the other who is *manifestly* other; and, on the other hand, anti-Semitism as hatred that someone experiences against another who is *imperceptibly* other?[6] So the distinction between racism and anti-Semitism would be their different attitudes in relation to a manifest alterity or else to a more discreet, more subtle, but nonetheless irreducible alterity.

L. P.: The difference is crucial. These are terms that go back to the period when the concepts of race and racism were first formed. That was when it was decreed that the Jews were a "race." All that is familiar. But as far as anti-Semitism is concerned, it seems probable that its first symptoms date from the forefather Abraham—that's all a matter of legend, but the fact remains that long ago there was someone to decree a ban on human sacrifices. You only have to open the Bible to see how far this ban was constantly trampled underfoot by the Hebrews themselves. So there was an intra-Jewish conflict; this again was the form in which Christianity separated off from Judaism nearly two millennia ago. So at the start there was a schism that was perpetuated, and we know that in all periods a Jew converting to Christianity was welcomed with open arms. That has nothing to do with the detestable concept of "race."

E. W.: Do you regard Jankélévitch's distinction as valuable or acceptable? Because falling back on the notion of "race" in this definition is problematic. If I have understood you correctly, you reject a usage of this kind because it suggests that "race" would have something to do with racism.

L. P.: Definitely. In the 1950s, you know, Jankélévitch took up a very distinctive position. He declared that it was not possible to pardon the Germans. My autobiography teaches you that I had a number of good reasons for adopting the opposite position. And in general the historian's approach is very different from the philosopher's. I am an aphilosophical spirit, if the truth be told. The most I have done, when I discovered Wittgenstein recently, was to say to myself: that's the philosopher for me. And you're a philosopher, you must certainly know all the games people get up to these days in philosophy.

E. W.: All the same, I think there's something very interesting going on in France at the moment. On this point, I would like to refer to a problematic you have elaborated on a number of times, in particular when you state that "to write the history of anti-Semitism is to write the history of a persecution that, in the bosom of Western society, was linked with the highest values of that society, for it was pursued in their name." You have also implicated the "immense responsibilities of philosophers."[7]

L. P.: I was only speaking about Enlightenment ones!

E. W.: What seems extremely interesting to me today is that in contemporary French thought there is a certain sensitivity in relation to questions that touch on Judaism, and this sensitivity goes together with a thinking about the notion of difference. So there is certainly a change . . . I don't know how much importance you grant this sensitivity.

L. P.: Together with a number of colleagues from various countries, I'm in the process of writing a fifth volume of the *Histoire de l'antisémitisme*, from 1945 onwards.[8] I worked on the Russian chapter and also the general introduction. But for the French chapter, I preferred to call on another French author, Christian Delacampagne—perhaps you know the name.[9] There are some things that annoy me. In particular—and it's an old story, the number of personalities, especially media personalities, who play games—even when it is widely accepted that they are Jewish, they pretend not to be. I don't like that game. Apart from that and in general, I don't think the French are on average anti-Semitic. They are less and less so, and I see a reflection of that in the difference that exists between [the daily newspaper] *Libération*—mainly read by young people—which, in my opinion, deals openly with these questions, and *Le Monde*, which is fairly hypocritical: for *Le Monde*, Vladimir Horowitz is a Russian, Nathan Milstein a Ukrainian, and Georges Charpak, the Nobel prizewinner, is a scholar of Polish origin. Having said that, anti-Semitism, bearing in mind the regrettable Vichy past, has become a very, very big media topic.

E. W.: Yes, the debate around the "revisionists" also demonstrated that.

L. P.: I was struck, for instance, by the fact that the Carpentras affair coincided with the Cannes film festival.[10] My wife and I had settled down at 8:30 in the evening to listen to Patrick Poivre-d'Arvor and Alain Delon on Channel 1. But the Carpentras news dispatch had just arrived, and the only thing being talked about was the Carpentras affair.

E. W.: Do you find that suspicious?

L. P.: No, but excessive, to say the least: something to give yourself and give the public a good conscience.

E. W.: There was a vast mobilization . . .

L. P.: Yes, of course, there were some excellent reactions, but that wasn't all. And that was why I preferred to relinquish my French chapter to someone French with French roots. As with my book on the traditional believers: I worked with a young and very brilliant French philosopher. She is very interested in Judaism. She was at the Rachi Center.[11] She said to me: "I can understand Judaic things better than you, because I am seeing it from the outside."

E. W.: Evidently you have often worked in collaboration with other researchers in the course of your work.

L. P.: Not as often as all that. It's just that I made that decision for this fifth volume, in the first place because I didn't have enough historical distance, and secondly, because in practical terms I could no longer be running around the libraries. Someone said to me: "I'm going to do the running for you," and I accepted. I mainly work at home.

E. W.: I'd like to come back to the question of difference. In 1977 you organized a Cerisy conference that was about the question of sexual difference.[12] You mentioned Freud several times, as you also approach questions from that angle. I'm sure I'm going to formulate the question too generally, but perhaps it can be nonetheless outlined in these terms: with the kinds of hatred mobilized in anti-Semitic hatred, are there parallels or analogies to be made—without wanting to blur the important differences—with the vast problematic of sexual difference? For instance, when we consider particular practices of torture or abuse that the Nazis indulged in, they were often accompanied by, strictly speaking, a form of sexual disparagement. It's a very delicate question . . .

L. P.: Yes, it is. What is more, among the superstitions that were rife about Jewish men in the Middle Ages, there were some claiming that they menstruated and had other very feminine attributes, which says a lot. But it is a very complex problem.

E. W.: Anti-Semitic propaganda has taken up these fantasies again in other forms . . .

L. P.: Yes. Again: I do feel the difference, myself, perhaps and above all because I continue to feel Russian. I spend time with lots of French Jews who are perfectly integrated; they are French going back several generations, claiming to follow the ideal of 1789, an ideal on the subject of which I permit myself one or two reservations. For some reason or other, there was certainly no identity crisis among the Jews in all the Christian countries in the Middle Ages—leaving aside Spain where they had already been assimilated for a long time. And the reason I mentioned these French friends to you was that I was thinking of these identity crises that were very powerful, particularly in the Germanic atmosphere, from Weininger to Wittgenstein, especially in Vienna. It's a very difficult question. I have friends who think that this is because of a certain analogy, basically, between Jews and Germans. I don't know what to think about it. With psychoanalysis you can end up with any conclusion at all . . .

E. W.: I'm sure you know Hermann Cohen's famous text[13] . . .

L. P.: Yes, but not only that. Nahum Goldmann was saying the same thing, I have a psychoanalyst friend, fairly well-known and very intelligent, who thinks the same way. . . . For myself, I will just say that both groups are very dynamic.

E. W.: But you, on the other hand, do wonder in your *Histoire de l'antisémitisme*, whether anti-Semitism wasn't always more marked and stronger in Germanic countries than elsewhere, and you ask the question whether Germanic culture wasn't perhaps more susceptible to yielding to it than Latin cultures.

L. P.: I stick to Luther's writings in old age, which are no longer in print but were much read in the nineteenth century, to the links between Protestantism and German idealist philosophy. The Germans were serious folk, for whom philosophy was the great key, dispensing the ultimate truths; so they read Kant, Fichte, Hegel, where they learned some beautiful ones. . . . And then there were the historical reasons: because of its division into small pieces, Germany was the only country from which the Jews had never been really expelled. That also made things more complicated . . .

E. W.: In a book of interviews with Georges Elia Sarfati, you express some fears in relation to the current situation of Germany. You write there that Chancellor Kohl "would like to base national prestige on a collective guilt-riddance."[14] The reasons for this, you say, are very complex, and they are not only electoral ones. How do you see this now, in view of the reunification that has taken place since then?

L. P.: It seems to me it has relegated the well-known "quarrel of the historians" to the background.[15] In addition, it has had some unfortunate consequences even as we watch, because since the second half of 1990, East German skinheads, followed by West German ones—more than five or six thousand of them in all—have begun to attack foreigners, even killing them and setting fire to their houses, but the police were slow to intervene on these occasions. The Jews were also targeted: so at Wuppertal, an industrial town on the Rhine, two local skinheads trampled a German so badly that he afterwards died, because they had mistaken him for a Jew. There have been other anti-Semitic attacks, and some Jews have already left Germany, while others are preparing to do so. It's because they constitute a perfect symbolic target.

Thinking about this, they always have been, but above all since World War II. As an Israeli, Zvi Rix, said to my friend Gunnar Heinsohn: "Auschwitz werden uns die Deutschen niemals verzeihen" [The Germans will never pardon us for Auschwitz].[16] In the same way, in 1982, during the Lebanese War, a section of the German media hastened to compare the Israelis to the Nazis. True, there were some of the French and other papers doing just the same. But there are some German milieux in which a delegitimation of the state of Israel is very pronounced.

E. W.: This debate divides the German left especially . . .

L. P.: Yes. In 1992, in Freiburg, a translation was published of a short book I had written in 1968 called *De l'antisionisme à l'antisémitisme* [From anti-Zionism to anti-Semitism], this time with a preface by Detlev Claussen, a brilliant polemicist from the left.[17] We can wonder whether there will ever be an end to these polemics: the most recent scandal exploded around Rudolf Augstein, who runs *Der Spiegel*, because it was discovered that half a century ago he had published a story in the Vienna edition of *Völkischer Beobachter*, a Nazi paper.[18] As for the delegitimation of the state of Israel, think too of the deliveries of toxic substances to Saddam Hussein's Iraq . . .

E. W.: Against the background of the Gulf War, your reflections on Islam at the start of your history of anti-Semitism were all the more striking to me. You point out that in Syria, Egypt, and Palestine, in the countries belonging to the Christian empire, the Jewish communities in the seventh century welcomed the invading Muslims with open arms, but also that at that time the notion of *jihad*, of holy war, was expressly reserved for polytheists—meaning, as you say, "Arab idolaters."[19] Today, this word, *jihad*, is surrounded by confusion. It is important to remember that in the beginning the word did not apply to the other monotheistic believers, Jews and Christians. How do you see present and future relations among these three monotheistic cultures?

L. P.: I wrote the volume you are referring to thirty years ago . . . At the moment, it can be said that the Western offshoot has established itself very badly among Arab peoples, and the only thing that has established itself well is anti-Semitism and, more precisely, the *Protocoles des sages de Sion*.[20] At any rate, this is not the moment for attempting forecasts.

E. W.: In general are you fairly pessimistic?

L. P.: No, not necessarily . . .

E. W.: My question refers to various passages in your writings where you approach the difficult problem of the relationship between Israel and the Arab countries. You write for instance that there has probably been a displacement from anti-Semitism toward anti-Zionism, or rather that anti-Semitism would nowadays call itself anti-Zionism.

L. P.: It is common knowledge that many Jews were militant on the anti-Zionist side and when, a century ago, the first Zionist congress took place at Basel, this was because the German *Protestrabbiner* had prevented it from being held in Munich. What is more, before launching the Zionist project, Theodor Herzl had dreamt of another: to lead all Viennese Jews to the Stephansdom (Cathedral of St. Stephen, in Vienna) for the purpose of a collective conversion. That's what Jewish contradictions can be like . . . It is also the case that Zionism was a revolutionary doctrine since, according to tradition, the Jews could only return to their "promised land" under the guidance of a messiah, a divine envoy. On this matter, I sometimes find myself taking pleasure in mystical speculations. But in reality, I am pro-Zionist and I have been to Israel about twelve times. And like all reasonable beings, I hope that a peace treaty between the Israelis and the Palestinians will eventually be signed.

E. W.: You have also worked on the question of bestiality. On that, I come back to what you write about the responsibility of philosophers, because one of the fundamental values of Western culture is certainly, from one point of view, the rigid distinction between humans and animals—but also, at the same time, the tendency, as you say, to bestialize the other.

L. P.: Yes. Here we see another of the differences between anti-Semitism and racism: blacks were generally bestialized, whereas Jews were generally seen as diabolical, which is certainly something else.

E. W.: Yes. However, in the *History of Anti-Semitism* you quote texts where animals' names are also applied to Jews.[21] It is significant that you conclude that this bestialization of the other is specific to Western culture. Elsewhere, the tendency would be more to anthropomorphize animals.[22]

L. P.: Yes, I was laying a lot of stress on the history of ideas and the responsibilities of science. From everything I know about it, there were countless clashes around the world between tribes and peoples, but conquests were carried out more through conversion than extermination. And the idea of destroying an entire human group existed already in embryo with polemicists like Voltaire who declared that there were harmful races and treated Jews, as he also did blacks, as animals. In the end, the Final Solution was a logical conclusion.

E. W.: Your pages on the bestialization of the other made me think of a passage by Theodor W. Adorno asking the question whether modern technology, by making possible all kinds of manipulations practiced on animals, and thus a certain transgression in relation to living things, was not also—even if in an extremely complex and mediated way—related to this transgression of taboos that reduces the other to bestiality.

L. P.: Yes, this is the problem of our times. Grillparzer, as you know, said it better: "Von der Humanität durch die Nationalität zur Bestialität" [From humanity to bestiality by way of nationality]. And we are right inside this at the moment.

E. W.: You were also acquainted with the Polish philosopher Leszek Kolakowski.

L. P.: Leszek Kolakowski was someone I briefly got to know at a Cerisy conference, when Gomulka had given permission for a group of Polish intellectuals to go to the West. We immediately found we had things in common. He's more a historian than a philosopher.

E. W.: And on one occasion it's in relation to historiography that you quote him: "The historian's work is always used for purposes of justification by people entrusted with power."[23] This diagnosis may be reminiscent of Walter Benjamin's: what we read is the history of the conquerors, because that is the one that gets transmitted. However, the same cannot be said of your work as a historian.

L. P.: I wouldn't put it like that, at least with regard to the beginnings. When I wrote my first book, *La Bréviaire de la haine* [Hatred's Breviary], which hasn't been translated into German, I gave it to a friend who was a very great philosopher, Alexander Kojève, and it was he who got it published [in French], by Calmann-Lévy, with the help of Raymond Aron.[24] At that time he said to me something like this: You are very shrewd. Instead of getting the victims to speak, you get the executioners to speak.

E. W.: That is true. However, even if you get the executioners to speak, that approach doesn't confirm Kolakowski's statement.

L. P.: In fact I took both aspects. I wrote that history of anti-Semitism: what that's about is the ideas people have of Jews; and I also wrote *Le Mythe aryen* [The Aryan Myth], which deals with the ideas that Western people have of themselves.[25]

E. W.: In *L'Auberge des musiciens*, you talk about the Nuremberg trial. You were present at it, as you were forty years later at the trial of Klaus Barbie in Lyon. Could you say something about this?

L. P.: It was fairly picturesque. Right after the liberation, in the fall of 1945, I started working at the Centre de documentation juive contemporaine [Contemporary Jewish Documentation Center] which . . . was short of documents. I found some through a combination of circumstances: one day I turned up at the national police headquarters, on the very day that the archives of the Gestapo in France had been discovered, but no one there knew German. So I became an unofficial translator, which made it possible for me to get to know this material very thoroughly. The French delegation at the Nuremberg trial didn't have one. So I was recommended to Edgar Faure, the former minister, who had to deal with war crimes there. I was even given a lesson in good manners, because I passed on a document to another attorney, M. Gerthoffer, who was dealing with lootings; M. Faure reprimanded me: "You came with me, you must only work for me!"

Once I got there, of course, it was very interesting to see Göring and the rest of them, but two or three days later it wasn't so interesting and, as Mme Lucie Faure very wittily said, "you end up thinking of them as relatives!" So instead of going into the public gallery, I dug about in the archives. That interested me more.

E. W.: Did you speak in the Barbie trial?

L. P.: At the Barbie trial, I wanted to get through a sort of message which, at the time, didn't get through and that I hope to get through soon. It's the story of the media again. . . . Around twenty years ago, Robert Faurisson was sending circulars out to a lot of people. I threw them in the bin myself, and I was against him being prosecuted. At an earlier meeting, I even said, "He's a clown, you're going to make him into a great man." But the lawyers insisted, the trial took place, and since then this solitary man has made a name for himself, as we know.[26] Jews, especially those who lost parents or grandparents in the Shoah, have every possible reason for insisting on the uniqueness of their case. But not everyone sees it that way. I found out about what is called the euthanasia program, which, until recently, was the ultimate secret of World War II (now, there are very worthy people working on it). It was in relation to this program that Hitler once said that, if necessary, he would have three-quarters of newborn German babies murdered so as to get a truly pure race. There he was, suggesting the idea of a genocide far more significant than that of the Jews, and, to top it all, an "autogenocide."

E. W.: Is this what you wanted to remind people of at the Barbie trial?

L. P.: Yes, but the press didn't pick up on it.

E. W.: But it does involve an important testimony. Why wasn't it picked up on?

L. P.: I don't know. Perhaps because I'm not a media type of witness. Neither the newspaper journalists nor the TV took any notice. But others will pick up on it, I hope.

E. W.: In your memoirs, you speak a little about Jacob Gordin, who is not well known nowadays[27] . . .

L. P.: Hardly at all. But he did originate a school of thought. He studied at Saint Petersburg, and was extremely well educated in Russian and European culture, but he was interested in orientalism, that was how he came to Jewish things. Then in 1933 he had to leave Berlin for Paris. He found a modest situation as a librarian at the Alliance isréalite universelle [Universal Israelite Alliance]. It was only under the Occupation, when he found himself in one of the communities organized by the Israelite boy scouts, that he became the intellectual master for young Jews, in particular for Léon Ashkenazi, called "Manitou," who was much better known than he was.[28] He went back to this teaching in 1945, but died from a terminal illness in 1947. He has been unjustly forgotten. He was behind the renewal of Jewish studies in France.

E. W.: Was it he who led you to have a particular interest in specifically Jewish questions?

E. W.: Yes, along with the circumstances of the time, of course.

E. W.: Did you attend his seminars?

L. P.: Not much, but occasionally.

E. W.: Did he also do readings of the Talmud?

L. P.: To get into the Talmud properly, you have to learn Aramaic, which isn't easy. A young Israeli scholar, Adin Steinsaltz, who began as a totally secular physicist, devoted himself to this task: he became an outstanding Talmudist and has translated parts of the Talmud into English.[29] So I started to have a slightly better understanding of what it is.

E. W.: Entering into those questions has never been one of your major interests.

L. P.: No, what attracted me in the Jewish tradition and the Talmud was first of all the sense of humor.[30] Let me give you an example. In one passage in the Talmud, it says that olives make you lose your memory. Another one mentions a Talmudist, dining at a rich man's house, who goes on eating them. So the rich man says to him: "But you know olives make you lose your memory!" So the Talmudist replies: "That's exactly why I'm eating them!" To me that is very neat.

E. W.: Yes. And in a letter from Freud's correspondence that you also quote, he writes that it is impossible simply to forget the Talmudic heritage. He presumably thought of himself as an heir . . .

L. P.: "Das talmudische Denken kann ja nicht plötzlich aus uns verschwunden sein!" [The Talmudic mode of thinking cannot have suddenly vanished from us!][31]

E. W.: Yes, we can see that especially in his book on jokes. And since you're talking about humor, could you describe a bit the importance of psychoanalysis for your work? I don't necessarily mean the personal aspect of psychoanalysis, but mainly its methodological contribution for the critique of Western systems of thought—a critique that you undertake as well.

L. P.: It's difficult for me to reply. In psychoanalysis, the point is to cure neuroses. As productive people are often neurotic, perhaps I would have been less productive if my analysis had been successful!

E. W.: Yes, but psychoanalysis also makes possible a certain way of looking at what we might call collective phenomena, like collective hatreds . . .

L. P.: Yes, of course. Ultimately, I use it cautiously, without using the technical terminology, and probably semi-consciously. I apply what I have learned semi-consciously. Of course, whatever its outcome, an analysis undoes the mind. Mine was pretty damaging.

E. W.: Yet you often speak sympathetically about Freud . . .

L. P.: On that too I'm a "Wittgensteinian": as my intellectual master wrote, Freud was a unique thinker of his kind, except that he was wrong about the label: what he was doing wasn't science but philosophy. Also, he was a great writer, unlike Lacan who was perhaps deliberately hermetic: I think that by trying to penetrate into the obscurities of an arcane, muddled text, you end up believing in it. At any rate, Alexander Kojève, who taught Lacan, said of him that he was a charlatan.

E. W.: You spent part of your youth in Germany, after 1921. Did that influence you?

L. P.: Initially, in 1920, in Paris, where I was put in the first year of Janson-de-Sailly high school, my only friends were foreigners like me. In Germany, religion was obligatory. In Berlin, at the Goetheschule, there were four classes to a year: three for the Protestants and the fourth for the Catholics and Jews.

E. W.: Mixed?

L. P.: Yes. And that is no doubt why I was immediately attached to a community, which is pleasant: I then spent three excellent years there.

E. W.: Have you been back to Germany subsequently?

L. P.: Yes, occasionally. Once in 1932, then at the Nuremburg trial, and two or three other times. The last time was for a conference on Nazism in 1989, at Hamburg.

E. W.: You also work with German scholars.

L. P.: Yes, absolutely. In the fifth volume of the *History of Anti-Semitism*, for the chapter on Germany, which is an important one, two authors collaborated with me, two friends. One of them is my translator, Professor Rudolf Pfisterer, the other is Klaus von Münchhausen, who first made a name for himself in journalism. He wrote a major article for *Die Zeit* on the relationship between the "Grand Mufti," who figures on the list of war criminals, and his nephew Yasir Arafat.[32]

E. W.: A moment ago you took your distance from philosophy. No doubt you recall the debate around Heidegger on the publication of Victor Farias's book, *Heidegger et le nazisme* [Heidegger and Nazism]?[33]

L. P.: First of all, with Wittgenstein, I thought I'd at last understood philosophy, while remaining a historian, which makes you tend toward skepticism. I read Farias's book with interest. But what mattered for me was a courageous article by Levinas in the *Nouvel Observateur*, in which he states the philosophical merits of Heidegger, and particularly his vision of the impasse that perhaps the whole human race finds itself in, through science, technology, etc.[34] These are terribly open questions.

E. W.: Has Levinas been an influence on you?

L. P.: We have been very good friends, we have discussed many things . . .

E. W.: Your approaches are certainly very different. But can you come back to one of my previous questions: what do you think about the growing interest in questions relating to Judaism which is very noticeable in France, but also in Germany?

L. P.: During a conversation with Pierre Vidal-Naquet, I pointed out to him that the story of Abraham or anyway what we call the birth of ethical monotheism is one of those mysterious things that can be compared, for instance, to the birth of language. We have no idea how it happened, but it is one of the decisive stages in the development of humanity.

E. W.: Do you think that this interest in these questions, which is after all relatively recent, is promising in the long term in one way or another for a change in anti-Semitic attitudes?

L. P.: In the West, certainly; but in former communist countries I fear there will be a long wait. And in general, the human race seems to me to be caught up in an impasse: first amongst them, the Christians or former Christians.

E. W.: How could this impasse be defined?

L. P.: Today, we can speak of a distressing disappearance of values. Previously, we placed all our hopes in the sciences. On this point, we now know that the further science advances, the more it gets lost in doubts, to the point that the astronomers' "big bang," a theory that verges on creationism, seems to me to be a mystical concept. As far as the traditional religions are concerned, they appear to me to be threatened not only by neopaganism and the proliferation of sects of all types, but also by the abandonment of the rites that used to serve as their foundation.

E. W.: Yet as far as the question of rites is concerned, your position, at least in what we read in some of your writing, seems to me to indicate that the fact of not being tied by religious ritual is one of the factors that have made possible the specificity of your approach as a historian.

L. P.: Recently I went back to the history of Jews in the Middle Ages.[35] And suddenly, through one book's reference to another one, I learned that at least two authorities have put forward the hypothesis that more Christians were converted to Judaism in the Middle Ages than Jews to Christianity! Which is most curious. There were all the persecutions, the torture (breaking on the wheel), the massacres, and so on, but also a certain inner balance, "they felt all right about themselves," unlike all these completely torn assimilated Jews, all those identity crises. Some people might be shocked by that.

E. W.: Is there an explanation for why more Christians were converted to Judaism than vice versa at this time?

L. P.: The primary factor is the lack of symmetry between Jews and Christians: Christians couldn't do without Jews theologically, even when it was they who determined their situation in real life. Christian society was oppressive to Jews—there were massacres, ritual murder trials, the distinctive badge—but it did tolerate them, in keeping with the doctrine of St. Augustine, respecting them in their lives and their culture. What is more, most of the time relations were excellent, all the more in that they lived on the same streets and willingly discussed things with each other. And then poor Christians could count on Jewish solidarity. Also, there have always been people with inquiring minds, even in modern times, who, by reading the Bible with care, observed for instance that in the Gospels Jesus says: "I have come to accomplish and not to abolish." Now in those days, people took sacred texts seriously, and there have always been individual or group conversions to Judaism. The most recent case, going back to the late 1930s, is that of an Italian village, San Nicandro, in the Apulia region, where all the inhabitants made themselves Jewish in their own way. After the war, they went off to live in Palestine. So that tendency has always been there.

E. W.: In recent years, you have also done a lot of work on the country you came from, Russia. We are seeing disturbing developments these days in the Soviet Union.[36]

L. P.: Of course, we are observing that well-known phenomenon, the Pamiat.[37] But behind that, there is a much more important cluster of intellectuals who don't go so far as to say that the *Protocols of the Learned Elders of Zion* are authentic, but who think it is a text with great predictive force and that the Russians have been humiliated—humiliated by other nationalities, and particularly the Jews. All that can lead to nasty developments, certainly. The journal *La Jeune Garde*, for instance, has been publishing extremely anti-Semitic articles for some years, including the wild imaginings of one Skourlatov who in 1976, in *Izvestia*, was already publishing a *Livre de Vless* [Book of Vless—Vless was the god of cattle and commerce for oriental Slavs], which claimed that the Russians were the beginning of European culture. On February 27, 1991, *La Jeune Garde* organized a meeting between journalists and representatives of public opinion. At the entrance to the room, two young men were distributing a twenty-nine-page pamphlet. Above the title, "La réponse russe à la question juive" [The Russian Response to the Jewish Question], was an eight-branch swastika. Some of the propositions in this publication went further than Hitler's ravings. Let me give you an example:

The Yids invented a new weapon, a dreadful weapon, for the purpose of annihilating the Goys. The Yids Albert Einstein and Robert Oppenheimer were the "fathers" of the atomic bomb; their task was completed by Edward Teller (hydrogen bomb) and Samuel Kogan (neutron bomb). The burned flesh of Japanese "pagans" and worshippers of the Sun was to terrorize the entire world and make it tremble. The assassination of the German leaders, at the Nuremberg trial accused in the first instance of persecuting the Yids, was fixed for October 16, 1946, in other words the day of the principal Jewish festival, the Great Pardon, the day of Jehovah's vengeance.

In the fifth volume of the history of anti-Semitism, I examine the meaning of ravings like this, such as the fact that military milieux do all they can to spread them.[38] In 1990, the journal of military history *Voïenno-Istoritcheskii Journal* published extracts from the *Protocols of the Learned Elders of Zion* and *Mein Kampf*, under the heading "documents." However, it should be added that an opinion poll carried out in Moscow with the help of the University of Houston and published in *Nouvelles de Moscou* suggests that anti-Semitism is a minority phenomenon that the majority regards with concern. Of those interviewed, 71 percent called it a "worrying social fact," 85 percent were sure that the majority of their fellow citizens were not anti-Semitic, although anti-Semites were in the majority according to 14 percent of those interviewed. Finally, for a good third, the situation was getting worse all the time . . .

E. W.: Have you had the chance of going back to the ex-Soviet Union?

L. P.: No. I have friends who go there, and my son does. I'm past the age of long trips . . .

E. W.: You haven't seen Saint Petersburg again, where you were born?

L. P.: No, never.

Massy
March 7, 1991

Before the Law, After the Law

JEAN-FRANÇOIS LYOTARD

ELISABETH WEBER: In your book *Heidegger and "the jews,"* you try to analyze what you call a paradox, even a scandal, and you describe it as follows: "This thought (Heidegger's), a thought so devoted to remembering that a forgetting (of Being) takes place in all thought, in all art, in all 'representation' of the world, how could it possibly have ignored the thought of 'the jews,' which in a certain sense, thinks, tries to think, nothing but that very fact? How could this thought forget and ignore 'the jews' to the point of suppressing and foreclosing to the very end the horrifying (and inane) attempt at exterminating, at making us forget forever what, in Europe, reminds us, ever since the beginning, that 'there is' the *Forgotten?*"[1] For some time, you have been trying to think through this figure of the Forgotten under various names: the *infans* [infant], the event, the state of being hostage, to name just those ones.

If the thinking of "the jews" reminds us that there is something Forgotten, it also at the same time introduces the law and a thinking of the law, a law of which, in a text on Kafka, you say that it is inscribed "on the body that does not belong to it . . . This inscription must suppress the body as savagery outside the law."[2] In other words, the law wants to make us forget life before the law: that is precisely what the alliance consists in. What, for you, is the relationship between the Forgotten to which the thinking of "the jews" would testify, and the law? The "first touch that touched me when I wasn't there" and which, for that reason, is absolutely forgotten—can't it be a sound, can't it be an appeal?[3]

JEAN-FRANÇOIS LYOTARD: Perhaps it is better not to make the Kafka text and my commentary on it the point of reference. Kafka's relation to the law cannot be considered as paradigmatic. It's a relationship that's itself extremely warped—off-course, I was going to say. There are singularities in the way that the law is present in Kafka and particularly in *The Penal Colony*. The extreme force and intensity with which the question of the body is posed, as well as the necessity for the law to come and, if one can put it this way, recover the body, reinscribe itself, by means of the needles of the machine, in the very body of the condemned man, who is condemned *a priori*—the guilt is original, it leaves no doubt, writes Kafka—all these things make this hardly an orthodox "reading" of the law. It is true, however, that in Jewish tradition there are a great many prescriptions applying to bodies, and that the concern to purify it, the concern for lustration, occupy an important place that engenders numerous rules. If we retain this fact of the necessity that the law be inscribed on the body (perhaps not as Kafka says, but certainly as the Pentateuch says), we have to balance it with another thing, the question of death, which I found very striking when I worked on Paul of Tarsus, Shaul. Having succeeded in bringing about his antirabbinic revolution, he of course asks himself what should be done in relation to the bodily prescriptions, such as alimentary ones, all the bodily prescriptions required by Hebraic tradition. On this point, Paul's position is fairly liberal: you should respect customs, not cause scandal. Which doesn't prevent him from being a very active militant. But it is striking to see the importance given by the message of the Christian Paul to the question of death; since death has been accentuated, highlighted, by Christ's passion. The death of the body immediately acquires an importance in the doctrine that it doesn't have in the Hebraic tradition. It's an essential part of the Christian revolution in relation to Jewish tradition, this stress on death as the moment of possible remission, the event of a transfiguration of bad, sinning flesh, into forgiven flesh. Now this valorization doesn't exist in the Jewish tradition, it seems to me, because it does not know the mystery of the Incarnation. In Jewish tradition, you would say that there is no separation between the body and the soul. It has to be St. Paul who decrees that there is a separation and that the body is bad, sinning, that the soul lets itself be seduced by the body, and so on. Everything Christians have learned and have taught us on this subject comes from him and is a break with traditional Jewish thought. Which all amounts to saying that the question of the body's relationship to the law is difficult to situate, and that you can't just follow Kafka's *Colony*. There are some texts by Levinas on this which are invaluable.[4]

You ask whether it is possible to consider this first touch of the law as an appeal and not simply as the cruel incision that Kafka describes. I would say, obviously! And I would even say that this appeal touches and changes the body. From having heard the appeal, Abram will become Abraham, his name will be changed. But also his body: he is ninety-nine, and he will have a son. And he will be required to sacrifice his son and that means that Abraham's ear hears an appeal, a horrible one, but he will try to respond to it. Same thing for Moses. Moses' miraculous capacity belongs to the same tradition. There is a listening, there is an alliance, it transfigures the body, it makes it possible for Moses' body to produce effects that are not natural.

Having said that, I understand your question more as an objection to my reading of Kafka's text. This reading says that there is first of all the body and that this body is immediately guilty (this is really the Christian tradition, but as you know Kafka is penetrated by that). This guilt is, so to speak, ontological, it is constitutive, so that the law always comes in second place, to try to sanction or blot out this wrongdoing. But your question suggests that perhaps the appeal of the law is anterior even to the body's guilt. Is that it?

E. W.: Yes. If on the one hand the thinking of "the jews" touches on the forgotten above all, if the forgotten—which for you, reading Kafka, would be the guilt—is at the heart of this thinking and, on the other hand, you also have a meditation on the law at the heart of this same thinking, then what is the relation between the two?

J-F. L.: You are quite right to ask this question. *Heidegger and "the jews"* was a first attempt—rapid, written too fast, impatient (for which I have been much reproached); the text on Kafka was written more patiently, but obviously under the law of Kafka himself, if I can put it like that. As a result, this text should be read with caution. But it is true that in what I thought at the time, there is a sort of confusion to do with what is forgotten. Is it the *infans*, is it that touch which is represented as one of guilt and misfortune in Kafka or which is represented for instance in Freud (who is also a Jewish thinker) as seduction? Seduction means that there is a very ancient guilt that will be forgotten, that will give rise to strange emotional events which will remain unassignable. Is it to do with this touch of scandal, or is it first of all to do with the appeal of the law? In other words with the fact that in Jewish tradition—this time the strictest, the most ordinary and accepted—the people hasten to forget the voice that has been addressed to it—an address that forces alliance—and to return to its golden calf. I would say that you can't have one without the other—and that is where the formulations I gave are not clear enough. First of all, it is very naive to want to date each of the two things, the moment of the guilt and the moment of the law. For there is only guilt because there is the law, otherwise there is pure and simple innocence, and this is the Adamic state. Both occur together, and to the extent that the Freudian problematic of unconscious affect belongs to this sphere of reflection—and I think it does—to want to date the moment of seduction and then the moment when the infant accedes to the law or, let's say, to the signifier, is very anthropological. Because that would mean you were supporting the idea of a temporal succession, a diachrony of these different touches, which can be indispensable in analytic practice, but obviously can't be so for thought. The idea of a temporal succession is instead quite alien to a real comprehension of the law and the guilt. I think the two moments have to be taken into account together, indissociable from one another.

E. W.: Gershom Scholem tells the story of a "touch," definitely not a "first" one, but that happens to a "people, an old communal apparatus already equipped, it is assumed, with the defense mechanisms and the controls of flow, economic and linguistic, without which it would not be a people."[5] The story recounted by Scholem concerns the discussion around the question of knowing what, at the time of the revelation of the Ten Commandments on Mount Sinai, was really heard by the people of Israel. Some say they all heard the divine voice uttering the Ten Commandments. For others, they only heard the first two commandments: "I am the Eternal thy God," and "Thou shalt have no other gods before me." The power of this experience exceeded the capacities of the people and only Moses heard the eight following commandments. According to Rabbi Mendel de Rymanóv, however, the people of Israel heard nothing more than the *aleph* at the beginning of the first word of the First Commandment, *Anochi*, "I." In Hebrew this aleph is just the inaudible consonant that precedes the vowel at the start of a word (like the *spiritus lenis* in Greek): so it's the source of all articulate sound. To hear the aleph is to hear nothing, but at the same time, the aleph constitutes the passage to all audible, articulated language: the aleph is the spiritual root of all the other letters of the alphabet.[6] So the aleph could be called the *quod* of language.

You have analyzed this "quod" on many occasions, the "*qu'*il arrive," "*that* it happens."[7] If there is a hostage-taking by a first touch, then there is also a hostage-taking by a voice, as you write of "this simple people . . . taken hostage by a voice that does not tell it anything, save that it (this voice) is, and that all representation and naming of it are forbidden, and that it, this people, only has to listen to its tone, to be obedient to a timbre."[8] Might not the thinking of "the jews" be exceptional from the fact that the too much of the first touch is recognized as the too much of language—the too much, in other words something outside the law?

J-F. L.: What do you mean by the "too much of language"? Is it language which is too much, is it language which is excessive in itself?

E. W.: It is language that exceeds, that exceeds itself. Like that aleph which is nothing and which already asks too much of the people. And which, as an inaudible sound, contains all articulated language.

J-F. L.: It doesn't contain it, it heralds it! I would see this aleph in the same way as the famous Rabbi Mendel de Rymanóv. Or rather, if I can put it like this, I would understand it, this almost inaudible aleph, as just what seems to me characteristic of the Jewish tradition, of its thought. Something is, I wouldn't say said, but heralded, and I think the aleph is a herald because what it is is the breath of the beginning that one doesn't *hear*: in one way, the people has heard nothing, except that something had been heralded. So perhaps it has heard the aleph as a heralding, but the aleph as a phenomenon is not heard. There will be a writing, not a voice. But there too, we should start again to examine what we understand by voice. There won't be a voice, in the good, plain sense of an oral utterance. I wonder what Moses might have heard. Who wrote the Tablets? There too, there are various stories! Some say, it was God himself and he handed them to Moses fully written; and others that it was Moses who wrote them to dictation. Never mind which, it is certain that the law will be written, and that is very important and very new. The law will be written, so there will be letters to bear witness to the aleph—in other words, to a heralding. A heralding whose timbre was strongly imperious. But the timbre won't be in the writing itself, and there will be dreadful difficulties for centuries and even millennia of the Jewish tradition in managing to *voice* the text, not only the Commandments, but the whole Torah.[9] An oral tradition will come to double the written tradition. And God knows what difficulties that will present. This people will have forgotten its language after the centuries of exile in Babylon. So the Torah will have to be *voiced* in another language, which will be Aramaic, and so on. The position of the voice means that the ontological status of what Christians call the Old Testament, in other words the Torah itself and the books appended to it, is utterly different from that of the New Testament, the Gospels and Epistles. The Gospels and Epistles are reports written from speeches *voiced* by someone who said he was the God incarnate, a God become human. There is no problem of the voice in the Christian tradition, but a charming simplicity that casts no doubts on elocution. Whereas in Jewish reason there is a vast suspicion as to what has spoken. Has he or it even spoken, since all that was heard was the inaudible aleph? So here is a people equipped, in fact, with written prescriptions, but no less equipped with a host of little, ordinary, and unlikely stories, of goatherds, shepherds, sheep, dromedaries, exchanges of women, thefts of land, exoduses, conflicts with the great empires, continual battles—and the people is going to have to hear the voice amid this disorder, hear the timbre of the eternal in the temporal, and "invent" what it has to do to be just amid this tempest of unpredictable circumstances that is called history. I think history in the sense of historicity begins with this aleph and with the fact that it isn't audible, that it doesn't clearly say what should be done. There is a historicity that begins with the obligation each time, step by step, to find where the law is, decide what has to be done. For that hasn't been said! It has been written, but this writing always gives rise to different readings: the Talmud. I would understand the aleph as that absolutely impalpable touch we were speaking of just now. But I can't say that it's a "too much," a too much in language . . .

　　E. W.: My question was whether this inaudible aleph could be put alongside the first touch. Because that would introduce a slight difference from your text on Kafka.

　　J-F. L.: Yes, you are right. That would be the Hebraic tradition. But I think it doesn't apply to Kafka's text. Kafka's text is basically . . . I was going to say pagan, pagan-Christian, pagan in the sense that Christianity has kept something essential of paganism. With the exception of revelation, which there is certainly no question of ignoring, Christianity keeps alive the notion of sacrifice that belongs to near-Eastern paganism. I'm well aware that there are sacrifices in Jewish tradition, but they are sacrifices of purification in the context of particular rites. The amazing thing is this: basically what you have is an address, an address in the American sense of the word, and which is an inaudible breath. This breath is practically a death-rattle, a little hum, it can be a feeble groan, a thin wailing, this is the way I hear it. God is lamenting, he is lamenting about this people that does nothing but stupid things. . . . Where is the crime? It lies in the fact that no one hears. What is being said will not have been heard. . . . So people will always be caught red-handed for not having understood, for not having been intelligent in the sense of the one who hears, in the sense of an understanding. So the Covenant is both absolutely inescapable, irrevocable—because to *revoke* you have to have the voice and here we are on the side of the voice—and it creates guilt immediately, since it is not and cannot be heard in the right way. There is something cruel in the problem of vocalization. I'm not the first to say it, all the interpreters know it. Square letters do after all have to be vocalized. People only succeeded in doing it in the eighth century—AD! Almost two millennia of hesitation to standardize the oral reading of the Torah. Standardization has in no way put a stop to the multivocity of the message.

E. W.: You show how Western humanism could only be constituted at the price of, and, at the same time, thanks to, a certain Forgotten. Jews, on the other hand, "testify that this misery, this enslavement to that which remains unfinished, is constitutive of the spirit," and that "thought harbors a lack it does not even lack." It is precisely this feeling of a lack that would be "the secret of thought" that the Final Solution sought to exterminate.[10] This feeling of a lack which is not even lacking, and which is at the heart of thought, this feeling whose heralding of lack we prefer to forget—would it be an explanation of Sartre's statement, cited by Pierre Vidal-Naquet and Richard Marienstras, to the effect that we can certainly do without Jews, but we can do even better without people?[11]

J-F. L.: Yes, but there is something that I find disturbing in Sartre's statement, which is that it's serious to say that Jews are simply the paradigm of humanity. If we can do without Jews, we will also be able to do without people . . .

E. W.: He says we will be *better* able to do without people . . .

J-F. L.: Meaning what? First, that Jews are people and that this notion of a diffuse feeling of lack that sets thought in motion only testifies, with the Jews, to a universal condition that defines humanity. Allow me to resist this philosophical humanism. It is to forget singularity once again.

E. W.: I understood this sentence more in an ironic mode—we could *better* do without people than Jews! At the heart of Western thought, there is a lack that is not perceived as lack, but which is nonetheless at the heart of this thought, and Jewish thought testifies in a very distinctive way to this lack. To wish to eliminate this lack (that is how you describe the National-Socialist program) would imply the elimination of the Jews but, by the same token, the elimination of the innermost element of thought.

J-F. L.: Yes, certainly that is what is at issue in this sinister "joke." All the same, what Sartre or the philosopher won't explain is why it is the Jews who have been *seized* and besieged. Why did the Nazis attack the Jews in such an exceptional way? It's something Sartre cannot conceive of, or that he can only conceive of. Someone deeply Sartrian and wholly admirable, like Robert Antelme, does in fact say that it was the species that was the issue in the camps, the species as Antelme admirably describes it in the process of discovering itself in the camps.[12] That's one thing. But why the Jews? And why extermination? It's not just the labor camp where people are worked to death. This is not at all to underestimate either the altogether admirable testimony or conduct of a Resistance writer like Antelme. But there is something else that isn't his concern.

We would have to go back to Jewish history, the text of that history. Hannah Arendt says some powerful things about it in "The Hidden Tradition."[13] This lack that is so unbearable that it is always ready to get itself forgotten, what is it, basically? A lack of legitimacy, a lack of foundation. The Jewish tradition in Europe cannot forget the *unfounded.* There are two ways of forgetting for Jews, for those who have "got" the aleph, who haven't really understood and who know that they will always be bad Jews. There are two ways: to shut yourself up in tradition, with all that implies about conformity and convention; or else to assimilate. Arendt observes that Jews are always in the process of hesitating between these two sides, tempted not to let tradition go but also to leave it behind, to make their lives not just livable, but actually open to what emerges in Europe at that point (I'm speaking about the period that begins at the end of the seventeenth century and lasts until the twentieth) as a movement toward liberty and emancipation. This to and fro between emancipation and the observation of tradition shows the extent to which this lack remains present: a chasm, an in-between. It's not a bridge but rather an abyss between two mistakes or two faults: to melt into modern civilization, or to become attached to the letter of tradition as though it were providing the rules for one particular ethnic custom among others. And this is a bit what has happened for the American Jewish community (as Harold Bloom shows in an excellent study of American Jews[14]). The United States is made up of minorities, it's a patchwork. There's the Irish tradition, the Italian one, the Indian, the Chicano, the Asiatic, and then the Jewish tradition . . . It's one way of disappearing! On the other hand, the old Jewish families of Germany, France, and England were deeply integrated, but they were completely destabilized and returned to their difference when fascism and Nazism came to power. They hardly still thought of themselves as Jewish. In France, the definition a Jewish man gave of himself was: I am a French citizen of Israelite faith. After Auschwitz, this "solution" became impossible. So there has been a reverse movement toward an emphasis on the faith, particularly with the arrival in France of Sephardic Jews, but even this return doesn't work, can't work. For the tradition is to be without tradition, in the strong sense, since it obliges Jews always to "invent" what the Law says. This tradition does not declare the Law, it transmits the duty of listening to it without understanding it.

Sartre speaks of "people," and forgets that the other people are Catholics, Protestants, Buddhists, agnostics, and that their relationship to the law cannot be compared to the Jewish lack of foundation.

E. W.: You have written of the Nazi attempt:

It would really be a question of eliminating an "other" thought, intimate and strange, not destined authentically to being the guardian of Being, but owed with regard to a Law, to which it is hostage.

One might expect that such a hypothesis dis-installs the position of philosopher . . . that it might lead him to suspect that the West is perhaps inhabited, unknowingly, by a guest, that it holds something hostage that is neither "Western" nor "its" hostage, but rather the hostage of something of which it is itself hostage. A thought . . . [t]hat has never told anything but stories of unpayable debt, transmitted little narratives, droll and disastrous, telling of the insolvency of the debtor soul.

This, you continue, is what Nazism "tried to definitively forget: the debt . . . it [. . .] tried to unchain the soul from this obligation, to tear up the note of credit, to render it debt-free forever."[15]

Nowadays would the only real philosophers be this sort—dis-installed, trying to discern the "foreclosure that is constitutive of Western thought"?[16] That would completely turn upside down the conception of the philosophical task. To pick up a passage from one of your most recent books, the philosopher would become the one who worries about the "Thing," and who as such, like the self, is "always naked as regards birth and death and thus as regards difference, sexual or ontological."[17] Does the Greek philosopher (in Heidegger's sense) have the means for this?

J-F. L.: *Heidegger and "the jews,"* which you quote, points out that if the philosopher is simply Greek, he or she does not have the means of this anxiety. He can certainly ask the question about ontological difference, but I think that when he calls it "ontological," then he does indeed presume that the question is that of being, he sets it in place. Which then corresponds to the Greek tradition, pre-Socratic and Aristotelian. But as to an irredeemable debt, it's obvious that that doesn't belong to Greek thought. The philosopher to be dis-installed is the one who, after Heidegger, has spoken about *Stellen, Gestell,* like my friend Philippe Lacoue-Labarthe— the one who continues to think that what is essential in tradition and thought for the West comes from Greece and has no other source.[18] It's a failure in thought, it's also a historical mistake, I would even say a historiographical one, because there is at least one other powerful and no less obvious tradition in the West, which is the Christian one, and that powerful and obvious Christian tradition itself derives from a revolution made within an even more ancient one, which is Jewish. Now this most ancient thought was present in the West—present, meaning observable, historically visible. It is true that it has been subject to hundreds of abominations since it infiltrated the West with Islam, but that curse is also visible. There is something there that I can't understand. Why do people shut their eyes to this, and especially when they are trying to deconstruct metaphysics? It is the case that the majority of elaborations of Western philosophical thought derive more or less closely from Christianity at least as much, if not more, than from Greek thought. They have borrowed many elements from it—but from a version of Greek thought that was "usable" for Christian thought, compatible, fitting in with it, very Latinized generally. The real father of Western metaphysics is St. Paul. He went and got from the Greeks what he needed to articulate his revolution. He's the one who reinvents the *pneuma*—in other words who begins the theory of spirit well before Descartes and Augustine, and quite differently. We can see what might be the relationship between St. Paul and Malebranche, even between St. Paul and Leibniz! Not to mention St. Paul and Lenin! He's a Lenin, that St. Paul! A crazy and admirable thinker. But how is it possible to deconstruct metaphysics without recognizing that besides the vast body of thought called Western metaphysics—born of the complex assimilation of the pagan, Greek tradition to the tradition of the Christian revelation, so that the question of God is asked as that of the name of being—another tradition of thought persisted? Even to say that there is being and that there is nothing that can be said about it still ultimately belongs not just to a certain pre-Socratic ontology, but to a current of the Christian tradition, that of mysticism. It's a very long tradition, dangerous, disturbing, readily heretical. But how can we not recognize that there was also this little trickle of voice and thought continuing to say: Listen, to be or not to be, that is not the question. What the question is, is: What has been asked of us? What can one do to be just with regard to this breath of which we are the guardians? We have been blown away![19]—in every sense.

I should add that I don't think this recognition means the end of philosophy. What is more, the West has always reflected on its end, has always thought of itself as an end—that is intrinsic to it. Plato was already the end. That's not the problem. But I think that the theme of the breath, the aleph as appeal, instead marks a leap in the thought of what we call the West. It was much in need of it.

E. W.: You characterize the work of writing, whether literature, poetry, painting, or music, as a recollection or anamnesis, both impossible and inevitable, "of the harm done to the soul by its unpreparedness, and that leaves it a child." There is no good way to be hostage to this unrepresentable, but one can be nothing else;[20] consequently, "the witness is always a bad witness, a traitor. But in the end, he or she does testify."[21] The same structure holds for Jewishness: "Every Jew is a bad 'jew,' a bad witness to what cannot be represented, just like all texts fail to reinscribe what has not been inscribed."[22] Perhaps you know Marina Tsvétayeva's phrase, quoted by Paul Celan: "All poets are Jews."[23] Would you say that all writers, according to your definition of writing, are Jews?

J-F. L.: With quotation marks, yes, I would say that, but with the proviso of the quotation marks. I think there is something absolutely fundamental here, and I'm not saying anything original there, because this work was started a long time ago. Think of Blanchot, Levinas, or Derrida.

Recently I was rereading Proust. I'm going to quote you an extraordinary bit of text. Listen:

> Do not forget: books are the work of solitude and the *children of silence*. The children of silence must have nothing in common with the children of speech, the thoughts born from the desire to say something, from a rebuke, an opinion, in other words an obscure idea.
>
> Do not forget: the matter of our books, the substance of our sentences must be immaterial, not taken just as it comes from reality, but our sentences themselves and the episodes too must be made of the transparent substance of our best minutes, when we are outside reality and the present. It is from those consolidated [*cimentées*] drops of light that the style and the story of a book are made.[24]

He knew what it was to write. Our best minutes . . . He knows it is going to be necessary to *cimenter*, cement, bind together, entering into representation, and that by entering into representation you're going to fall back into speech. But all the same, the book as child of silence has nothing in common with the child of speech. And a book is not written from desiring to say something. It's an admirable observation. There are opinions, rebukes—these exist, but don't make books. It may bear the name *book*, but it isn't book. A book is a child of silence. That's one way, much more "elegant" than mine, of speaking of this anamnesis—both impossible, because it is forced into words and representations, and absolutely inevitable. I think I have invented nothing. I think one could find wholly comparable sentences in the most unlikely writers, saying the same things quite differently. I'm thinking, for instance, of someone like Diderot, taken to be a great pagan, crazy, a libertine, et cetera, but if you carefully reread *Rameau's Nephew* or *The Paradox of the Actor* or even *Jacques the Fatalist*, after all a very Jewish narrative in one way, full of little stories that contradict each other, that are crazy, that come to a halt—if you reread Diderot in that light, you will see that basically nothing else interests him but to succeed in making books of silence, that render homage to the Thing. That Diderot at least—I know he has other faces. But even the materialism of *D'Alembert's Dream* is immaterial in the highest degree, as Proust would say.

E. W.: You sometimes speak of painting as of a genre of writing. In a text on Barnett Baruch Newman, you describe the picture as a messenger. It seems to me close to what you have just said about silence: "The message (the painting) is the messenger; it 'says,' 'Here I am'; in other words, 'I am yours' or 'Be mine.' . . . Or . . . 'Listen to me.'"[25] This is also the response of numerous biblical figures to God's call.

In another text, you write: "Every writing worthy of its name wrestles with the Angel and, at best, comes out limping."[26] This wrestling with the Angel changes the one who was engaged in it, even changing his name. Wrestling like this will have dislocated Jacob's hip (Jacob will become Israel)—in other words, as you say of the event, it will have opened "a wound in the sensibility. You know this because it has since reopened and will reopen again, marking out the rhythm of a secret and perhaps unnoticed temporality. This wound ushered you into an unknown world, but without ever making it known to you."[27] Would you say that in spite of its claim to make known all possible worlds, philosophical interrogation also originates in a wound of sensitivity like this?

J-F. L.: I think so, yes. For painters, at least for Barnett Baruch Newman, the case is clear, because he gave a clear account of it. He wrote some quite admirable texts. (I have meant for a long time to get them published in French. . . . The French know nothing about them, but they are there in English.) He was very well versed in all that. He was more or less pious himself, in the Jewish tradition, and he read the texts on the sublime. He was well aware of what he was doing. He is probably the one who knew all that best, perhaps even better than Rothko, who was from the same tradition. But one can cite names that belong less directly to this tradition of thought. At the moment I'm working on Sam Francis, who wasn't born into this tradition.[28] His canvases arise from his love of impressionism and fauvism, of light and color, then they throw the principle off course. They are canvases for Proust, apparently, the Proust of the *Jeunes filles*.[29] But I assure you that it is impossible to understand what is happening when you look at these canvases if you don't attend to the fact that this marvelous event, this visual seduction, the splendor of the colors, is upheld by the knowledge that there is nothing. And that it is to this night that homage must be given. To give homage to colors is to pay the debt to the nothing from which they come. There is something there that is a constant for all great visual artists. It's not a question of the period. It marks out a secret temporality that has nothing to do with the history of art. I have the greatest respect for art historians. They are such erudite, scholarly people, capable of pursuing a motif for three centuries across an unbelievable quantity of individual paintings. It's a very important and very useful kind of work. But what is at issue in this corpus, and makes it enigmatic, is obviously something else, that you can find just as much in Piero della Francesca as in Barnett Newman.

As for philosophers, it is certain that philosophy wouldn't even get started without the wound. Kierkegaard speaks of his spine in the flesh. This is an instance that supports my idea, you will say. But there are wounds in Descartes: dreams are wounds, and the great Deceiver. Pascal's wound stares you in the face. And even in Hegel the wound is exhibited in his early text on skepticism, a text of grief, where it is said that you can't philosophize if you haven't been through the experience of nihilism. A grief that Hegel shares with Hölderlin and Schelling. The hurt is there for philosophers, too, a secret grief that makes their greatness, their determination. But also, to the extent that they are philosophers according to the tradition of *consolatio*, they try to scar it over. Hegel says that the wounds of the spirit always become scars. It is essential to the spirit to be consoled. For Hegel that is called dialectics, use of the sophistry of paradoxes for rational ends, and so on. But the wound we are speaking of, more of the soul than the spirit, bleeds all the time and certainly asks to be tended, but also not to be tended—to be respected, like the aleph. It is the paradox, the *oxymoron* of writing itself.

E. W.: At the beginning of your book *The Differend*, you write: "In writing this book, the A. [author] had the feeling that his sole addressee was the *Is it happening?* [*Arrive-t-il?*] It is to it that the phrases which happen call forth. And, of course, he will never know whether or not the phrases happen to arrive at their destination, and by hypothesis, he must not know it. He knows only that this ignorance is the ultimate resistance that the event can oppose to the accountable or countable [*comptable*] use of time."[30] This book takes as its point of departure the differend between "revisionists" like Faurisson and the survivors of the Nazi extermination camps. It engages strongly in this affair, the stakes of which are nothing less than memory. Could you explain the sentence that says that the sole addressee of the book was the *Is it happening?*

J-F. L.: When I said that this book was only dealing with the *Is it happening?*, I was thinking primarily of the camps, of Auschwitz. That is where the book begins. For Auschwitz preeminently belongs to the order of the event. It *is* the question: *Is it happening?* First of all, we never finish establishing that it did happen [*c'est arrivé*] and it's over *that* having happened that these pathetic revisionists have been expending all their efforts, in an effort to demonstrate that it was not possible to establish it (which is an absolute counter-truth in terms of historical science). But above all, secondly, Auschwitz is the event because we don't succeed [*arrive*] in establishing its *meaning*. Therein lies the difficulty. We don't know how to think extermination. It is that which resists thought, par excellence. The "explanations" that can be given of it, be they economic, political, or ideological, provide absolute no *reason*. You have the impression here of having to do with the event, with all the monstrosity of what occurs without reason. Something that is there, but doesn't succeed [*arrive*] in being there because it cannot be integrated into a network of themes and arguments; it isn't open to question, doesn't supply matter for discussion. In this sense—and please don't let what I am saying be taken the wrong way—there is in Auschwitz something reminiscent of the aleph. Something has touched, we don't know what that means, we don't know *what* that asks of us, we know that that always *asks* of us, and that thus it is never forgotten. But as we don't know *what*, it gets forgotten, we don't know *how* to remember it. There is a frightening debt, we won't manage to pay it off.

E. W.: In *The Inhuman* (1988), you write that we don't pay off the "debt to childhood. But it is enough not to forget it in order to resist it and, perhaps, not to be unjust. It is the task of writing, thinking, literature, arts, to venture to bear witness to it."[31] A few years before (in 1983), you were assigning this task of bearing witness to politics as well, even if this was in the attenuated mode of a "perhaps." I quote from *The Differend*: "What is at stake in a literature, in a philosophy, in a politics perhaps, is to bear witness to differends by finding idioms for them."[32]

This hope, however faint it was, in relation to politics—do you still have it? And if it was linked to the statement in the same book that "Marxism has not come to an end, as the feeling of the different," as "silent feeling that signals a different [and that] remains to be listened to," is there still today, would you say, a political idiom for the "suffering due to capital" which for Marx *is* suffering *tout court*?[33]

J-F. L.: The "perhaps" is very important. Indeed, probably I wouldn't still say it now. But you have to make qualifications. Some time ago, I had written some texts on the so-called end of Marxism (again a rather shorthand thing), at least as instituted doctrine and regime.[34] The reflections put forward in these texts have turned out to be right. I say that without boasting; it was predictable, comprehensible, it wasn't a case of divination. *How* it happened, no one could predict. I remember a discussion with Claude Lefort,[35] he was saying to me: for the most part, we weren't wrong, but we hadn't foreseen the way that Stalinist totalitarianism collapsed. In other words that it was dismantled from within, and not by a massive revolt. However that may be, it happened that a certain type of politics—with which I was associated as a member of "Socialisme ou Barbarie," in other words a critical group that was not Trotskyite, I want to be clear about that, because there's always confusion, critical not just of Stalinism and Trotskyism, but also critical of capitalism—that that type of politics is over. That way of existing of the differend is over with. The real question now is to know where the differend or differends that necessarily involve and shake up every society are going on. Nicole Loraux, for instance, categorizes them under the concept of *stasis* as the division, the separation that perpetually threatens a human community, especially one that is democratically organized.[36] For a democracy leaves a lot of room for conflicts. In contemporary societies there is a vast surplus of conflicts, perhaps more overwhelmingly than ever, but they don't look at all the same as they used to. It wasn't too long ago that these conflicts essentially centered on the position of workers, and they appeared to be bearers of an alternative to the capitalist organization. There was another possible form of life, that was the program and the promise of the *Communist Manifesto*. For a good century and a half people lived and acted with this idea of a general alternative to the organization of the system, of capital. Today things are quite different. All these "small" conflicts—which are not so small as all that—about women, education, all these extremely important questions, like that of knowing who is a citizen, who isn't; who is a foreigner, who isn't; what an immigrant is; and so on; all these population movements in the world that create a sociopolitical universe that is deeply unbalanced, fascinating and impassioned, dangerous— how can they be ignored? They supply the proof that societies are always marked by a differend, and that we shouldn't calmly rely on capitalism's expanding cycles of reproduction. Capitalism is certainly maintaining its

health very well across all these conflicts. It has always created crises and
been threatened by its own crises, it has always lived and progressed through
crises. There is certainly no reason to panic because there is "a crisis"—it's at
least the fifth crisis I've seen in my life. At any rate, "the crisis" will never
again be as far-reaching and deep-seated as the one at the end of the 1920s
that finished in 1950. I don't want to, and I can't engage politically in contemporary conflicts to the same extent that I was able to engage in the Marxist differend, for a very simple reason: we now know (even "the left" knows
it, in spite of itself) that there is no universal alternative to capitalism, and
that these conflicts will have to be regulated from within the capitalist system. As a result their dimension as differend is much less strong than their
"litigious" dimension.[37] Litigations can be extremely violent: wars like that
of ex-Yugoslavia, like the Gulf War. They are very important indeed, and obviously our duty as citizens, as just citizens if possible, is to take a position.
I'm not even speaking of intellectuals, because I think there are no more intellectuals in Voltaire's, Zola's, or even Sartre's sense. (Sartre, moreover, is in
my opinion the worst of all, not by chance, because it's not his fault if he was
too late.) No one any longer expects intellectuals to lend justice their voice as
Voltaire, Michelet, Hugo, or Zola could, when the world was still in the general frame of emancipation. Nowadays we are no longer living in this kind of
frame. We are living in one of development and growth, and really the problems are always problems of the sharing of growth. That's true of Germany,
it's what matters broadly speaking for feminism—not the only thing, but
broadly speaking—it's obviously what matters for the immigration question, as for education, and of course for all the poor countries. The sharing
of growth always means the integration of the underprivileged into the cycle
of capitalist development. That is why these conflicts are litigations, even if
something of a quite different order may be operating beneath their surface.
Which is clearly the case for feminism, particularly. So we do have to intervene there as *citizens*. (Which I did do, with others, for instance during the
Gulf War, causing a small scandal. It's not considered good taste on the left
to intervene to say that there has to be a war, even if there *must* be, in every
sense.)[38] We have to take up positions to defend those whom we consider to
be the ones oppressed and under attack. But these interventions take place
within the framework of the system, not with the idea of destroying it, only
of making it less unjust. I don't like the arrogance, the pretentiousness, the
air of false tragedy in the issues involving contemporary "minoritarians." I'm

quite happy to take up a position, but please don't say to me: it's that or death! That's not true. When the workers were involved in the Paris Commune, it really was that or death. Who is ready to die for politics nowadays? Muslim fundamentalists . . . But their motivation isn't political in the Western sense, it's a religion that teaches that it is holy to die in war. In what is called the developed world, no one any longer feels the obligation to die for a political cause. Especially not out of solidarity. For a living Marxism, class solidarity was *the* sign that a struggle, even a distant one, even one about making demands for a particular group, was understood by all the exploited as an appeal for their emancipation. That is no longer the case. This is the sense in which I would no longer say that politics is "perhaps" a means of testifying to a radical wrong. And that's better! Because for two centuries it was thought that it was, from the French Revolution to Nazism, and these were two centuries of massacres. Without precedent in history. I am wary of those who are nostalgic for politics as tragedy.

Irvine, California
October 18, 1991

7

Born in 1943

LUC ROSENZWEIG

ELISABETH WEBER: Right at the start of the 1980s, you published a collection of interviews called *La jeune France juive* [Young Jewish France], a title that is both provocative and ironic, since it alludes indirectly to the title of an extremely anti-Semitic book, Edouard Drumont's *La France juive* [Jewish France] (1886).[1] On the flyleaf—so, literally at the opening—you then put the following sentence from Bernard Lazare's work *Le Fumier de Job* [Job's Dung]: "You want to get to know a people? You have to look at them in the magnifying glass of their Jews." Three pages further on, you look through the magnifying glass of a Jewish friend, Pierre Goldman—or, to be more precise, the magnifying glass of his death—not only at a people but a "period": a period that too easily "got rid of its guilt." And you go on: "By killing Pierre Goldman, his murderers, whoever they are, tried to set a definite end to a history France drags along like a millstone: that of the collective cowardice of a people that agrees to send 'its' Jews to death."[2] What would you say today when you look at France through the magnifying glass of its Jews?

LUC ROSENZWEIG: At any rate, and I am telling you this right away, it would be more nuanced than the response I was formulating at the time. It would be more nuanced because at the time I was writing this book and, with some friends, the *Catalogue pour des Juifs de maintenant* [Catalog for Today's Jews][3]—we were still reacting to Goldman's murder.[4] That's the context. It was at a time when already—and this seems a bit prophetic to me now—a whole generation of young Jews who had been influenced by involvement in the communist ideal had taken their leave of it. We had a double relationship to Goldman: on the one hand the wish to see him as a martyr, and on the other, for us who were leaving that ideal, a kind of retrospective admiration for someone who would never have left it and wanted to live it right to the furthest limits. This character, and I'm speaking here for all the people I discussed it with, was in a way for everyone the rediscovery of something denied: we had denied Judaism for the sake of universality. The history of that whole Parisian and French generation that had taken part in the Communist Students' Union, in May 1968—well, in all those things—had turned out a bit orphaned, and when you are an orphan, what do you set out to find? Your daddy and your mummy. So, since you're a bit bombastic, you try to make and remake a universal history out of an individual one. Having said that, on the core of the affair, the quotation from Bernard Lazare seems to me still worth taking into consideration, because if you think about French Jewishness today, then France is a country where it has never been so easy to be Jewish. French Israelites, as I call them, are returning in force—the way French Jews fit into this society, this Republic, has never been stronger. They are spread out through every shade of political opinion or economic status, naturally with some pronounced areas of distribution: for instance there have always been more of them in the media than in agriculture, but there are historical reasons for that. At any rate, the attachment of this French Jewish society to the fundamental values of this Republic has never been as strong as today. It perhaps expresses this attachment with more emphasis and more lyricism than others: in that sense it's a question of a magnifying glass. To the extent that you've left behind the revolutionary ideal, your relationship to the nation is one of tenderness and love. It is true that by looking at French Jews, one can get an idea of French society (even if not in its totality). If you think about everything that French people feel represents them, then many things are expressed by Jews in terms that are linked to their personal history. That's why I find everything that is said about anti-Semitism a bit incantatory. It's true, it does exist. And France has never been exempt from anti-Semitism, at least the sort declared in words. But that has never stopped Jews from feeling fine there and from being impossible people when they're abroad—even more impossible than non-Jewish French people in that they defend all its values, everything that they think makes this country the pinnacle of

humanity, with even more conviction. The second thing is that French Judaism brings together the West and the East. For example, when I was
young, there were no Sephardic Jews in France.

E. W.: The arrival of the Sephardic Jews is a very important moment
for the French Jewish community.

L. R.: Very. I saw them arrive; I remember, I was fifteen, it was between 1959 and 1962.

E. W.: During the Algerian War.

L. R.: It was connected to the Algerian War, yes. I was in high school,
and then we saw a bunch of kids turn up who were much less uptight than
we were, who had a way of behaving that was both oriental and Mediterranean, and this was a sort of liberation. We all called them Choukroun,
Abitbol, and so on. We were saying to each other: who are these people? It
was about our relationship to the Middle East. French Judaism reunited
the north-Rhine-Strasbourg side of France with the Mediterranean side.

E. W.: The day after the murder of Pierre Goldman, you wrote in the
newspaper *Libération* a "Kaddish for Pierre," which ends with a sort of
promise: "Jews bowed down never again. Your hatred of anti-Semites,
which we sometimes found excessive and untimely, we take up again entirely and totally in our names."[5] At the beginning of your book of interviews, you speak of Goldman and his death. Reading *Le Mystère Waldheim*
[The Waldheim Mystery], which you wrote later on with Bernard Cohen,
I felt that here was an echo or response to that promise, a carrying out of
that promise.[6]

L. R.: Yes, well, I wouldn't put it in such a moving way as you do. As
to that Waldheim affair, I was sent to Austria by *Le Monde*. It was absolutely
necessary to write something.[7] Because it wasn't just about finding that
grassroots Austria is anti-Semitic, everyone knew that, but because there was
a danger of a general effacement of memory. It's certainly the least that this
generation owes the preceding one—for me for instance, born in 1943. My
generation suffered relatively little directly from the persecution, and the
minimum of grateful recognition with regard to the preceding generation
consists in saying: just because you are no longer there to denounce and to
say what it was like doesn't mean that we have to pass on to today's agenda.
It is a kind of moral duty, or I would say even more than that, it's something

quite natural, that gets us enemies, because there is a force of forgetting that is relatively powerful. I am not against amnesty, since guilt must not be carried over onto subsequent generations. But the forgetting of the facts and of the truth as revealed so manifestly by a character like Waldheim had to be denounced. The least we could do was to make that public. At that point I worked with a Sephardic Jew who was even more excited than I was. It was I who had to calm him down. Well, he's a very good friend.

E. W.: Let's continue with the question of memory since you're broaching it. It's significant that the introduction to the book on Waldheim is entitled "The Duty of Memory," and the title of your conclusion echoes this: "The Duty of Democracy." So the chances of democracy would be inseparable from a fidelity that is called memory. In this conclusion, you observe, however, that in democratic countries there is a growing indifference in relation to war criminals: "There is hardly any indignation left in affluent countries, with the exactitude of journalistic revelations becoming inversely proportional to the collective emotion that they were intended to elicit."[8] How then can a journalistic project's chances of success be evaluated nowadays? You tell the story of how during the period when you and Bernard Cohen were presenting the Waldheim material in your respective papers, *Le Monde* and *Libération*, the mail you were receiving was bursting with threats and insults, including insults that referred to your Jewish-sounding names . . .

L. R.: The unfortunate thing in this affair is that if we aren't there to take care of it, I think that no one *will* take it on. I don't mean to be rude about my colleagues, but in the end, let's say that the fact of being concerned . . . I return to the question of "memory and democracy," which seems to me very important, all the more in that now, with the liberation of the Eastern bloc countries where democratic forms exist, the liberation of communism—especially in the Polish case—can also bring with it the extinction of memory, along the lines of: We suffered because we were under the communist yoke, so we are absolved from any need to reflect, in particular from any return to our history, and—to summarize this crudely—we can be anti-Semitic with no problems. Having been to Poland a number of times, I can tell you I'm not exaggerating. I would call this the archaic form of anti-Semitism, arising from ancient, pre-Vatican II Christianity, and having nothing whatever in common with the exterminating anti-Semitism of the Nazis. I see it more as a continuation of Christian European archaism. Having said that, the way you accept the other—not only the other as foreigner but, in this case, the other within oneself—is also a measure of the degree of democracy. To have spent four years abroad sent me back to my home country and, in the end, the way things have happened up till now in France could perhaps be worse. I know American society a bit, where you have several communities living adjacent to each other with few links between them. It's a society of juxtaposition, not integration. That makes a big difference. If there are formal things about democracy—like, for instance, free elections—there is also the way a society behaves in relation to those who don't form part of the majority group. This behavior has to be based on a whole historical memory and consists in remembering the mistakes and crimes that were committed when this question was not at the center of moral, ethical, and political reflection.

E. W.: *Le Mystère Waldheim* isn't just the result of lengthy research on Waldheim's life and activities, but also a reflection on memory. For in this affair, everything happens "as if, at the end of this century, memory had become suspect, and as if it had to be submitted to a morality inquest . . . when it presented itself to testify at the witness-box of the court of history." And you add: "What is more, Vietnam, Cambodia, or yet other traumas have for a long time shut down that chamber of justice that intellectuals frequented with great delight twenty years ago."[9] I hear this sentence as a barb against "intellectuals." Yet the work of some contemporary French philosophers rests on a persistent reflection on memory, on its paradoxes, and on the immense difficulty of remembering the very thing whose excessiveness challenges human imagination, namely the Shoah. Haven't some intellectuals withdrawn from the big trials and public declarations to work in more depth on the vast questions that arise in our century?

L. R.: You're right. And I have a friend, Annette Wieviorka, who wrote a thesis on the first testimonies, the first stories from the camps.[10] You've got to realize that at the time when we published the book on that affair—it was 1986—the revisionist debate was at its height. Who are you thinking of when you ask the question?

E. W.: I'm thinking for instance of philosophers like Jean-François Lyotard or Emmanuel Levinas.

L. R.: I see. At any rate, they are not the ones at the forefront of the intellectual-media scene. At the time we were confronted with other types of media intellectuals—I'm thinking especially of Bernard-Henri Lévy or André Glucksmann, or all those people who were also in a way twisting memory for the sake of testimony, which aroused a kind of uneasiness in us, given that they situated themselves halfway between journalism and ethical and philosophical reflection. We, at least Bernard and I, we stay in our domain, which is more straightforwardly that of journalism, which I call the constant, in-depth study of the surface. I don't want it to be said that it's to do with anything else.

E. W.: But it's still an extremely meticulous kind of work . . .

L. R.: It doesn't preclude meticulousness, but we are in fact technicians of the surface, a bit like cleaners. Obviously, you always run the very unpleasant risk of being taken for a pain in the neck. And it's true, to come back to the readers' letters, that when you touch on these things a little bit you awaken their anti-Semitism in people who've buried it in the depths of themselves. Some Jews, in the tradition of the "French Israelites" of the time of the Dreyfus affair, prefer to keep quiet when faced with manifestations of anti-Semitism, on the pretext of not attracting attention, fearing that the integration for which they have paid a high price will be challenged once more. Their motto is don't awaken the sleeping monster, we're perfectly at ease. But on the other hand, one shouldn't make a mistake in the evaluation of things, either. The importance of someone like Waldheim on the international scene is *nil*. He has done his six years, Austria has been a bit shoved to one side, but it's not a crucial event in world history. However, I hope my children will do the same thing in similar circumstances and will say no, no, that won't do. That book is made up, in a sense, of a bit of work, a bit of passion, a kind of passion for the truth, a truth that's certainly a subjective one too, but which means that you don't turn the page, you don't pass on to today's agenda.

E. W.: Let me go back to the journal *Recherches*, where in 1979 you brought together and presented a certain number of texts under the title *Catalogue pour des Juifs de maintenant* [Catalog for Today's Jews]. In the introduction you write: "The majority of contributors to this issue belong to a generation that has not had to set itself the problem of its survival. The specter of Auschwitz is present, of course, but nowadays it functions more like an a priori category of knowledge, indispensable for any Jew reflecting on the Western world, than as a specter to be conjured away."[11] As regards the a priori category of knowledge, you are very close, for instance, to philosophers like Adorno, Hannah Arendt, or Lyotard. However (and I think you have already referred to this) isn't there a danger nowadays of a quasi-rhetorical use of the reference to Auschwitz that would run the risk of removing from memory the unimaginable and immeasurable aspect of what happened and so of destroying that memory?

L. R.: Yes, take the example of the Carmelite monastery. In his book on the affair, Théo Klein recounts all the negotiations with the Catholic Church at the time of this idiotic episode of the Carmelite monastery.[12] The Christianization of the Shoah is something I find physically intolerable, even if the others tell you: what else do you want, we're praying for you, you should be pleased! I know Cardinal Lustiger well, we have talked about it at length.[13] He is completely stuck in this affair. What's dangerous, in the event, with this contentless incantation of Auschwitz, is that people even end up presenting the Enlightenment—in other words the Haskalah—as the mother of totalitarianism. The Christianization of the Shoah refers everything in the category of liberation and humanism to a matrix from which the horror is said to have issued and, moreover, not just that horror, but also, later, the horror of communism. "Auschwitz" today is perhaps no longer a material, physical memory of actually lived suffering, but it's a concept whose preservation as real memory remains important for the determination of the future. We see every day that relativizations, the Christianization of the Shoah, not to mention the brutality of negation, are things that endanger humanist and lay values taken together—the values of the Haskalah for Jews and of the Enlightenment for non-Jews, which give us the capacity to identify with this civilization. In 1979 we weren't thinking of those things, because events like the Auschwitz Carmelite affair hadn't yet taken place. What we were thinking of at the time was revisionist history, which was gathering momentum. It is up to our generation to find words and responses, because the victims' generation can only express—how can I put this?—a horrified silence in the face of these phenomena.

E. W.: In contemporary French thought, interrogation of the Jewish tradition seems to me to have been more and more important for some

years; and we notice—at least this is my impression, perhaps it only ap-
plies to a few intellectuals—a growing sensitivity to questions touching on
Judaism. What do you think of this phenomenon?

L. R.: There is one thing I notice, which is that more and more people likely to be heard declare their Jewish loyalties in various ways. That is
true of my fellow Strasbourgian Benny Lévy (he lives here too), who has
become a neo-Talmudist . . . [14]

E. W.: And who took part in your political struggles . . .

L. R.: Yes, yes, he's an absolutist, as always, he's becoming absolutely
kosher . . . and it extends to people like Finkielkraut who refer in their
philosophical writing to the Jewish tradition, and try to link it to the Enlightenment.[15] So the Jewish tradition is much more present as a reference
for this generation, which has abandoned the claim to adhere to a mode of
thinking the universal, and which integrates the particular—which means
that having started from a completely ghettoized minority, that tradition is
now an element in the French intellectual and moral landscape. With all
the phenomena that that can create: the supporters of Le Pen, and the ex-
clusive Far Right are putting their finger on it and asking whether this
component of the national mind is justified or not. Having said that,
nowadays it is much easier and simpler to refer to Jewish tradition because
you have no claims to make . . .

E. W.: Easier than twenty years ago?

L. R.: Yes, there is a kind of discrediting of effective anti-Semitism,
meaning separating off, whether by law or through measures that led to
death. It's now true that in France the Jewish component has become something totally natural, through its numbers, in fact it is the principal community in Europe apart from the USSR,[16] and with a different status than
in America. Naturally, there are still anti-Semites in France, but that's nor-
mal, so to speak, and anyway it's not the majority. . . . Having said that,
now we are reaching a time—and here I really do wonder about what's going on—when becoming aware of the death of nonreligious universals
brings people back to positions that might possibly provoke a new confrontation with Catholicism. In France, Jews and Protestants, representing
minorities, have most often been grouped under the Jacobin banner, thus
contributing to the reinforcement of the central state against local feudal

loyalties. They have in common the experience of how the Republic guarantees them access to powers and positions of responsibility more in the name of "Republican elitism," in other words, the priority of academic performance over birth. The whole ancient historical memory of French Judaism appears again in this moment of theoretical and ideological uncertainty. Politics—should you engage in it, should you not engage in it? Problems like that. But we're lucky to be able to wonder about them rather than being confronted with the problem of survival. What position should one take in the debate on assimilation? You can be totally assimilated and still claim an adhesion and a filiation that needn't necessarily be a problem for others! I myself am more and more French.

E. W.: Your father, a Communist Jew, fled Germany in 1933; you tell the story in that issue of *Recherches*. Your grandparents fled Berlin *in extremis* in 1940. Your grandfather went back there in 1952 and in 1979 he celebrated his ninety-second birthday there.[17] You have lived for several years in West Germany yourself. What are the thoughts of a French Jew of German origin about the reunification of Germany and the fact that the city from which his grandparents had to flee to save their lives is once again the German capital? Do you think this end of the post-war could lead the Germans to wipe clean the slate of history—or to put it another way, to act as if the trauma of the annihilation of European Jews by Nazi Germany had never existed?

L. R.: When the wall came down, I really had divided feelings, totally divided feelings. In one way, I had no regrets, as I knew East Germany well through having lived there too for a year, in 1964.

E. W.: In Berlin?

L. R.: No, in Leipzig. As far as the relation to memory is concerned, it was still the most amnesiac state in that region of the world. West Germany had at least engaged in a quiet work, had taken on the inheritance. Austria, it's more a *wir wurschteln uns durch* [We muddle through!] kind of thing. With the East Germans, it was: Don't know about it. So no regrets about it. Second, there was the just idea that justice was done by history. I was sure, when I got there, that unity would happen, of course I didn't know it would happen while I was there, but I was sure it would happen because you can't go against those kinds of things. So I took it both as something that had to occur and, on the other hand, as something that would lead me to have some fears, in that in some social circles I moved in, this reunification was taken as a sort of endpoint: now we are going on to something else, you're not going to bug us with that history any more. Or else, they suggested parallels: we suffered from communism. . . . Now, with a bit of hindsight and more reason than sentiment, I'm thinking, in the end, it's East Germany being taken over again by a West Germany that's settled its relation to the past in what we could call a relatively satisfying way. Now they have to impose it on people who have been completely set outside that thing, and as a consequence the reactionaries speak up. Think for instance of those Leipzig or Dresden skinheads who say, The communists maintained that the Nazis were evil, the communists always lied, therefore the Nazis were good. It's difficult to straighten these things out again. At present, my relationship to Germany is not principally a German Jew's relationship, it's the relationship of a French person, a French French person, to Germany, with the real fear—I work in a Franco-German sector, I experience this every day and I fight over it—that this country's excessive power may be imposing certain kinds of reflection and action, and that the face of this Europe of which I feel I am a sort of representative or citizen might have features that are too Germanic.[18] There are a number of values that come out of the French tradition that need to be preserved in this Europe that's in the process of being constructed, and that I adhere to. My job is to represent them, with the feeble means I have—I feel a bit like the representative of the French enlightenment. So as well as my commitment to Franco-German cooperation, I also have—and this is what I wrote in *Die Zeit*—the peaceful certainties of a father of French Jews. There's my identity.

In addition, from having lived a long time in Germany, what I more feared was a cloying philo-Semitism, rather than anti-Semitism, in other words being set apart through philo-Semitism. It's true that my family's relationship to Germany was very odd—at any rate my grandparents were convinced that France was chaos, that nothing worked there. They were more Germanic than anyone. They always believed that to be German put you at the highest point of humanity from the outset, and that to be a German Jew put you at the highest point of Germanness.

E. W.: When you came to the end of your period as *Le Monde*'s Bonn correspondent, in the farewell piece you've just mentioned that appeared in *Die Zeit*, you write: "If I have learned anything from my time in the German Federal Republic, it is this: to mistrust all moralizing discourse, to flee like the plague all excessive compassion that forces you to feel you are responsible for all the ills of the world. It doesn't look good to be male, white, well off, and even a bit of a *bon vivant* in a society that regularly denounces precisely those characteristics. It's a pity, because in fact the people who most vehemently defend that type of moral order seem to me ideologically the closest: they have gone through a part of the century that resembles mine."[19] In that article, you also took your distance from German pacifists. In spite of the reservations that can be expressed about them, couldn't one think that it's precisely German pacifists who keep alive the memory of a history that might otherwise risk falling into oblivion, especially today?

L. R.: They don't give a damn about it. Not quite all of them, but in general, that's not their problem. Their problem is, they prefer trees to people. They will mobilize to defend any old willow that's dying. Man must master nature, for me that's one of the fundamental values. By the way, Judaism includes a relationship to nature. The memory of history you are speaking of is completely foreign to them. I've spent hours and hours discussing with the Greens, the ex-Left. With Cohn-Bendit, who's an old friend, it's different, I agree with him 99 percent.[20] But this return to natural mysticism, this paganism, this pantheism, this idolatry—let's go for it—for me they mean very, very dangerous things. I spoke about this more specifically in a paper I wrote at the time of the Gulf War, because some pacifists living opposite the Israeli embassy in Bonn had unrolled a banner that said [in English] "Israel keep cool." That blindness can go a very long way. At the beginning, really, was May '68, and that generation was formed in its rising up against the parents' silence about the past, but afterwards, we saw that transformation happen. In the end, what it produced was a left version of the resurgence of German nationalism's desire for sovereignty.

And to take the example of the relations between the sexes, German feminism is completely unbearable. By wanting to transform every relative truth into an absolute truth, you slip very rapidly toward a totalitarianism of truth. I try to make fun of them, but there I really feel the difference in relation to the Germans. This difference is made of Jewish roots and French roots that were mixed up without even being able to tell which was which.

E. W.: Could one formulate the following hypothesis: When people on the left in Germany, including the generation of 1968, wondered about the question of fascism, they omitted, so to speak, the Jewish question?

L. R.: Yes, because it doesn't come naturally to them. Apart from a certain number of people (there are thirty thousand Jews in Germany), no party on the left, not the Social Democrats or the Greens, has for instance opened up again that question so fundamental for German identity, the question of blood as the basis of nationality. Which is to say that there is a belonging based not on diversity, but on tribalism. Those who do try to challenge it remain voices that are completely without any public response, because the public can't hear them. You only have to have been born in the remotest part of Kazakhstan of a German family that left to go there two hundred years ago to be straightaway accepted as German by the German authorities. So it's a country of tribes. The left, the far left, have never really raised this issue. Whereas even if reactions of rejection sometimes get expressed in France, you can't impinge on the *ius soli* (citizenship by place of birth) without questioning its identity as defined by Fernand Braudel: France is the last country where everyone ends up, because the great migrations, since the Neolithic period, have always been from east to west.[21] When migrating populations arrived on the Atlantic coast, they came to a halt, cohabited, and mixed with the ones that were there already. So you have to get on with the other, to accept them. It's because blood-right isn't questioned in Germany that there can't be credibility.[22] The relationship to the Jews is thought of in the mode of an eternal guilt. It's as if they were saying something like: we kill trees through pollution, and then we killed the Jews, it's equivalent. What follows is a generalized equivalence of a kind of protectiveness: not to destroy anything of the future, neither Jews nor trees. Of course, I'm exaggerating a bit. But you can make long speeches about guilt, and these long speeches don't change any of the fundamentals of the matter.

E. W.: You have spoken about Israel. I would like to ask you a question that you put to a number of your interlocutors in your collection of interviews. In the introduction to that book, you speak of "the love of Israel that animates me nowadays, that 'Ahavat Israel' without which speaking of the Jews is just stupidly doing sociology."[23] What's the relationship between that "Ahavat Israel" that has no need of a state and your feelings with regard to the state of Israel?

L. R.: I go through highs and lows all the time. Fundamentally, it's unthinkable for me—I was born more or less with this state—that one day it might disappear as a Jewish state. Always with the bad conscience of being a Zionist on the outside, you can live with it. In fact, I don't think that in this century there can be a continuation of Jewish identity and a Jewish message without the State of Israel. It's fundamental. As far as I'm concerned, the political ups and downs of the development of this state often—you can imagine it—plunge me into such depressions that I wonder: What's the point of it? When you see on TV what's going on in the occupied territories, for instance, you wonder: do we really have to continue to fight for that? And finally, at the end of the day, the response is yes all the same. There are so many links being woven between people from there and people from here that even if you don't go there, it's still something that remains. Not that I am tempted in the least by what's called double loyalties. Those aren't the terms of the problem: the void would be too great if this state didn't exist. If the Zionist/anti-Zionist debates as they were set up in the nineteenth century are over now, we still have to take account of this state, defend it, give it as large a human and lay dimension as possible and try to guarantee that for it. It's still there to be defended. Flaubert would say: "Israel: defend it."[24]

E. W.: In that context, I'd like to mention an article you have perhaps read by the German Jewish philosopher Ernst Tugendhat, which appeared right in the middle of the Gulf War, on February 22, 1991, in *Die Zeit* [pp. 61ff.]. In it, he reproached the Germans for not consciously working through their feeling of guilt toward the Jews and, in particular, toward Israel. This shortfall would have, according to Tugendhat, the following effect: doing everything that the other, for instance the representatives of Israel, might think it necessary that you do. Consequently, said Tugendhat, the Israelis could play on this underlying feeling of guilt, "as on a piano." In other words, the result of the feeling of guilt, if it wasn't clarified, would be a paralysis of the autonomy of judgment. And it's this paralysis of the moral judgment that Tugendhat observed in West Germany during the Gulf War.

L. R.: I wouldn't agree with that position, because I think Germany should still for some time steer clear of having a judgment, or let's say a position, like that of other nations as regards things to do with Israel. Should Germany have condemned the Gulf War? I say no. I think a certain restraint is desirable—but in the end, Germany doesn't hesitate to give its opinion. The justification—because nations are also moral beings—the legitimacy of appearing like a moral being or nation in these matters, doesn't seem to me to have been acquired yet—if only because not all those who played a role under the National Socialists are dead. Second, I think that Germany, for some time still to come, is coresponsible for the existence of a state it contributed to creating, to bringing into existence. In my view, Tugendhat's position is not appropriate to the situation.

Strasbourg
December 16, 1991

Notes

Introduction

1. Théodore Reinach, *Histoire des israélites depuis l'époque de leur dispersion jusqu'à nos jours* [History of the Israelites from the Period of their Dispersal to Present Times] (Paris, 1895), quoted from Pierre Birnbaum, *Les Fous de la République: Histoire politique des Juifs d'état, de Gambetta à Vichy* (Paris: Fayard, 1992), p. 157. Théodore Reinach's brother Joseph was one of Léon Gambetta's collaborators and closest friends. The Reinach family dedicated themselves to the State and the republican ideal for several generations, and played a major role in the Third Republic. Théodore's son Julien Reinach was excluded from public office in 1940 because of the "Statute on the Jews" (see p. 9). In 1943 he was deported from Drancy to Bergen Belsen, where he was liberated in 1945 by the Allied troops. His brother Léon was murdered with all his family at Auschwitz. See also Birnbaum, *The Jews of the Republic: A Political History of State Jews in France from Gambetta to Vichy,* trans. Jane Marie Todd (Stanford: Stanford University Press, 1996), pp. 7–19.

2. Birnbaum, *Les Fous,* p. 157.

3. See Maurice Szafran, *Les Juifs dans la politique française de 1945 à nos jours* [Jews in French Politics from 1945 to the Present] (Paris: Flammarion, 1990), p. 19.

4. Cited in Birnbaum, *Les Fous,* p. 143.

5. Birnbaum, *Les Fous,* p. 144. The majority of the centenary speeches collected by Benjamin Mossé in the book *La Révolution française et le rabbinat* [The French Revolution and the Rabbis] (Avignon, 1890) end with a patriotic prayer. That of chief rabbi Moïse Weil begins by asking for "our France, our beloved mother" to be blessed, then expresses the wish that "our generous and magnanimous country" will continue to prosper, and finishes by asking for the protection of Judaism and the blessing of humanity.

6. Mossé, pp. 59, 135–36, 228.

7. Pierre Birnbaum, *Anti-Semitism in France: A Political History from Léon Blum to the Present* (1988), trans. Miriam Kochan (Oxford: Basil Blackwell, 1992), p. 16.

8. Mossé, pp. 100, 152.

9. Quoted in Birnbaum, *Les Fous*, p. 148.

10. The deputy Ferdinand Dreyfus, quoted in Birnbaum, *Les Fous*, p. 156.

11. See pp. 9–11.

12. Quoted in Szafran, p. 41.

13. Szafran, pp. 41–43.

14. On this, see Paula E. Hyman, "The French Jewish Community from Emancipation to the Dreyfus Affair," in *The Dreyfus Affair: Art, Truth, and Justice*, ed. Norman L. Kleeblatt (Berkeley: University of California Press, 1987), pp. 25–36, esp. pp. 28–29.

15. Hyman, p. 28.

16. Some of the extremely anti-Semitic caricatures referring to the Dreyfus affair give them a German accent. See, for instance, Kleeblatt, pp. 91, 161, 184.

17. Hyman, p. 28.

18. Ibid., p. 27.

19. Birnbaum, *Les Fous*, p. 8. The following paragraph draws on Birnbaum, *Anti-Semitism*, pp. 6, 11.

20. Birnbaum, *Anti-Semitism*, pp. 11–12.

21. Ibid., pp. 14, 15.

22. Ibid., pp. 17, 20.

23. Birnbaum, *Les Fous*, p. 159.

24. Reproductions of posters bearing this slogan, which were widely circulated, can be found in Kleeblatt, pp. 58, 170.

25. Drumont, cited in Birnbaum, *Les Fous*, p. 159.

26. Here we can only sketch out the decisive events of the affair. As there is a more than abundant literature on this subject, we will only mention the following works: Jean-Denis Bredin, *L'Affaire* [The Affair] (Paris: Julliard, 1983); Bruno Weil, *Der Prozess des Hauptmanns Dreyfus* [The Trial of Captain Dreyfus] (Berlin: W. Rothschild, 1930); Émile Zola, *L'Affaire Dreyfus: La vérité en marche* [The Dreyfus Affair: Truth on the March] (1896–1900; Paris: Garnier-Flammarion, 1969); Charles Péguy, *Notre jeunesse* [Our Youth] (Paris: Gallimard, 1933); Kleeblatt, *The Dreyfus Affair*; Rolf Schneider, *Süss und Dreyfus* (Göttingen: Steidl, 1991). [In English, see also Émile Zola, *The Dreyfus Affair: "J'accuse" and Other Writings*, ed. Alain Page, trans. Eleanor Levieux (New Haven: Yale University Press, 1996).—Tr.]

27. Bruno Weil, p. 56.

28. A reminder that the title is Georges Clemenceau's.

29. Bredin, p. 549 (declaration of September 21st, 1899).

30. As described in Schneider, p. 107.

31. One of the best-known anti-Dreyfus men, Maurice Barrès, gave the title *La Parade de Judas* [The Parading of Judas] to his memoirs on Dreyfus's dishonorable discharge, at which he had been present. During the executive military parade, which Dreyfus himself described as "worse than death," the public responded to his

protestations of innocence with "Death to the Jews!" "Death to Judas!" "Traitor!" "Coward! Judas! Filthy Jew!" See Bredin, pp. 11ff. See further Kleeblatt, pp. 156, 160, and Eugen Weber's preface to this, p. xxvi; and Bruno Weil, p. 65.

32. Péguy, pp. 10–14. Péguy does also identify the "derepublicanization" movement with the "dechristianization" of the French state (p. 14).

33. Maurice Blanchot, "Les intellectuels en question" [Intellectuals in Question], *Le Débat* 29 (March 1984): 8ff. Since then, the affair has been involved in another turn of events with the publication, in February 1994, of a report entitled "L'affaire Dreyfus d'après le SHAT [Service historique de l'armée de la terre]" [The Dreyfus Affair According to SHAT (the historical department of the territorial army)]. The newspaper *Libération* (February 5–6, 1994) summarized this "dubious lesson from the army" as follows: "Apart from an accumulation of lies, this text is described by the lawyer and writer Jean-Denis Bredin as 'a caricature' that 'shows the persistence of the old anti-Dreyfus mentality'." Following this publication, the head of SHAT had to resign from his post (see *Le Monde*, February 10, 1994, p. 9).

34. Birnbaum, *Anti-Semitism*, p. 17.

35. Michael R. Marrus and Robert O. Paxton, *Vichy France and the Jews* (New York: Basic Books, 1981), p. 3. Regarding the whole of this paragraph, see also Birnbaum, *The Jews*, pp. 338ff.; and also Serge Klarsfeld, *Vichy-Auschwitz 1942: Le rôle de Vichy dans la solution finale de la question juive en France* [Vichy-Auschwitz: The Role of Vichy in the Final Solution of the Jewish Question in France] (Paris: Fayard, 1985). See also *Memorial to the Jews Deported from France, 1942–1944* (1978), edited by the lawyer Serge Klarsfeld (New York: Beate Klarsfeld Foundation, 1983). This includes alphabetical lists, by convoy, of Jews deported from France, a historical recapitulation of the deportation initiatives, and an alphabetical list of Jews who were summarily executed or beaten in France.

36. See Marrus and Paxton, p. 3.

37. Ibid., p. 5.

38. Birnbaum, *The Jews*, p. 340.

39. Ibid.

40. Birnbaum, *Les Fous*, p. 154.

41. See the title Birnbaum gives his chapter in *Les Fous* on Vichy: "Vichy: The State's Betrayal," p. 442.

42. Annette Wieviorka, *Déportation et génocide: Entre la mémoire et l'oubli* [Deportation and Genocide: Between Memory and Forgetting] (Paris: Plon, 1992), pp. 167ff. See too Szafran, p. 33.

43. Szafran, pp. 34ff.

44. Quoted in Szafran, p. 35.

45. Kriegel's books include *Aux origines du communisme français, 1914–1920* [At the Origins of French Communism, 1914–1920] (Paris: Flammarion, 1964); *Les internationales ouvrières, 1864–1943* [International Workers' Organizations, 1864–1943] (Paris: P.U.F., 1964); *Les Juifs et le monde moderne: Essai sur les logiques de l'émanci-*

pation [Jews and the Modern World: Essay on the Logics of Emancipation] (Paris: Éditions du Seuil, 1977).

46. Szafran, p. 56.

47. Robert O. Paxton, *Vichy France: Old Guard and New Order, 1940–1941* (New York: Knopf, 1972).

48. Robert Paxton, in an interview with *Libération*, July 16, 1992, p. 3.

49. See *Libération*, June 17, 1992, p. 26.

50. All quotations are taken from Philippe Rochette's article, "Le fardeau du silence officiel sur les crimes de Vichy" [The Burden of Official Silence about the Crimes of Vichy], *Libération*, July 11–12, 1992, p. 23.

51. *Libération*, July 16, 1992, p. 2; and July 15, 1992, p. 8.

52. See the article by Sydney Chouraqui, honorary lawyer and voluntary Resistance combatant, in *Libération*, November 24, 1992, p. 5.

53. In *Libération*, November 14–15, 1992, p. 36; see also *Libération*, November 13, 1992, p. 23.

54. See Pierre Grundman, "Mitterrand institue l'anniversaire du Vel'd'Hiv jour de commémoration", *Libération*, February 4, 1993, p. 48.

55. On Chirac's speech see the discussion between Nathalie Heinich and the historian Henry Rousso published in *Le Débat* 89 (March-April 1996).

56. See Joseph Lévy and Yolande Cohen, *Itinéraires sépharades: L'odyssée des Juifs sépharades de l'Inquisition à nos jours* [Sephardic Itineraries: The Odyssey of Sephardic Jews from the Inquisition to the Present] (Paris: Grancher, 1992), pp. 14, 60ff.

57. Apart from liturgical differences, the Ashkenazi code is for instance stricter with regard to food prohibitions, but more liberal with regard to interpersonal relationships between Jews and their non-Jewish neighbors: see, for instance, Lévy and Cohen, pp. 15ff.

58. André Chouraqui, *Histoire des Juifs en Afrique du Nord* [A History of Jews in North Africa] (Paris: Hachette, 1985), pp. 285ff. See also the much abbreviated English translation, *Between East and West: A History of the Jews of North Africa*, trans. Michael M. Bernet (Philadelphia: The Jewish Publication Society of America, 1968), p. 114.

59. Lévy and Cohen, p. 22.

60. Cited from Chouraqui, *Between East and West*, p. 143. See also Chouraqui, *Histoire*, p. 288.

61. Chouraqui, *Histoire*, p. 288.

62. Ibid., 283.

63. Claude Tapia, *Les Juifs sépharades en France* [Sephardic Jews in France] (Paris: L'Harmattan, 1986), pp. 36ff.

64. See Lévy and Cohen, p. 116. To achieve these aims, the AIU also founded schools; the first of these opened in Tunisia in 1878. See Chouraqui, *Histoire*, p. 383; and *Cent ans d'histoire: L'Alliance israélite universelle et la renaissance juive*

contemporaine (1860–1960) [A Hundred Years of History: The Universal Israelite Alliance and the Contemporary Jewish Renaissance] (Paris: Presses universitaires de France, 1965).

65. Pierre Nora, *Les Français en Algérie* [The French in Algeria] (Paris: Julliard, 1961), p. 138. For the text of the Crémieux decree, see Chouraqui, *Histoire*, p. 293.

66. Tapia, p. 39.

67. See Nora, pp. 138ff.

68. Ibid., p. 101; and Chouraqui, *Histoire*, p. 295.

69. See Tapia, p. 74; and Nora, pp. 140ff.

70. On the Algerian War, see the set of articles by Jean-François Lyotard that appeared from 1956 to 1963 in *Socialisme ou barbarie*, collected under the title *La Guerre des Algériens: Ecrits, 1956–1963* (Paris: Galilée, 1989). [*Political Writings*, trans. Bill Readings and Kevin Paul (Minneapolis: University of Minnesota Press, 1993).]

71. Figures given in the sources vary between 120,000 and 150,000.

72. Quoted in Szafran, p. 132.

73. Quoted by Tapia, p. 40.

74. See Chouraqui, *Histoire*, pp. 438ff.

75. Chouraqui, *Between East and West*, p. 437. The dilemma of "dual allegiance" that the Jewish community found itself in became apparent from the mistrust harbored toward it from both the Arab and the French sides. "A symbol: in a Lévy family from Algiers, the father was murdered by the OAS because he was showing sympathy for the FLN, and the son was killed by the FLN because he was suspected of belonging to the OAS." The OAS—the Organisation Armée Secrète—was a French clandestine movement that employed torture, murder, and other forms of violence (such as the strategy of "scorched earth") to oppose the struggle for Algerian independence from 1961 to 1963. But Jacques Derrida maintains that the great majority of Algerian Jews were in favor of a French Algeria, and so hostile to the nationalist aspirations of the FLN [verbal communication].

76. Chouraqui, *Histoire*, p. 438.

77. See Tapia, p. 407.

78. Claude Lanzmann, in Bernard Cuau et al., *Au sujet de "Shoah," le film de Claude Lanzmann* [On the Subject of Claude Lanzmann's film *Shoah*] (Paris: Belin, 1990), p. 295.

79. Emmanuel Levinas, *Otherwise than Being or Beyond Essence* (1974), trans. Alphonso Lingis (Pittsburgh: Duquesne University Press, 1998).

80. Jacques Derrida, "Passages—from Traumatism to Promise," in *Points . . . : Interviews, 1974–1994*, ed. Elisabeth Weber, trans. Peggy Kamuf et al. (Stanford: Stanford University Press, 1995), p. 382.

81. Levinas, p. 121 and p. 197, note 26.

82. Derrida, p. 389.

83. Robert Faurisson and Henri Roques are the two best-known representatives of the French revisionist school that denies the existence of Nazi gas cham-

bers and the Nazis' murder of millions of European Jews. See interview with Pierre Vidal-Naquet, below pp. 30–32.

84. Pierre Vidal-Naquet, *Les Juifs, la mémoire et le présent* [Jews, Memory and the Present], vol. 2 (Paris: La Découverte, 1991), p. 10. [*The Jews: History, Memory, and the Present*, ed. and trans. David Ames Curtis (New York: Columbia University Press, 1998). This quotation is not in the English translation of *Les Juifs*, a single volume in which the editor (in his own words) "compiled a representative selection."]

85. Léon Poliakov, preface to the German edition of *A History of Anti-Semitism* (*Geschichte des Antisemitismus*), vol. 1, trans. R. Pfisterer (Worms: Verlag Georg Heintz, 2nd edn., 1979), pp. x–xi.

86. Ibid.

87. Yosef Hayim Yerushalmi, *Zakhor: Jewish History and Jewish Memory* (Seattle and London: University of Washington Press, 1982), p. 101.

88. Yerushalmi, pp. 93, 95.

89. See Hannah Arendt, "The Jew as Pariah: A Hidden Tradition," in *The Jew as Pariah: Jewish Identity and Politics in the Modern Age*, ed. Ron H. Feldman (New York: Grove Press, 1978), pp. 67–90.

90. See Rita Thalmann, "Une lacune dans l'historiographie" [A Historiographical Lacuna], in *Les Juifs dans la Résistance et la libération: Histoire, témoignages, débats* [Jews in the Resistance and the Liberation: History, Testimonies, Debates], ed. Association pour la recherche sur l'histoire contemporaine des Juifs (Paris: Scribe, 1985), pp. 89ff.

91. "Être juif," *Les Dossiers de l'écran*, broadcast by Armand Jammot, June 11, 1991, Channel 2, Paris, p. 17 of the brochure. In contemporary French thought, attempts to reassess the place of women in the Jewish tradition in a new and critical way are multiplying. See for instance Annie Goldmann, *Les Filles de Mardochée: Histoire familiale d'une émancipation* [The Daughters of Mardochea: The Family History of an Emancipation] (Paris: Denoël, 1979); Janine Gdalia and Annie Goldmann, *Le Judaïsme au féminin* [Judaism in the Feminine] (Paris: Balland, 1989); Catherine Chalier, *Les Matriarches: Sarah, Rebecca, Rachel, et Léa* [The Matriarchs: Sarah, Rebecca, Rachel, and Leah] (Paris: Le Cerf, 1986).

92. Vidal-Naquet, pp. 10, 11.

93. Jean-François Lyotard, *Lectures d'enfance* [Childhood Readings] (Paris: Galilée, 1991), p. 66.

94. This is the title of Yosef Hayim Yerushalmi's book, first cited in note 86.

95. Klaus Barbie was the SS officer in charge of the Gestapo in Lyon, France, from November 1942 to August 1944. Known as "the butcher of Lyon" for torturing and killing over 26,000 people, Barbie was brought to trial on May 11, 1987 in a French court for crimes against humanity related to his role in executing Hitler's Final Solution. After having been sentenced to death *in absentia* twice previously, Barbie was sentenced to life imprisonment. He died of cancer in prison in 1991.

96. *Le Monde*, May 2, 1987, p. 9.

97. Yerushalmi, "Reflections on Forgetting," in *Zakhor*, foreword by Harold Bloom, with a new preface and postscript by the author (New York: Schocken Books, 1989), p. 117. It is only recently that the French judicial system has proved that these two terms were not antonyms, despite the slowness and scandalous delays of the procedures. Paul Touvier, regional head of the second division of the Rhône militia in 1944 and intelligence officer in the struggle against the Resistance, was sentenced to death on April 20, 1994, for complicity in a crime against humanity. Through the intervention of numerous bishops of the French Church, he had escaped both death sentences passed against him *in absentia,* in 1946 and 1947, and he had received a pardon from President Georges Pompidou on November 23, 1971. It was only following complaints lodged in 1973 and 1974 that he was arrested, in 1989, and charged with five major crimes, including the murder of the Basch couple and the execution of seven people, all Jewish, at Rillieux-la-Pape (in the Ain region at the time). The case was dismissed on April 13, 1992, but this was partly revoked on November 27 of that year; and he was referred to the courts at Versailles, where the trial opened in March 1994.

It had not been possible to put on trial René Bousquet (responsible for the deportation of 59,000 of the 76,000 deported French Jews, acting in the name of a politics of state collaboration), who was murdered in June 1993. Maurice Papon, a high-ranking official under the Nazi puppet regime of Marshal Pétain and later prefect of police under Charles de Gaulle, was sentenced in 1998 to ten years of imprisonment for complicity in crimes against humanity. However, he was released on September 19, 2002, due to poor health.

Because of the history of the Bousquet and Papon cases, the Touvier trial was given a symbolic function that it was perhaps not in a position to fulfill, despite the weight of the charges against the accused. These were not entirely representative of what national memory demanded a judgment of: the complicity of Vichy in the "Final Solution." See Eric Conan and Henry Rousso, *Vichy, un passé qui ne passe pas* [Vichy, a Past that Does Not Pass] (Paris: Fayard, 1994).

98. Luc Rosenzweig, *La jeune France juive* [Young Jewish France: Conversations with Jews of Today] (Paris: Libre-Hallier, 1980), p. 185. See also Edmond Jabès, *Je bâtis ma demeure* [I Build My Dwelling]: "To all questions, Jews reply with a question" (Reb Léma).

99. Jacques Derrida, "Adieu," in *Adieu: To Emmanuel Levinas*, trans. Pascale-Anne Brault and Michael Naas (Stanford: Stanford University Press, 1999), pp. 11–12.

Chapter 1: Pierre Vidal-Naquet

1. Pierre Vidal-Naquet, *Les Juifs, la mémoire et le présent*, vol. 1 (Paris: La Découverte, 1981), P. 78.

2. Alain Schnapp and Pierre Vidal-Naquet, eds., *Journal de la commune étudi-*

ante: Textes et documents, novembre 1967–juin 1968 [Journal of the Student Commune: Texts and Documents, November 1967 to June 1968].

3. Pierre Vidal-Naquet, ed., *Les Crimes de l'armée française* [The Crimes of the French Army] (Paris: Maspero, 1975), pp. 5, 6.

4. Pierre Vidal-Naquet, "Du bon usage de la trahison," preface to Flavius Josephus, *La Guerre des Juifs* [The Jewish War] (Paris: Minuit, 1976).

5. The book was published in Paris by La Découverte four days before this interview: Pierre Vidal-Naquet, *Les Juifs*, vol. 1; *Les Juifs, la mémoire et le present*, vol. 2 (Paris: La Découverte, 1991). *The Jews: History, Memory, and the Present*, ed. and trans. David Ames Curtis (New York: Columbia University Press, 1998). See Introduction, note 84, above. When the French edition is quoted, it is because the text is not in the English version.

6. See Marek Edelman and Hanna Krall, *Mémoires du ghetto de Varsovie: Un dirigeant du ghetto de Varsovie raconte* [Memories of the Warsaw Ghetto: Narrated by a Warsaw Ghetto Supervisor] (Paris: Editions du Scribe, 1983). This book is in two parts, the first of which, "The Ghetto Struggles," was published in Lodz in 1945, and the second, "Beating the Good Lord to It," in Warsaw in 1977. See also Vidal-Naquet, *The Jews*, pp. 127ff.

7. Directed by Marcel Ophuls (born in Frankfurt in 1927, emigrated to France in 1933 and to the United States in 1941). The film is subtitled: "Chronicle of a French Town Under the Occupation." Marcel Ophuls is also the director of the film *Hôtel Terminus: Klaus Barbie, sa vie et son temps* [Hotel Terminus: The Life and Times of Klaus Barbie], 1988.

8. Directed by Claude Lanzmann.

9. In Yosef Hayim Yerushalmi, *Zakhor: Jewish History and Jewish Memory* (Seattle and London: University of Washington Press, 1982).

10. The Ninth Av, Tisha be-av, is the day of fasting in memory of the destruction of the first and second temples in Jerusalem.

11. See "Paulus, Thrasybulos und Mielke: Was tun mit der Vergangenheit, mit der Stasi-Elite? Vorschläge des französischen Althistorikers Pierre Vidal-Naquet," interview by A. Smoltczyk, *Die Tageszeitung*, June 22, 1991.

12. Vidal-Naquet refers here to the question, after the reunification of Germany, of whether and how to put on trial former East German officials who, along with other crimes, had ordered the shooting of people trying to flee the communist German Democratic Republic.

13. Pierre Vidal-Naquet, foreword to Miguel Benasayag, *Utopie et liberté: Les droits de l'homme: une idéologie?* [Utopia and Freedom: Human Rights: An Ideology] (Paris: La Découverte, 1986), pp. 13–14.

14. See Pierre Vidal-Naquet, *L'Affaire Audin (1957–1978)* [The Audin Affair (1957–1978)] (1958; Paris: Minuit, 2nd edn., 1989). The French mathematician Maurice Audin, a member of the Algerian communist party, was arrested in June 1956 in Algiers. He was never seen again after his arrest. The military authorities

said he escaped while he was being taken to the place of interrogation. The contradictions and discrepancies in the official reports raised the suspicion that he had been murdered under torture, and an "Audin committee," whose members included Pierre Vidal-Naquet, Jacques Panijel, Michel Crouzet, Luc Montagnier, and Laurent Schwartz, was set up with the aim of making a judicial enquiry. On April 20, 1962, on the pretext of an amnesty for all participants in the Algerian insurrection, the case was dismissed, in spite of its obscurities and the questions that the army's evidence had failed to clarify. This affair was an issue in the opposition to French politics in Algeria.

15. "Lyotard et Vidal-Naquet: parler encore de la guerre d'Algérie" [Lyotard and Vidal-Naquet: To Speak Some More About the Algerian War], *Libération*, November 9, 1989, pp. 30–31.

16. See Vidal-Naquet, *L'Affaire Audin*, p. 126n9. Charles Hernu served as the prime minister for defense under François Mitterrand from 1981 to 1985. Hernu died January 17, 1990.

17. In August 1961, Bernard Chenot took over as minister of justice from Edmond Michelet, who was thought too liberal.

18. The Sorgue is a river in Provence.

19. Vidal-Naquet, *Les crimes de l'armée française*, p. 13.

20. See Pierre Vidal-Naquet, *Assassins of Memory: Essays on the Denial of the Holocaust* (1987), trans. Jeffrey Mehlman (New York: Columbia University Press, 1992), e.g., p. 24, where the revisionist method is described as being "in our spectacle-oriented society, an attempt at extermination on paper that pursues in another register the actual work of extermination. One revives the dead in order the better to strike the living."

21. Vidal-Naquet, *Assassins*, p. 20.

22. Aeschylus, *Eumenides*, lines 970ff.; cf. also lines 885ff.

23. Robert Faurisson is seen as *the* French revisionist historian. He claimed in 1974 that the "Holocaust story" was a collection of contradictory eyewitness testimonies mounted against a backdrop of wartime hate propaganda. To him the Shoah is so unbelievable that he does not believe it. For example, on the basis of a German letter discovered in 1960, he claimed that no one had been gassed to death at Dachau. Faurisson was dismissed from the University of Lyon for his accusations, and he has been convicted under the Fabius-Gayssot Law of 1990.

24. The letters from Michel de Boüard to Henri Roques were first published during the summer of 1991 (August–September) by the *Revue d'histoire révisionniste* [Review of Revisionist History] (no. 2, pp. 46–49), and then in an anonymous letter signed by the Vieille Taupe [Old Mole] in September 1991, under the title: "Le doyen Michel de Boüard et les chambers à gaz homicides" [Dean Michel de Boüard and the Homicidal Gas Chambers].

25. Vidal-Naquet, *Assassins*, p. 98.

26. *Ibid.*, p. 57.

27. *Esprit,* April 1979, pp. 119–21.

28. Raymond Kilbansky, Erwin Panofsky, and Fritz Saxl, *Saturn and Melancholy: Studies in the History of Natural Philosophy, Religion, and Art* (London: Nelson, 1964).

29. Pierre Vidal-Naquet, preface to Arno J. Mayer, *La "solution finale" dans l'histoire,* trans. M.-G. and J. Carlier (Paris: La Découverte, 1990), p. x. *Why Did the Heavens Not Darken? The "Final Solution" in History* was published in 1988 (New York: Pantheon).

30. Amos Funkenstein, "Theological Interpretations of the Holocaust," in *Unanswered Questions: Nazi Germany and the Genocide of the Jews,* ed. François Furet (New York: Shocken, 1989), pp. 275–303.

31. An ultraorthodox, anti-Zionist movement, whose Israeli branch is known under the name *Natourei Karta,* the "guardians of the city."

32. Gershon Weiler, *Jewish Theocracy* (New York: Brill, 1988).

33. Pierre Vidal-Naquet, *La Démocratie grecque vue d'ailleurs* [Greek Democracy Seen from Elsewhere] (Paris: Flammarion, 1990). A. Marchand's French translation, with Vidal-Naquet's preface, of Karl A. Wittfogel, *Oriental Despotism: A Comparative Study of Total Power* (New Haven: Yale University Press, 1959) was published in 1964.

34. A painting of 1901, in the Österreichische Galerie, Vienna.

35. Isaac Deutscher, "The Jewish Tragedy and the Historian," in Isaac Deutscher, *The Non-Jewish Jew and Other Essays,* ed. Tamara Deutscher (London: Oxford University Press, 1968), p. 163–64.

36. Claudine Vegh, *I Didn't Say Goodbye,* with an afterward by Bruno Bettelheim, trans. Ros Schwartz (New York: E. P. Dutton, 1984).

37. Vidal-Naquet, *Assassins,* p. 96.

38. Ibid.

39. Simha Guterman, *Le Livre retrouvé* [The Rediscovered Book], ed. with an introduction by Nicole Lapierre (Paris: Plon, 1991).

40. Vidal-Naquet, *Les Juifs,* vol. 1, p. 46; *The Jews,* p. 22.

41. See Jean-François Lyotard, *The Differend: Phrases in Dispute* (1983), trans. Georges Van Den Abbeele (Minneapolis: University of Minnesota Press, 1988), p. 105.

42. Lyotard, p. 100.

43. Vidal-Naquet, *Les Juifs,* vol. 1, p. 124. (The text does not appear in the English translation.)

44. Nicole Loraux, *L'Invention d'Athènes: Histoire de l'oraison funèbre dans la "cité classique"* [The Invention of Athens: A History of the Funeral Oration in the "Classical City"] (Paris: EHESS, 1981); and "Mourir devant Troie, tomber pour Athènes" [To Die Before Troy, to Fall for Athens], in G. Gnoli and J.-P Vernant, eds., *La Mort, les morts dans les sociétés anciennes* [Death and the Dead in Ancient Societies] (Paris: Maison des Sciences de l'Homme, 1982), pp. 27ff.

45.   German reunification took place officially on October 3, 1990, as the culmination of a series of events that included: the opening of the borders between West and East Germany, November 9, 1989; the beginning of the systematic destruction of the Berlin Wall, June 13, 1990; the removal of Checkpoint Charlie, June 22, 1990; the monetary union between West and East Germany, July 1, 1990; the signing of a treaty concerning the final settlement of Germany by the four former occupying powers, September 12, 1990.

46.   Pierre Vidal-Naquet, foreword to Karl Jaspers, *La Culpabilité allemande* [German Guilt] (Paris: Minuit, 1990), p. 22.

47.   *Historikerstreit*: See the conversation with Rita Thalmann, pp. 71–72.

48.   Christian Meier is a professor of history in Munich and president of the Deutsche Akademie für Sprache und Dichtung. Author of *From Athens to Auschwitz*, he is one of the few German historians to retain a view of history as a whole, daring to explore European history at the turn of the twenty-first century and ask what that history means for Europeans today in terms of the special responsibilities contemporary individuals have within historical processes.

49.   Pierre Vidal-Naquet, ed., *Atlas historique de l'humanité, de la préhistoire à nos jours* [Historical Atlas of Humanity from Prehistory to the Present] (1987; Paris: Hachette, 2nd edn., 1992).

50.   Hillgruber is author of *Zweierlei Untergang: die Zerschlagung des deutschen Reiches und das Ende des europäischen Judentums* [Double Destiny: The Destruction of the German Reich and the End of European Judaism] (Berlin: Siedler, 1986).

51.   "Maintenant que la guerre est lancée, il vaut mieux la gagner" [Now that the war has begun, it is better to win it], interview between Pierre Vidal-Naquet and Anne Guthmann, *Libération*, January 28 1991, pp. 13–14.

52.   "Reportage: un peuple étranglé. Treize personnalités françaises s'expriment sur la Palestine" [Report: A Strangled People: Thirteen French Figures Say What They Think About Palestine], in *Pour la Palestine* (*Bulletin des amitiés franco-palestiniennes*), no. 34, 3rd term, 1991.

Chapter 2: Jacques Derrida

1.   Jacques Derrida, "Violence and Metaphysics: An Essay on the Thought of Emmanuel Levinas," *Writing and Difference* (1967), trans. Alan Bass (London: Routledge & Kegan Paul, 1978), pp. 90–91.

2.   Jacques Derrida, *Glas* (1973), trans. John P. Leavey and Richard Rand (Lincoln: University of Nebraska Press, 1986); *The Post Card* (1980), trans. Alan Bass (Chicago: University of Chicago Press, 1987); "Shibboleth: For Paul Celan" (1986), trans. Joshua Wilner, in *Wordtraces: Readings of Paul Celan*, ed. Aris Fioretos (Baltimore and London: Johns Hopkins University Press, 1994); "Circumfession," in Geoffrey Bennington and Jacques Derrida, *Jacques Derrida* (1991), trans. Geoffrey Bennington (Chicago: University of Chicago Press, 1993).

3. Derrida, "Circumfession," p. 70. On the *pharmakos*, see Jacques Derrida, *Dissemination* (1972), trans. Barbara Johnson (Chicago: University of Chicago Press, 1982) passim, esp. "Plato's Pharmacy."

4. Derrida, "Circumfession," p. 202, tr. mod.

5. Derrida, "Shibboleth," p. 99. This passage does not appear in the English translation.

6. See "Circumfession," p. 190: "the last of the Jews that I . . . am."

7. For example in "Circumfession," p. 88.

8. Derrida, "Shibboleth," p. 65.

9. Jacques Derrida, *Given Time: 1, Counterfeit Money* (1991), trans. Peggy Kamuf (Chicago: Chicago University Press, 1992), pp. 91–92.

10. Paul Celan quoting Marina Tsvétayeva, cited in "Shibboleth," p. 54.

11. In seminars given at the École normale supérieure and the École des hautes études en sciences sociales in Paris.

12. See Jacques Derrida, *Psyche: Inventions de l'autre* [Psyche: Inventions of the Other] (Paris: Galilée, 1987), pp. 10, 31.

13. Jacques Derrida, "Force of Law: The Mystical Foundation of Authority," in *Deconstruction and the Possibility of Justice, Cardozo Law Review* (October 1990); see also " *Geschlecht*: Sexual Difference, Ontological Difference" (1987), trans. Ruben Berezdivin, in Peggy Kamuf, ed., *Between the Blinds: A Derrida Anthology* (New York: Columbia University Press, 1991), pp. 378–402; and " *Geschlecht II*: Heidegger's Hand" (1987), trans. John P. Leavey, Jr., in John Sallis, ed., *Deconstruction and Philosophy: The Texts of Jacques Derrida* (Chicago: University of Chicago Press, 1987), 161–96.

14. See Hermann Cohen, "Germanité et judéité" [Germanness and Jewishness], trans. M. B. de Launay, in *Pardès*, 5 (1987); and Jacques Derrida, "Interpretations at War: Kant, le Juif, l'Allemand," in *Phénoménologie et politique: Mélanges offerts à Jacques Taminiaux* [Phenomenology and Politics: Mixtures Presented to Jacques Taminiaux] (Brussels: Ousia, 1990), pp. 209–92. ["Interpretations at War: Kant, the Jew, the German," trans. Moshe Ron, in *Acts of Religion*, ed. Gil Anidjar (New York and London: Routledge, 2002), pp. 137–88].

15. Derrida, *Glas*, pp. 162, [61].

16. Ibid., p. 166.

17. Ibid., p. 187, quoting Hegel, *The Phenomenology of Spirit.*

18. Jacques Derrida, *Spurs* (1978), trans. Barbara Harlow (Chicago: University of Chicago Press, 1979).

19. Jacques Derrida, *Mémoires: for Paul de Man*, trans. Cecile Lindsay, Jonathan Culler, and Eduardo Cadava (New York: Columbia University Press, 1986), p. 73.

20. See, for instance, Derrida, *The Post Card*, pp. 3, 19, 23–24, passim.

21. Ibid., p. 175.

22. Jacques Derrida, *Memoirs of the Blind: The Self-Portrait and Other Ruins*

(1990), trans. Pascale-Anne Brault and Michael Naas (Chicago: University of Chicago Press, 1993), pp. 102–4.

23. Jacques Derrida, *Of Spirit* (1987), trans. Geoffrey Bennington and Rachel Bowlby (Chicago: University of Chicago Press, 1989), pp. 109–13.

24. On the notion of *différance*, see for instance Jacques Derrida, *Speech and Phenomena and Other Essays on Husserl's Theory of Signs* (1967), trans. David B. Allison (Evanston: Northwestern University Press, 1973), pp. 98ff; and *"Différance,"* in *Margins of Philosophy* (1972), trans. Alan Bass (Chicago: University of Chicago Press, 1984), pp. 1ff.

25. Jacques Derrida, *Of Grammatology* (1967), trans. Gayatri Chakravorty Spivak (Baltimore: Johns Hopkins University Press, 1976); *Speech and Phenomena*, p. 115.

26. Derrida, "Circumfession," p. 75.

27. Derrida, *The Post Card*, p. 97; and "Circumfession," pp. 58, 248, 288, 293.

28. Bennington and Derrida, "Curriculum vitae," in *Jacques Derrida*, 325–36.

29. Paul Celan, "Conversation in the Mountains," in *Collected Prose*, trans. Rosemarie Waldrop (Manchester: Carcanet Press, 1986), p. 17.

30. Derrida, "Shibboleth," p. 54.

31. Derrida, "Circumfession," p. 190.

32. Ibid., pp. 191–92.

33. Charles Michel Épée (1712–89) founded a school for deaf-mutes.

34. Derrida, "Circumfession," pp. 98, 20.

35. Derrida, *Memoirs*, p. 122.

36. Jacques Derrida, *Ulysse gramophone: Deux mots pour Joyce* (Paris: Galilee, 1987). ["Two Words for Joyce," trans. G. Bennington, in *Post-Structuralist Joyce: Essays from the French*, eds. Derek Attridge and Daniel Ferrer (Cambridge: Cambridge University Press, 1984); and "Ulysses Gramophone: Hear Say Yes in Joyce," trans. Tina Kendall and Shari Benstock, in *James Joyce: The Augmented Ninth*, ed. by Bernard Benstock (Syracuse: Syracuse University Press, 1988).]

Chapter 3: Rita Thalmann

1. Nationalsozialistische Deutsche Arbeiterpartei, i.e., the Nazi Party.—Tr.

2. Rita Thalmann, *Être femme sous le IIIe Reich* (Paris: Laffont, 1982), p. 68.

3. Ibid., p. 13.

4. Gunnar Myrdal (1898–1987) was a Swedish economist and political scientist and winner of the Nobel Prize in Economics in 1974 who analyzed the connection between racism and sexism, most notably in *The American Dilemma*.

5. See Rita Thalmann, "Sexism and Racism," in Gill Seidel, ed., *The Nature of the Right: Feminist Analysis of Order Patterns* (Philadelphia: John Benjamins Publishing Company, 1988), pp. 153–60.

6. The Web site of the United States Holocaust Memorial Museum, Washing-

ton, D.C., http://www.ushmm.org/wlc/article.php?ModuleId=10005342, has the following entry on Gurs:

The Gurs camp was one of the first and largest camps established in prewar France. It was located in the Basque region of southwestern France, just to the south of the village of Gurs. The camp, about 50 miles from the Spanish border, was situated in the foothills of the Pyrenees Mountains northwest of Oloron-Sainte-Marie.

The French government established the Gurs camp in April 1939, before war with Germany and well before the occupation of France in June 1940. Originally, Gurs served as a detention camp for political refugees and members of the International Brigade fleeing Spain after the Spanish Civil War.

In early 1940, the French government also interned about 4,000 German Jewish refugees as "enemy aliens," along with French leftist political leaders who opposed the war with Germany. After the French armistice with Germany in June 1940, Gurs fell under the authority of the new collaborationist French government, the Vichy regime.

Conditions in the Gurs camp were very primitive. It was overcrowded and there was a constant shortage of water, food, and clothing. During 1940–1941, 800 detainees died of contagious diseases, including typhoid fever and dysentery.

In October 1940, German authorities deported about 7,500 Jews from southwestern Germany across the border into the unoccupied zone of France. Vichy officials then interned most of them in Gurs. Of this group, 1,710 were eventually released, 755 escaped, 1,940 were able to emigrate, and 2,820 men were conscripted into French labor battalions.

Between August 6, 1942 and March 3, 1943, Vichy officials turned over 3,907 Jewish prisoners from Gurs to the Germans; the Germans sent the majority of them to the Drancy transit camp outside Paris in northern France. From Drancy, they were deported in six convoys to the extermination camps in occupied Poland, primarily Auschwitz.

Vichy authorities closed the Gurs camp in November 1943. Almost 22,000 prisoners had passed through Gurs, of whom over 18,000 were Jewish. More than 1,100 internees died in the camp. In 1944, Gurs was reopened briefly to intern political prisoners and resistance fighters arrested by Vichy police. After the Allied liberation of France in August 1944, French officials used Gurs to house German prisoners of war and French collaborators. At the end of 1945, officials of the postwar French republic closed the Gurs camp for the last time.

7. Gabrielle Mittag, ed., *Gurs, Deutsche Emigrantinnen im französischen Exil* [Gurs, German Women Emigrants into French Exile] (Berlin: Argon Verlag, 1990).

8. Maria Antonietta Macciocchi, a leading Italian feminist and member of the European Parliament, was awarded the French Legion of Honor in 1992 by President François Mitterrand for her work as writer, professor, and journalist.

9. Maria Antonietta Macciocchi, *Séminaire Paris VIII: Les Femmes et leurs*

maîtres [Seminar at Paris 8 University: Women and Their Masters] (Paris: Christian Bourgeois, 1978), p. ii.

10. Ibid., pp. xix, xx, emphasis Weber's. The rally in question took place on October 6, 1943. This is the passage of Himmler's quoted by Macciocchi: "The following question has been put to us: 'What do we do with the women and children?' I have taken the decision to find a completely clear solution in that case too. In fact I did not feel I had the right to exterminate men—say, if you like, to kill them or have them killed—and to let the children grow up who would take their revenge on our children and our descendants. It was necessary to take the grave decision to make this people disappear from the Earth." See further Heinrich Himmler, *Geheimreden 1933 bis 1945* [Secret Speeches, 1933–45], eds. B. F. Smith and A. F. Peterson (Frankfurt: Propyläen Verlag, 1974), p. 169.

11. In the commentary by the editors of the "Secret Speeches," p. 301n16.

12. The conference took place March 12–13, 1991.

13. Rita Thalmann, "Zwischen Mutterkreuz und Rüstungsbetrieb: Zur Rolle der Frau im Dritten Reich" [Between the Maternity Cross and the Armaments Industry in the Third Reich], in K. Bracher, H. A. Jacobsen, M. Funke, eds., *Deutschland 1933–1945: Neue Studien zur nationalsozialistischen Herrschaft* [Germany 1933–1945: New Studies on Nazi Government], Bonn Studies in Politics and History (Düsseldorf: Droste, 1992), pp. 198–217. The maternity cross was given to women who had given birth to a large number of children.

14. Alfred Rosenberg, *Der Mythus des 20. Jahrhunderts* [The Myth of the 20th century] (Munich: Hoheneichen Verlag, 1st edn., 1930).

15. Emmi Göring was the wife of Hermann Göring, who under Hitler served as head of the Gestapo, commander-in-chief of the Luftwaffe, minister for economic affairs, and field marshal of the German army. In September 1939 Hitler officially designated Hermann Göring as his successor.

16. Pierre Durand, *La Chienne de Buchenwald* (Paris: Temps actuels, 1982).

17. Irma Grese was a woman guard in Auschwitz who sought out shapely Jewish women and cut their breasts open with a whip. She then brought her victims to an inmate doctor and watched, cheeks flushed, foaming at the mouth, while the doctor performed a painful operation. Grese was condemned to death with ten members of the SS by a British military tribunal and executed in 1945. See *Law Reports of Trials of War Criminals*, vol. 2 (London, 1947), pp. 153ff. Quoted by Raul Hilberg, *The Destruction of European Jews*, vol. 3 (New York and London: Holmes and Meier, rev. edn., 1985), pp. 904, 1095.

18. Thalmann, *Être femme*, pp. 35, 39.

19. See Max Domarus, *Hitler: Reden und Proklamationen, 1932–1945*, vol. 1, *Triumph (1932–1938)* (Würzburg: Schmidt, 1962), p. 450; see also B. Classen and G. Geottle, " Le Juif nous a volé la femme" [The Jew Has Stolen the Woman from Us], in Macciocchi, *Séminaire*, p. 17.

20. Mathilde von Kemnitz (1877–1966), a prolific *völkisch* writer, was married

to General Erich Ludendorff in 1926. Together they founded a "combat-alliance" against the "supranational powers" (the Catholic Church, Jesuits, Jews, and Freemasons), and the "Tannenberg Alliance for the German Cognition of God."

21. Pia-Sophie Rogge-Börner, a *völkisch* feminist, edited *Die Deutsche Kämpferin* [The German Woman Warrior] from 1933 to 1937. The journal was considered critical of National Socialism and was forbidden in 1937.

22. Cited from Liliane Crips, in *La Tentation nationaliste* [The Nationalist Temptation], ed. Rita Thalmann (Paris: Deux Temps Tierce, 1990), p. 168.

23. Lida Gustava Heymann (1868–1943) was a journalist and advocate of women's rights. From 1914 to 1919, she was editor in chief of the publication of the "Alliance for Women's Voting Rights," in which she called for an immediate end to World War I. At the beginning of 1933, she organized in Munich a rally for peace against Hitler's party, the Nationalsozialistische Deutsche Arbeiterpartei [the German National Socialist Workers' Party] (NSDAP). After the Nazis seized power on January 30, 1933, Heymann and her life-long companion, Anita Augspurg, went into exile in Switzerland. All their belongings were confiscated by the Nazis. From Zurich, Heymann wrote articles opposing the Nazi regime. In 1941, Heymann and Augspurg wrote a joint autobiography, *Erlebtes—Erschautes: Deutsche Frauen kämpfen für Freiheit, Recht und Frieden 1850–1940* [Experiences and Visions: German Women Fight for Freedom, Justice, and Peace 1850–1940]. Lida Gustava Heymann died in Zurich in 1943.

Anita Augspurg (1857–1943) was a lawyer and advocate of women's rights. In 1902, she cofounded the German Association for Women's Voting Rights, of which she became president. During World War I (in 1915), she was one of the conveners of the International Women's Conference for Peace in The Hague. On that occasion the International Committee for an Enduring Peace was founded. It was renamed in 1918 International Women's League for Peace and Freedom, with Augspurg as one of its leading figures. Augspurg was coeditor, with Lida Gustava Heymann, of the feminist and pacifist periodical *Woman in the State*. In 1933, she went with Heymann into exile in Switzerland. She died in Zurich, five months after her companion's death.

24. Helene Stöcker (1869–1943) was cofounder, in 1902, with Minna Cauer, Lida Gustava Heymann, and Anita Augspurg, of the German Association for Women's Voting Rights. In 1905, together with representatives of the proletarian women's movement, she founded the Alliance for the Protection of Mothers and Sexual Reform, which worked to improve the legal and social position of single mothers and their children. From 1905 to 1932, she was editor in chief of the journal *Mutterschutz* [Protection of Mothers] (since 1908: *Die neue Generation* [The New Generation]), the official publication of the Alliance for the Protection of Mothers. In this journal, Stöcker advocated her ideas of a "new ethics" based on women's rights over their bodies and sexuality. In 1908 she petitioned the General Assembly of the Alliance of German Women's Associations (BDF) to debate the

legalization of abortion, but her proposal was rejected by a majority of delegates. In 1910, she participated in an international conference in The Hague where she defended women's right to contraception. The BDF rejected a petition to admit the Alliance for the Protection of Mothers for membership, due to the Alliance's "mission to pursue sexual reforms." During World War I, Stöcker became a radical pacifist. She was a delegate at the International Women's Conference for Peace in The Hague. After the Nazis' takeover, Stöcker emigrated to Zurich. The files of the Gestapo (*Geheime Staatspolizei*—the Nazis' infamous secret state police) show that Stöcker's doctoral degree was revoked in 1937, and the Nazis confiscated and destroyed the boxes containing her manuscripts. In March 1938, Stöcker lost her German citizenship. In 1940, she moved to Sweden and in 1941 emigrated via the USSR to the United States. She died in New York in February 1943.

25. Camilla Jellinek (1860–1940) was a German advocate of women's rights.

26. Thalmann, "Jewish Women Exiled in France After 1933," in Sibylle Quack, ed., *Between Sorrow and Strength: Women Refugees of the Nazi Period* (Cambridge: Cambridge University Press, 1995), pp. 51–62.

27. Her name was Hania Mansfeld, alias Hélène Kro. See Rita Thalmann, "Une Lacune dans l'Historiographie," in Association pour la recherche sur l'histoire contemporaine des Juifs (RHICOJ), ed., *Les Juifs dans la Résistance et la libération* (Paris: Editions du Scribe, 1985), pp. 89–94.

28. Thalmann, "Les voix du silence: Les femmes juives du Reich ou l'opposition silencieuse à la déhumanisation" [The Voices of Silence: Jewish Women of the Reich or the Silent Opposition to Dehumanization], in Thalmann, ed., *La Tentation nationaliste*, pp. 207ff.

29. Leonore Siegele-Wenschkewitz, *Verdrängte Vergangenheit, die uns bedrängt: Feministische Theologie in der Verantwortung für die Geschichte* [Excluded Past that Oppresses Us: Feminist Theology in the Justification of History] (Munich: Kaiser, 1988).

30. Thalmann, *Être femme*, p. 47.

31. Ibid., p. 15.

32. Gertrud Bäumer (1873–1954) was a politician and a conservative advocate of women's rights. During World War I, she founded the National Women's Service, designed to organize women's support of the war. During the Weimar Republic, she led the cultural-political division of the interior ministry and was responsible for school curricula and the welfare of the youth. From 1930 to 1932 she was a parliamentary delegate for the German State Party. She was relieved of her functions after the National Socialist seizure of power in 1933. In spite of her exclusion in the following years, she moved closer ideologically to Nazi policies on women's issues.

33. Agnes von Zahn-Harnack (1884–1950) was the author of *Die Frauenbewegung—Geschichte, Probleme, Ziele* [The Women's Movement—History, Problems, Goals] (Berlin, 1928).

34. Alice Schwarzer, born in 1942, is a feminist journalist and editor in chief and publisher of *Emma*, a famous German journal "written by women for women," founded in 1977. *Emma* is worldwide the only autonomous feminist periodical with a wide circulation. Schwarzer is also the author of, among other works, *Simone de Beauvoir. Rebellin und Wegbereiterin* (1999) [Simone de Beauvoir: Rebel and Pathbreaker], and of *Der große Unterschied. Gegen die Spaltung von Menschen in Männer und Frauen* (2000) [The Big Difference: Against the Division of Human Beings into Men and Women].

35. Prof. Dr. Rudolf von Thadden, born in 1932, is a renowned German historian, one of the official representatives of the German government in relation to Franco-German cooperation. He is the author of books on the history of Prussia, on European integration, and on recent German history.

36. In general, Germany follows not the principle of *ius soli* (citizenship by place of birth) but that of *ius sanguinis* (citizenship according to citizenship of the parents). Under the citizenship law that went into effect on January 1, 2000, an exception is made for children born after December 31, 1999 to foreign parents who had been living in Germany for at least eight years. As a rule, German citizenship is either automatically acquired by birth (or adoption) through at least one German parent, or else may be obtained through naturalization.

37. Quoted in Siegele-Wenschkewitz, pp. 47, 57.

38. Macciocchi, p. vi.

39. *Choisir* [Choice] was founded in 1971 by Gisèle Halimi, Simone de Beauvoir, Christiane Rochefort, and other women. Its aim was the legalization of abortion, which was achieved in 1975 through the "Simone Weil law." Further objectives for securing women's social, economic, and political equality were put forward in 1974. See Gisèle Halimi, *La Cause des femmes* [Women's Cause] (Paris: Gallimard, 1973 and 1992). Rita Thalmann was secretary-general of *Choisir* from 1971 to 1977.

40. The Web site of the Wilhelm Reich Museum, http://www.wilhelmreich-museum.org/index.shtml, has the following entry on Wilhelm Reich:

Wilhelm Reich (1897–1957) was a physician-scientist whose investigation of energy functions in human emotions led to the discovery of an unknown energy which exists in all living matter and in the cosmos. He called this energy *orgone*.

Born in 1897 in the Austrian province of Galicia, Reich graduated from the medical school of the University of Vienna in 1922. A student of Sigmund Freud, he became one of the great psychoanalytic pioneers before his clinical studies led him into the laboratory and to investigations of the energy processes in nature.

Reich came to the United States in 1939 where he continued to study the manifestations and laws of orgone energy and to invent ways to make this energy usable. In 1954, the Federal Food and Drug Administration obtained an injunction by default which ordered Reich's literature to be banned and destroyed. As a result, several tons of Reich's published books and journals were burned, constituting one of the most heinous acts of censorship in U.S. history. In his defense, Reich asserted to the Court that "Man's right to know, to learn, to inquire, to make bona fide errors, to investigate human emotions must, by all means, be safe, if the word *freedom* should ever be more than an empty political slogan." The Court rejected this defense and Reich was convicted of contempt of court and imprisoned in Lewisburg Penitentiary where he died on November 3, 1957.

In 1930, Reich founded the Deutscher Reichsverband für proletarische Sexualpolitik (German Association for Proletarian Sexual Politics), or "Sexpol," which was closely associated with the German Communist Party.

Among Reich's best-known books are *Character-Analysis* (1933) and *Die Massenpsychologie des Faschismus* [The Mass Psychology of Fascism], 1933 (the first English translation was pblished in 1946; a revised translation was published in 1970: New York, Farrar, Straus & Giroux).

41. There are 577 elected representatives in the Assemblée nationale (the French parliament). At the June 16, 2002 general elections, 71 women were elected, as opposed to 30 in December 2002. (The interview with Thalmann was conducted in August 1991.)

42. Hesse is one of Germany's federal states. The CDU is one of the two biggest political parties in Germany.

43. Rita Thalmann, ed., *Femmes et fascismes* (Paris: Tierce, 1986), p. 7.

44. Thalmann, *Être femme*, p. 13.

45. Thalmann, ed., "Judaïsme, antijudaïsme, antisémitisme" [Judaism, Anti-Judaism, Anti-Semitism], *Austriaca: Cahiers Universitaires d'Information sur l'Autriche* 31 (December 1990).

46. See the Vidal-Naquet interview, note 23.

47. On this "battle of the historians," see Rita Thalmann, *"Historikerstreit": Die Dokumentation der Kontroverse um die Einzigartigkeit der national-sozialistischen Judenvernichtung* [The Battle of the Historians: The Documentation of the Controversy Around the Singularity of the National-Socialist Annihilation of the Jewish People](Munich: Piper, 1987).

48. See pp. 124–26.

49. Rita Thalmann and Emmanuel Feinermann, *Die Kristallnacht* (Bodenheim: Athenäum Verlag, 1988), p. 6.

50. This debate was published in *Les Nouveaux Cahiers* 105 (Summer 1991). Alfred Grosser, born in 1925 in Frankfurt, is a leading sociologist and political scientist. He emigrated to France in 1933 and has been a French citizen since 1937. He is professor emeritus at the Institut d'études politiques, Paris, and has received a number of prestigious prizes in France and Germany, including the Grand Prix de l'Académie des Sciences morales et politiques (1998) and the Friedenspreis des deutschen Buchhandels (1975), for his work of "mediation between French and German people, believers and nonbelievers, Europeans and people from other continents."

51. *Matériaux pour l'histoire* [Materials for History] is published by the Biblio-thèque de documentation internationale contemporaine de Paris at Nanterre (Université de Paris 10).

52. The Berlin Wall came down on November 9, 1989. "Crystal Night" was the night of November 9–10, 1938.

53. See *Die Tageszeitung* 3452, July 10, 1991, p. 4; and 3456, July 15, 1991, p. 6. Ravensbrück was a camp for women near Furstenberg (about fifty-six miles north of Berlin). Of 132,000 who passed through the camp, about 92,000 died. The Nazis' original intent was to rent the female labor supply to the industrial farms located in the area. The camp women worked primarily on the production of SS uniforms. Ultimately, the camp furnished cheap labor throughout a large part of Germany. Once a price was agreed upon, a business would receive 500 to 1,000 women along with guards supplied with dogs and clubs. Dead or dying workers were replaced with fresh ones at no additional cost to the client. More than twenty barracks were assigned to the work command at the nearby Siemens factory. The camp was notorious for its medical experiments on women. In late March 1945, it was ordered to evacuate, and 24,500 prisoners were put on the road to Mecklenburg. At the end of April 1945, the camp was liberated by Soviet forces.

54. See *Die Tageszeitung* 3452, July 10, 1991, p. 4; and 3655, March 13, 1992, p. 5. One of the buildings of the former camp Sachsenhausen has indeed been, since 1993, home of the *Finanzamt* [tax office] of the district of Oranienburg.

55. The transfer of the ashes of the Prussian kings took place on August 17, 1991. See *Die Tageszeitung* 3365, March 25, 1991, p. 2. The article describes plans for the transfer on the 205th anniversary of Frederic the Great's death.

56. SA: The infamous *Sturm-Abteilung* [Storm Section], Hitler's private army founded in 1921. The SA were also known as stormtroopers or brownshirts. Their primary mission was to disrupt the meetings of political opponents and to protect Hitler from attacks. The SA grew from 70,000 members in 1931 to 700,000 in 1933. In 1934, between 60 and 400 high-ranking members of the SA—including their leader Ernst Roehm—were purged during the Night of the Long Knives by men of the SS (*Schutzstaffel:* Hitler's personal bodyguard) and in Hitler's presence for having fomented a conspiracy against the Nazi leadership.

57. In 1923, in Rita Thalmann's hometown of Nuremberg, Julius Streicher (1885–1946) founded the periodical *Der Stürmer*, which became notorious for its anti-Semitic and pornographic features. Already in 1938, in one of his publications he called for the "total extermination" of the Jews.

58. Theodor W. Adorno and Max Horkheimer, *Dialectic of Enlightenment* (1947), trans. John Cumming (New York: Continuum, 1972), p. 183.

59. Issue 61 (September–October 1990) of the journal *Le Débat* contained an article by the sociologist Paul Yonnet, entitled "La machine Carpentras: histoire et sociologie d'un syndrome d'épuration" [The Carpentras Machine: History and Sociology of a Purification Syndrome], in which the author objected to media

"manipulation" (before and after the desecration of the Carpentras cemetery on May 9–10, 1990) of the question of anti-Semitism, which he claimed had been and was then over-dramatized, while creating the "fantasy" of the "irresistible rise" of the National Front. Paul Yonnet went on to argue that by making Jean-Marie Le Pen the "scapegoat of desecration," without having any real evidence, the media and political circles were triggering a "mechanism" belonging to a "purification syndrome." The article was hotly contested.

60. During the first round of the French presidential elections on May 5, 2002, 5.5 million people voted for the candidate of the far right Front Nationale, Jean-Marie Le Pen. During the second round, Jacques Chirac won the run-off with Le Pen.

Chapter 4: Emmanuel Levinas

1. Emmanuel Levinas, in *God, Death, and Time*, trans. Bettina Bergo (Stanford: Stanford University Press, 2000), p. 70.

2. Levinas, *God, Death, and Time*, p. 72.

3. For instance, Emmanuel Levinas, *Totality and Infinity: An Essay on Exteriority* (1961), trans. Alphonso Lingis (Pittsburgh: Duquesne University Press, 1961); and *Otherwise than Being or Beyond Essence* (1974), trans. Alphonso Lingis (Pittsburgh: Duquesne University Press, 1988).

4. A concept taken from the philosophy of Martin Heidegger.

5. Levinas, *God, Death, and Time*, p. 72, translation slightly modified.

6. This coinage of Levinas's feminizes the usual French word for the past, *le passé*; because English does not gender nouns, the distinction cannot be made in translation—"la passée" is translated as "the past" by Lingis.—Tr.

7. Levinas, *Otherwise*, p. 169; and *En découvrant l'existence avec Husserl et Heidegger* [Discovering Existence with Husserl and Heidegger] (Paris: Vrin, 4th edn., 1982), p. 208.

8. "Now"; literally, "hand-holding," from *main* [hand] and *tenir* [to hold]. —Tr.

9. *Begreifen* means "to grasp," "to understand." *Eingreifen* is used for instance in military or police language for "intervene." It also means "make a clear-cut decision," "take energetic measures."

10. *Cahier de l'Herne*, "Emmanuel Levinas," ed. Catherine Chalier and Miguel Abensour (Paris: l'Herne, 1991), p. 74.

11. For instance Levinas, *Otherwise*, pp. 81–97; *En découvrant*, p. 195.

12. Emmanuel Levinas, interview with Christian Descamps in *Le Monde*, November 2, 1980, pp. xv–xvi.

13. The concept of *conatus essendi*, taken from Spinoza's philosophy, expresses the effort by which "each thing endeavors to persist in its own being." Baruch Spinoza, *The Ethics and Selected Letters*, trans. Samuel Shirley; ed., with introduc-

tion, Seymour Feldman (Indianapolis: Hackett Publishing Company, 1982), p. 109.

14. Vassili Semenovitch Grossman, *Life and Fate*, trans. Robert Chandler (New York: Harper and Row, 1956).

15. Interview with Christian Descamps, *Le Monde*.

16. Emmanuel Levinas (1983), *Time and the Other*, trans. Richard A. Cohen (Pittsburgh: Duquesne University Press, 1986), see especially pp. 84–94.

17. Interview with Christian Descamps, *Le Monde*.

18. For instance, in *Otherwise than Being*.

19. See Emmanuel Levinas, (1987), "Dying for . . ." in *Entre Nous: Thinking of the Other*, trans. Michael B. Smith and Barbara Harshav (New York: Columbia University Press, 2000), pp. 207–18.

20. *The Jerusalem Bible* (London: Dartman, Longman and Todd, 1966), p. 120.

21. *Cahier de l'Herne*, pp. 28, 74.

22. "Emmanuel Levinas se souvient" [Emmanuel Levinas Remembers], *Les Nouveaux Cahiers*, special issue on "Emmanuel Levinas," 82, Autumn 1985, p. 32.

23. Micah, 6:8: "*ahavat chesed.*"

24. *Le Bible de Jérusalem*, French translation supervised by the École biblique de Jérusalem. The 13th edition, completely revised and expanded (Paris: Cerf, 1990), translates the relevant words *aimer la bonté*, as "loving goodness." [The 1966 Jerusalem Bible in English has "to love tenderly" (p. 1505).—Tr.]

25. *La Bible*, translated and introduced by André Chouraqui (Paris: Desclée de Brouwer, 1985), p. 1075.

26. See Salomon Malka, *Monsieur Chouchani: l'Énigme d'un maître du XXe siècle: Entretiens avec Elie Wiesel suivis d'une enquête* [Mr. Chouchani: The Enigma of a 20th-Century Master: Interviews with Elie Wiesel and an Investigation] (Paris: J.-Cl. Lattès, 1994). Salomon Malka is also the author of *Lire Levinas* [Reading Levinas] (Paris: Cerf, 1984).

27. See for instance "A Religion for Adults" (1963), in Emmanuel Levinas, *Difficult Freedom: Essays on Judaism*, trans. Sean Hand (Baltimore: Johns Hopkins University Press, 1997).

28. J. W. von Goethe, *Hermann and Dorothea*, trans. Daniel Coogan (New York: Frederick Ungar, 1966), see especially Book VI (Clio), lines 1–17, pp. 93–97.

29. J. W. von Goethe, *The Autobiography of Johann Wolfgang von Goethe*, trans. John Oxenford (New York: Horizon, 1969), see p. 90.

Chapter 5: Léon Poliakov

1. Léon Poliakov, *L'Auberge des musiciens: Mémoires* [The Musicians' Inn: Memoirs] (Paris: Mazarine, 1984), p. 185.

2. Léon Poliakov, *History of Anti-Semitism* (New York: Vanguard Press, 1964–1989): vol. 1, *From the Time of Christ to the Court Jews* (1964); vol. 2, *From*

Mohammed to the Marranos (1974); vol. 3, *From Voltaire to Wagner* (1975); vol. 4, *Suicidal Europe 1870–1933* (1989). Other related, translated texts by Poliakov include *Harvest of Hate: The Nazi Program for the Destruction of the Jews of Europe* (New York: Holocaust Library/Shocken Books, 1979); and *The Aryan Myth: A History of Racist and Fascist Ideas in Europe*, trans. Edmund Howard (New York: New American Library, 1977).

3. Léon Poliakov, *L'Épopée des vieux-croyants: Une Histoire de la Russie authentique* [A History of Authentic Russia] (Paris: Perrin, 1991).

4. *Ni Juif, ni Grec* [Neither Jewish nor Greek: Conversations on Racism], Actes du colloque du 16 au 20 juin 1975 au Centre culturel international de Cerisy-la-Salle [Proceedings of Cerisy Conference of June 16–20, 1975] (Paris: La Haye, 1978).

5. Léon Poliakov, Christian Delacampagne, and Patrick Girard, *Le Racisme* [Racism] (Paris: Seghers, 1976), p. 13.

6. Vladimir Jankélévitch and Béatrice Berlowitz, *Quelque part dans l'inachevé* [Somewhere in the Unfinished] (Paris: Gallimard, 1978), pp. 138ff.

7. Poliakov, *History*, vol. 2, p. vii; *L'Auberge des musiciens*, p. 188.

8. This has since been published: Léon Poliakov, ed., *Histoire de l'antisémitisme*, vol. 5, *1945–1993* [A History of Anti-Semitism, 1945–1993] (Paris: Seuil, 1994).

9. Christian Delacampagne is a contributor to the book section of the newspaper *Le Monde*; see also note 5. With Robert Maggiori, he has also edited *Philosopher: Les interrogations contemporaines* [Doing Philosophy: Contemporary Interrogations] (Paris: Fayard, 1980). See Poliakov, *Histoire de l'antisémitisme*, vol. 5, pp. 121ff.

10. The desecration of the Jewish cemetery at Carpentras took place during the night of June 9–10, 1990. (It is also referred to in the interview with Rita Thalmann; see p. 75.)

11. The Rachi Center (Centre Rachi-CUEJ [Centre universitaire d'Études juives]), for advanced Jewish studies in Paris, was founded in 1973.

12. *Le Couple interdit: Entretiens sur le racisme: La dialectique de l'altérité socioculturelle et la sexualité* [The Forbidden Couple: Interviews on Racism: The Dialectic of Sociocultural Alterity and Sexuality], Actes du colloque de mai 1977 au Centre culturel international de Cerisy-la-Salle [Proceedings of Cerisy Conference, May 1977] (Paris: La Haye, 1980).

13. Hermann Cohen, "Germanité et judéité" [Germanness and Jewishness], translated and introduced by M. B. de Launay, in *Pardès* 5 (Paris: J.-Cl. Lattès, 1987), esp. pp. 69–70. This text culminates in the declaration that Germany is the "mother country" of all the Jews in the whole world. Short extracts have been translated in *Reason and Hope: Selections from the Jewish Writings of Hermann Cohen*, trans. Eva Jospe (New York: Norton, 1971).

14. Léon Poliakov, *L'Envers du destin: Entretiens avec Georges Elia Sarfati* [*The Other Side of Destiny: Interview with George Elia Safarti*] (Paris: Fallois, 1989), p. 273.

15. The following lines, and the reply to the next question, were added to the interview when Léon Poliakov reread it in December, 1992.

16. Gunnar Heinsohn, *Was ist Antisemitismus?* [What Is Anti-Semitism?] (Frankfurt: Eichborn, 1988), p. 115.

17. Léon Poliakov, *De l'antisionisme à l'antisémitisme* (Paris: Calmann-Lévy, 1969).

18. Rudolf Augstein, born in 1923, was from 1947 to his death in 2002 publisher of the political weekly *Der Spiegel*, with a circulation in Germany of over a million. He published a response to the accusations made against him by the Viennese monthly *Forum*, as well as the original article: "In eigener Sache. Rudolf Augstein zu einem Artikel der Wiener Zeitschrift *Forum*," in *Der Spiegel* 52, December 21, 1992, pp. 76, 77.

19. Poliakov, *History*, vol. 2, p. 27.

20. See Léon Poliakov, *De Moscou à Beyrouth: Essai sur la désinformation* [From Moscow to Beirut: An essay on misinformation] (Paris: Calmann-Lévy, 1983), pp. 26ff.

21. "Marrano," for example, signifies "pig": see *Hommes et bêtes. Entretiens sur le racisme* [Men and Beasts: Interviews on Racism], Actes du colloque du 12 au 15 mai 1973 au Centre culturel internationale de Cerisy-la-Salle [Proceedings of the May 1973 Cerisy Conference] (Paris: Mouton, 1975), p. 174; one medieval poem describes Jews as "evil and cruel as dogs," apostrophizing them as "stinking dogs" (Poliakov, *Histoire*, vol. 1, p. 142), another source as "deceitful scumdogs" (ibid).

22. See for example *Le Couple interdit*, p.19; Poliakov, *L'Auberge*, p. 220.

23. Quoted in Poliakov, *L'Auberge*, p. 211.

24. Poliakov, *Le Bréviaire de la haine: Le IIIè Reich et les Juifs* (Paris: Calmann-Lévy, 1951) [*Harvest of Hate: The Nazi Program for the Destruction of Jews in Europe*, foreword by Reinhold Niebuhr (Philadelphia: The Jewish Publication Society of America, 1954)].

25. Léon Poliakov, *The Aryan Myth: A History of Racist and Fascist Ideas in Europe*, trans. Edmund Howard (New York: New American Library, 1977).

26. See the interview with Pierre Vidal-Naquet, pp. 30–32.

27. Jacob Gordin (1896–1947), philosopher, born at Dunabourg (Daugavpils), in Latvia. In 1917 he fought for the Russian Revolution. A few years later, disappointed by Soviet communism, he left the USSR to study Hermann Cohen's philosophy in Germany and to join the Akademie für die Wissenschaft des Judentums [Academy for Studies in Judaism]. He published numerous articles, including some in the *Encyclopédie juive* [Jewish Encyclopaedia] and, in 1929, his book *Das unendliche Urteil* [The Endless Judgment]. At the same time he worked on the Kabbalah. In 1933 he emigrated to France. Under the German occupation, he worked for the Resistance and took part in the rescue of many Jewish children. He taught philosophy and Jewish thought to Jewish boy scouts in one of their communities, at Beaulieu (in Corrèze). After the war, he taught at the Orsay school, founded by Robert Gamzon, for the training of Jewish boy scouts. Gordin made a decisive im-

pression on postwar Jewish French thought. See also for instance Emmanuel Levinas, "Jacob Gordin," in *Difficile Liberté* [Difficult Freedom] (Paris: Albin Michel, 1963–76), pp. 219–24; Jacob Gordin, *Ecrits: le renouveau de la pensée juive en France* [Writings: The Renewal of Jewish Thought in France] (Paris: Albin Michel, 1995).

28. Léon Ashkenazi was one of Gordin's best-known students at the École d'Orsay. He continued the teaching method initiated by Gordin for twenty years after his death; his pupils included Jean Zacklad and Eliahou Abitbol. See, e.g., "Tradition et modernité" [Tradition and Modernity] and "L'Exil" [Exile], in *Tradition et modernité dans la pensée juive* [Tradition and Modernity in Jewish Thought], ed. Emil Weiss (Festival international de la culture juive, Paris, 1983), pp. 1ff, 33ff.

29. *The Talmud: The Steinsaltz Edition*, ed. and trans. Rabbi Israel V. Berman, with a commentary by Rabbi Adin Steinsaltz (New York: Random House, 1989); and *The Talmud: The Steinsaltz Edition: A Reference Guide by Rabbi Adin Steinsaltz* (New York: Random House, 1989).

30. See Gérard Haddad, *L'Enfant illégitime: Sources talmudiques de la psychoanalyse* [The Illegitimate Child: Talmudic Sources of Psychoanalysis] (Paris: Desclée de Brouwer, 1996), section 3, ch. 1B.

31. Sigmund Freud and Karl Abraham, *Correspondance 1907–1926*, ed. Hilda C. Abraham and Ernst L. Freud (Frankfurt: Fischer, 1965–80), "Abraham et Freud" [Abraham and Freud], p. 48. Sigmund Freud and Karl Abraham, *A Psycho-Analytic Dialogue: The Letters of Sigmund Freud and Karl Abraham 1907–1926*, ed. Hilda C. Abraham and Ernst L. Freud and trans. Bernard Marsh and Hilda C. Abraham (New York: Basic Books, 1965). The quotation is from Abraham's letter to Freud, May 11, 1908, p. 36.; tr. mod.

32. See Klaus von Münchhausen, "Der Traum vom grossen Arabien. Aus dem Leben des Grossmufti [The Dream of Great Arabia: From the Life of the Great Mufti]," *Die Zeit*, September 7, 1990, pp. 45ff; von Münchhausen and Rudolf Pfisterer, "L'Antisémitisme en Allemagne [Antisemitism in Germany]," in Poliakov, ed., *Histoire*, vol. 5, pp. 33–96. In this chapter, the first section, "Le Miroir brisé [The Broken Mirror]," is by von Münchhausen, the second, "Un mal incurable? [An Incurable Evil?]" by Pastor Rudolf Pfisterer.

33. Victor Farias, *Heidegger and Nazism*, ed. Joseph Margolis and Tom Rockmore and trans. Paul Burrell and Gabriel R. Ricci (Philadelphia: Temple University Press, 1989).

34. Emmanuel Levinas, "Comme un consentement à l'horrible," *Le Nouvel Observateur* 1211, January 22–28, 1998.

35. Poliakov, *Histoire*, vol. 5, p. 294.

36. At the time of this interview (March 1991), the Soviet Union was still in existence.

37. "Having captured press attention several years ago, NPF-Pamiat (National Patriotic Front-Memory) is one of many groups that form the extra-parliamentary

opposition to the government in Russia today. The vileness and violence of their attacks on Jews and other groups has repeatedly drawn Western attention to this organization. The atmosphere of near-anarchy in Russia has allowed informal groups such as NPF-Pamiat and several other so-called political parties to step out of the shadows to express the most irrational and dark sentiments of an unstable society." Charles R. Sauer, "Life on the Russian Extreme: Letter from Moscow," in *East/West Letters*, vol. 1, no. 4 (Fall 1992).

38. Poliakov, *Histoire*, vol. 5, p. 295.

Chapter 6: Jean-François Lyotard

1. Jean-François Lyotard, *Heidegger and "the jews"* (1988), trans. Andreas Michel and Mark S. Roberts (Minneapolis: University of Minnesota Press, 1990), p. 4.

2. Jean-François Lyotard, *Lectures d'enfance* [Childhood Readings] (Paris: Galilée, 1991), p. 40.

3. Ibid, p. 39.

4. For instance, "Intentionnalité et métaphysique" [Intentionality and Metaphysics], and "Intentionnalité et sensibilité" [Intentionality and Sensitivity], in Emmanuel Levinas, *En découvrant l'existence avec Husserl et Heidegger* [Discovering Existence with Husserl and Heidegger] (Paris: Vrin, 4th edn., 1987), pp. 137–62.

5. See Lyotard, *Heidegger*, p. 21; tr. mod.

6. See Gershom Scholem, *The Kabbalah and its Symbolism*, trans. R. Manheim (New York: Shocken Books, 1965), p. 30.

7. For instance in Jean-François Lyotard, *The Inhuman: Reflections on Time* (1988), trans. Geoffrey Bennington and Rachel Bowlby (Stanford: Stanford University Press, 1991), p. 82.

8. Lyotard, *Heidegger*, p. 21.

9. Lyotard invents the word *voiser*, from the noun *voix* (voice) to suggest the disjunction between the written and the oral. English has available the existing verb "voice," so the point is not made so graphically.—Tr.

10. Lyotard, *Heidegger*, p. 27.

11. See Pierre Vidal-Naquet, *Les Juifs, la mémoire et le présent*, vol. 1 (Paris: La Découverte, 1981), p. 125 [*The Jews: History, Memory, and the Present*, ed. and trans. David Ames Curtis (New York: Columbia University Press, 1998), p. 192]; and Richard Marienstras, *Être un peuple en diaspora* [Being a People in Diaspora] (Paris: Maspero, 1975), p. 60.

12. Robert Antelme, *The Human Race*, trans. Jeffrey Haight and Annie Mahler (Chicago: Northwestern University Press, 1998).

13. Hannah Arendt, "The Jew as Pariah: A Hidden Tradition," in *The Jew as Pariah: Jewish Identity and Politics in the Modern Age*, ed. Ron H. Feldman (New York: Grove Press, 1978), pp. 67–90.

14. Harold Bloom, "The Pragmatics of Contemporary Jewish Culture," in

John Rajchman and Cornel West, eds., *Post-Analytic Philosophy* (New York: Columbia University Press, 1985), pp. 108–26.

15. Lyotard, *Heidegger*, pp. 83–84.

16. Ibid., p. 56.

17. Lyotard, *Lectures d'enfance*, p. 79.

18. Philippe Lacoue-Labarthe, *Heidegger, Art, and Politics: The Fiction of the Political*, trans. Chris Turner (Oxford: Blackwell, 1990).

19. *Nous avons été soufflés.* The verb *souffler*, to breathe on, has a number of different meanings, including (theatrical) prompting, whispering or breathing the words to be said, blowing out (a flame), and inspiring. "Être soufflé," continuing the "souffle" [breath] of the previous sentence, means to be breathed or blown on in both literal and metaphorical senses. It can also mean to be blown away, flabbergasted.—Tr.

20. Lyotard, *Lectures*, pp. 47, 34.

21. Ibid., p. 62.

22. Lyotard, *Heidegger*, p. 81.

23. Quoted by Paul Celan as epigraph to "Und mit dem Buch aus Tarussa" [And with Tarussa's Book], *Die Niemandsrose* [Nobody's Rose] (1963). See also note 10 in the Derrida interview.

24. Marcel Proust, *Contre Sainte-Beuve* [Against Sainte-Beuve] (Paris: Gallimard, 1954), p. 303. The word *cimentée* is omitted in this edition, since its legibility is equivocal, according to the editors. But it does figure in an edition of 1954, in which, however, the two instances of "Do not forget" are missing. Marcel Proust: "Contre Saint-Beuve," in *On Art and Literature*, trans. Sylvia Townsend Warner (New York: Meridian Books, 1958), p. 272, tr. mod.

25. Lyotard, *The Inhuman*, p. 81.

26. Lyotard, *Heidegger*, p. 34.

27. Lyotard, *The Postmodern Explained: Correspondence, 1982–1985*, ed. Julian Pefanis and Morgan Thomas; trans. Don Barry, Bernadette Maher, Julian Pefanis, Virginia Spate, and Morgan Thomas (Minneapolis and London: University of Minnesota Press, 1992), p. 91.

28. Jean-François Lyotard, *Sam Francis: Lessons of Darkness—Like the Paintings of a Blind Man* (Los Angeles: Lapis Press, 1993).

29. Marcel Proust, *À l'ombre des jeunes filles en fleur* [In the Shadow of Young Girls in Bloom], from *Remembrance of Things Past*, trans. C. K. Scott Moncrieff and Terence Kilmartin (New York: Random House, 1981).

30. Jean-François Lyotard, *The Differend* (1983), trans. Georges Van Den Abbeele (Minneapolis: University of Minnesota Press, 1988), p. xvi.

31. Lyotard, *The Inhuman*, p. 7.

32. Lyotard, *The Differend*, p. 13.

33. Ibid., p. 171.

34. See for instance Jean-François Lyotard, "Afterword: A Memorial of Marx-

ism: For Pierre Souyri" (1982), trans. Cecile Lindsay, in *Peregrinations: Law, Form, Event* (New York: Columbia University Press, 1988), pp. 45–75.

35. Claude Lefort was, with Cornelius Castoriadis, editor of the journal *Socialisme ou barbarie* (1948–1966), which regularly published contributions by Lyotard. See for instance Claude Lefort, *Democracy and Political Theory*, trans. David Macey (Minneapolis: University of Minnesota Press, 1988); *L'Invention démocratique: Les Limites de la domination totalitaire* [The Democratic Invention: The Limits of Totalitarian Domination] (Paris: Fayard, 1981).

36. Nicole Loraux, "Le lien et la division" [The Tie and the Division], *Cahier du Collège International de Philosophie* 4 (November 1987): 101ff; and "L'oubli dans la cité" [Forgetting in the City-state] in *Le Temps de la réflexion* 1 (1980): 213–42. *Stasis* is the Greek word for internal warfare, "the division turned into tearing apart" of the city-state.

37. On the difference between "litigation" and "differend," see *The Differend,* p. 9: "The plaintiff lodges his or her complaint before the tribunal, the accused argues in such a way as to show the inanity of the accusation. Litigation takes place. I would like to call a *differend* [*différend*] the case when the plaintiff is divested of the means to argue and becomes for that reason a victim. . . . A case of differend between two parties takes place when the 'regulation' of the conflict that opposes them is done in the idiom of one of the parties, while the wrong suffered by the other is not signified in that idiom."

38. *Il le faut* implies at once lack, necessity, and moral obligation.—Tr.

Chapter 7: Luc Rosenzweig

1. Luc Rosenzweig, *La jeune France juive: Conversations avec des Juifs d'aujourd'hui* [Young Jewish France: Conversations with Jews of Today] (Paris: Libre-Hallier, 1980). Drumont's *La France juive* is subtitled *Essai d'histoire contemporaine* [An Essay in Contemporary History].

2. Luc Rosenzweig, *La jeune France*, pp. 9–10.

3. *Catalogue pour des Juifs de maintenant* [Catalog for Today's Jews], edited with an introduction by Luc Rosenzweig, *Recherches, Revue du Cerfi* 38 (September 1979).

4. Pierre Goldman, born in Lyon in 1944, was from 1963 a member of the Union des étudiants communistes [Communist Students' Union] (UEC) at the Sorbonne. In 1968 he joined a revolutionary group in Venezuela, spending fourteen months in hiding in the company of rebels, but he returned to Paris in September 1969 after the rebel movement failed. In December 1969 he was arrested and in December 1974 he was sentenced to life imprisonment for double murder and armed robbery. During his first years in prison, he studied for a philosophy degree and an MA in Spanish literature, and wrote his famous *Souvenirs obscurs d'un Juif polonais né en France* [Obscure Memories of a Polish Jew Born in France,*

trans. Joan Pinkham (New York: Viking Press, 1977)]. These were both memoirs and defense; according to the author, they could prove his innocence in the double murder of which he was accused if he were granted a second trial: this opened on May 1, 1976 at the Somme region court of assizes in Amiens. "By benefit of doubt," Goldman was declared innocent of the double murder, but guilty of the three armed robberies, for which he returned to prison for six months. He was freed in December, 1976. On September 20, 1979, he was murdered by two men in the 13th arrondissement of Paris. An unknown commando group called "Honneur de la police" [Police Honor] claimed responsibility in the name of the law that the French authorities were unable, so they said, to enforce. Fifteen thousand people went in silence to Pierre Goldman's funeral, including Jean-Paul Sartre, Simone de Beauvoir, Samuel Beckett, and Yves Montand. See *Libération*, September 21, 27, and 29, 1979.

5. *Libération*, September 21, 1979: 4.

6. Luc Rosenzweig and Bernard Cohen, *Le Mystère Waldheim* (Paris: Gallimard, 1986), translated as *Waldheim* by Josephine Bacon (London: Robson Books, 1988).

7. Kurt Waldheim was secretary-general of the UN from 1972–82. In March 1986, the Austrian magazine *Profil* speculated about the role he had played in World War II. The World Jewish Congress was asked to undertake some investigations. Despite the documents brought to light, Waldheim denied having been a member of three Nazi organizations, only acknowledging that he belonged to the cavalry corps of the SA. But additionally, Waldheim had been appointed in 1943 as second in command of Group 1a at the headquarters of the Wehrmacht, with the Eleventh Italian Army, and posted to Arsakli (near Salonika, in Greece). He had to carry out information-gathering missions there, and make daily summary reports for the secret services. He followed the Jewish deportation operations and was responsible for "special missions," a common euphemism for execution. Although Waldheim's lies were clearly established, he won the June 1986 election for the Austrian presidency. In 1988, an international commission of historians submitted its report to the chancellor, Franz Vranitsky. They concluded that, while he had not participated directly in the war crimes, Kurt Waldheim was certainly aware of the atrocities, which he had always denied.

8. Rosenzweig and Cohen, p. 186.

9. Ibid., p. 11.

10. Annette Wieviorka, *Déportation et génocide: Entre la mémoire et l'histoire* [Deportation and Genocide: Between Memory and History] (1992; reprinted Paris: Pluriel, 1995).

11. Rosenzweig, *Catalogue*, p. 7.

12. Théo Klein, *L'Affaire du carmel d'Auschwitz* [The Auschwitz Carmelite Monastery Affair] (Paris: J. Bertoin, 1991).

13. His Eminence Jean-Marie Cardinal Lustiger of the Archdiocese of Paris was

born in Paris in 1926, the son of Polish Jewish immigrants. He converted to the Catholic faith in 1940, but he has never ceased to identify with his Jewish background and experience, including the death of his mother in Auschwitz. He is the author of some twenty books, a member of the Académie Française, and a major figure in Christian-Jewish dialogue. His books include his autobiography, *Le Choix de Dieu* (1987; translated in 1991 as *Choosing God—Chosen by God*); *Dieu merci—les droits de l'homme* [Thank God—Human Rights] (1990); and *Pour l'Europe: Un Nouvel art de vivre* [For Europe: A New Art of Living] (1999).

14. Benny Lévy, born in Cairo in 1946, came to France in 1963, and attended the École Normale Supérieure, where he was Louis Althusser's student. He joined the Union des jeunesses communistes (marxistes-léninistes) [Communist Youth Union (Marxist-Leninist)] (UCJml). In 1968 he founded the Gauche prolétarienne [Proletarian Left]; in 1974, Jean-Paul Sartre invited him to become his secretary. In 1983, Benny Lévy left Paris with his family to go and live in Strasbourg in an orthodox Jewish community. His books include *Le Nom de l'homme* [The Name of Man] (Lagrasse: Verdier, 1984) and *Le Logos et la lettre* [The Logos and the Letter] (Lagrasse: Verdier, 1988).

15. Alain Finkielkraut, born in Paris in 1949 to a Polish Jewish family. His books include *The Imaginary Jew*, trans. Kevin O'Neill and David Suchoff (Lincoln: University of Nebraska Press, 1994); *La Réprobation d'Israël* [Israel's Reprobation] (Paris: Denoël, 1983); *Remembering in Vain: The Klaus Barbie Trial and Crimes Against Humanity*, trans. Roxanne Lapidus with Sima Godfrey (New York: Columbia University Press, 1992); *The Wisdom of Love*, trans. Kevin O'Neill and David Suchoff (Lincoln: University of Nebraska Press, 1997).

16. At the time of the interview, the USSR still existed.

17. Rosenzweig, *Catalogue*, p. 117.

18. At the time of the interview, Luc Rosenzweig was director of the European culture television channel Arte, based in Strasbourg.

19. Rosenzweig, *Die Zeit*, July 5, 1991: 5.

20. Daniel Cohn-Bendit, born in 1945, was the spokesperson and leader of the May Revolution in Paris (1968). Expelled from France in 1968, he went to Frankfurt and became active in the counter-culture movement. In 1976 he was the managing editor and publisher of the *Pflasterstrand* magazine; from 1989 to 1996, he was an honorary city councilor at the "Amt für Multikulturelle Angelegenheiten" (Office for Multicultural Affairs). From 1994 to 1999, he was a member of the European Parliament for Bündnis 90/Die Grünen (German Green Party), and from 1994, he was the host of the Swiss TV show "Literaturclub." Since 1999, he has been member of the European Parliament for the French Green Party.

21. See Fernand Braudel, *The Identity of France*, trans. Sîan Reynolds (New York: Harper and Row, 1988).

22. On this issue, see the interview with Rita Thalmann, note 36.

23. Rosenzweig, *La jeune France*, pp. 8ff.

24. Since this conversation, Luc Rosenzweig has published two texts on this question: a book co-written with the Israeli ambassador to France, Elie Barnavi, *France et Israël: une affaire passionelle* [France and Israel: A Passionate Affair] (Paris: Perrin 2002); and an article "Comment je suis devenu sioniste" [How I Became a Zionist], *L'Arche* 539–40, January–February 2003, pp. 20–23.

Cultural Memory | in the Present

Ban Wang, *Illuminations from the Past: Trauma, Memory, and History in Modern China*

James Phillips, *Heidegger's People: Between National Socialism and Poetry*

Frank Ankersmit, *Sublime Historical Experience*

István Rév, *Prehistory of Post-Communism*

Paola Marrati, *Genesis and Trace: Derrida Reading Husserl and Heidegger*

Krzysztof Ziarek, *The Force of Art*

Marie-José Mondzain, *Image, Icon, Economy: The Byzantine Origins of the Contemporary Imaginary*

Cecilia Sjöholm, *The Antigone Complex: Ethics and the Invention of Feminine Desire*

Jacques Derrida and Elisabeth Roudinesco, *For What Tomorrow: A Dialogue*

Elisabeth Weber, *Questioning Judaism: Interviews by Elisabeth Weber*

Jacques Derrida and Catherine Malabou, *Counterpath: Traveling with Jacques Derrida*

Martin Seel, *Aesthetics of Appearance*

Jacques Derrida, *Eyes of the University: Right to Philosophy 2*

Nanette Salomon, *Shifting Priorities: Gender and Genre in Seventeenth-Century Dutch Painting*

Jacob Taubes, *The Political Theology of Paul*

Jean-Luc Marion, *The Crossing of the Visible*

Eric Michaud, *The Cult of Art in Nazi Germany*

Anne Freadman, *The Machinery of Talk: Charles Peirce and the Sign Hypothesis*

Stanley Cavell, *Emerson's Transcendental Etudes*

Stuart McLean, *The Event and its Terrors: Ireland, Famine, Modernity*

Beate Rössler, ed., *Privacies: Philosophical Evaluations*

Bernard Faure, *Double Exposure: Cutting Across Buddhist and Western Discourses*

Alessia Ricciardi, *The Ends Of Mourning: Psychoanalysis, Literature, Film*

Alain Badiou, *Saint Paul: The Foundation of Universalism*

Gil Anidjar, *The Jew, the Arab: A History of the Enemy*

Jonathan Culler and Kevin Lamb, eds., *Just Being Difficult? Academic Writing in the Public Arena*

Jean-Luc Nancy, *A Finite Thinking*, edited by Simon Sparks

Theodor W. Adorno, *Can One Live after Auschwitz? A Philosophical Reader*, edited by Rolf Tiedemann

Patricia Pisters, *The Matrix of Visual Culture: Working with Deleuze in Film Theory*

Andreas Huyssen, *Present Pasts: Urban Palimpsests and the Politics of Memory*

Talal Asad, *Formations of the Secular: Christianity, Islam, Modernity*

Dorothea von Mücke, *The Rise of the Fantastic Tale*

Marc Redfield, *The Politics of Aesthetics: Nationalism, Gender, Romanticism*

Emmanuel Levinas, *On Escape*

Dan Zahavi, *Husserl's Phenomenology*

Rodolphe Gasché, *The Idea of Form: Rethinking Kant's Aesthetics*

Michael Naas, *Taking on the Tradition: Jacques Derrida and the Legacies of Deconstruction*

Herlinde Pauer-Studer, ed., *Constructions of Practical Reason: Interviews on Moral and Political Philosophy*

Jean-Luc Marion, *Being Given That: Toward a Phenomenology of Givenness*

Theodor W. Adorno and Max Horkheimer, *Dialectic of Enlightenment*

Ian Balfour, *The Rhetoric of Romantic Prophecy*

Martin Stokhof, *World and Life as One: Ethics and Ontology in Wittgenstein's Early Thought*

Gianni Vattimo, *Nietzsche: An Introduction*

Jacques Derrida, *Negotiations: Interventions and Interviews, 1971–1998*, ed. Elizabeth Rottenberg

Brett Levinson, *The Ends of Literature: The Latin American "Boom" in the Neoliberal Marketplace*

Timothy J. Reiss, *Against Autonomy: Cultural Instruments, Mutualities, and the Fictive Imagination*

Hent de Vries and Samuel Weber, eds., *Religion and Media*

Niklas Luhmann, *Theories of Distinction: Re-Describing the Descriptions of Modernity*, ed. and introd. William Rasch

Johannes Fabian, *Anthropology with an Attitude: Critical Essays*

Michel Henry, *I am the Truth: Toward a Philosophy of Christianity*

Gil Anidjar, *"Our Place in Al-Andalus": Kabbalah, Philosophy, Literature in Arab-Jewish Letters*

Hélène Cixous and Jacques Derrida, *Veils*

F. R. Ankersmit, *Historical Representation*

F. R. Ankersmit, *Political Representation*

Elissa Marder, *Dead Time: Temporal Disorders in the Wake of Modernity (Baudelaire and Flaubert)*

Reinhart Koselleck, *The Practice of Conceptual History: Timing History, Spacing Concepts*

Niklas Luhmann, *The Reality of the Mass Media*

Hubert Damisch, *A Childhood Memory by Piero della Francesca*

Hubert Damisch, *A Theory of /Cloud/: Toward a History of Painting*

Jean-Luc Nancy, *The Speculative Remark: (One of Hegel's bon mots)*

Jean-François Lyotard, *Soundproof Room: Malraux's Anti-Aesthetics*

Jan Patočka, *Plato and Europe*

Hubert Damisch, *Skyline: The Narcissistic City*

Isabel Hoving, *In Praise of New Travelers: Reading Caribbean Migrant Women Writers*

Richard Rand, ed., *Futures: Of Jacques Derrida*

William Rasch, *Niklas Luhmann's Modernity: The Paradoxes of Differentiation*

Jacques Derrida and Anne Dufourmantelle, *Of Hospitality*

Jean-François Lyotard, *The Confession of Augustine*

Kaja Silverman, *World Spectators*

Samuel Weber, *Institution and Interpretation: Expanded Edition*

Jeffrey S. Librett, *The Rhetoric of Cultural Dialogue: Jews and Germans in the Epoch of Emancipation*

Ulrich Baer, *Remnants of Song: Trauma and the Experience of Modernity in Charles Baudelaire and Paul Celan*

Samuel C. Wheeler III, *Deconstruction as Analytic Philosophy*

David S. Ferris, *Silent Urns: Romanticism, Hellenism, Modernity*

Rodolphe Gasché, *Of Minimal Things: Studies on the Notion of Relation*

Sarah Winter, *Freud and the Institution of Psychoanalytic Knowledge*

Samuel Weber, *The Legend of Freud: Expanded Edition*

Aris Fioretos, ed., *The Solid Letter: Readings of Friedrich Hölderlin*

J. Hillis Miller/Manuel Asensi, *Black Holes/J. Hillis Miller; or, Boustrophedonic Reading*

Miryam Sas, *Fault Lines: Cultural Memory and Japanese Surrealism*

Peter Schwenger, *Fantasm and Fiction: On Textual Envisioning*

Didier Maleuvre, *Museum Memories: History, Technology, Art*

Jacques Derrida, *Monolingualism of the Other; or, The Prosthesis of Origin*

Andrew Baruch Wachtel, *Making a Nation, Breaking a Nation: Literature and Cultural Politics in Yugoslavia*

Niklas Luhmann, *Love as Passion: The Codification of Intimacy*

Mieke Bal, ed., *The Practice of Cultural Analysis: Exposing Interdisciplinary Interpretation*

Jacques Derrida and Gianni Vattimo, eds., *Religion*